The São Paulo Law School and the Anti-Vargas Resistance (1938–1945)

JOHN W. F. DULLES

The São Paulo Law School and the Anti-Vargas Resistance (1938–1945)

UNIVERSITY OF TEXAS PRESS, AUSTIN

Printed in the United States of America

First Edition, 1986

Library of Congress Cataloging-in-Publication Data
Dulles, John W. F.
The São Paulo Law School and the anti-Vargas resistance (1938–1945).
Includes index.
1. Universidade de São Paulo. Faculdade de Direito.
2. Law students—Brazil—São Paulo—Political activity.
3. Law teachers—Brazil—São Paulo—Political activity.
4. Brazil—Politics and government—1930–1954. I. Title.
KHD201.S275D85 1986 340'.07'118161 85-15069
ISBN 0-292-77599-7

Contents

Introduction

Brazil is not one of those nations (such as Portugal, Spain, and the Soviet Union) where authoritarian governments continued to prevail after 1945; nor is it to be classed among those whose dictatorships were terminated with the help of invading forces. The collapse in 1945 of the Brazilian dictatorship, known as the Estado Novo, was an internal affair, determined largely by the widespread discontent that influenced military leaders and persuaded highly placed civilians to abandon plans to retain the authoritarian constitution of November 1937 in modified form.

During the Estado Novo (1937–1945), the voice of resistance was lifted courageously at different times and places, as the documents of the dictatorship's National Security Tribunal make clear. But its persistence with clarity was nowhere as great as at the São Paulo Law School. Luís Arrobas Martins, one of the *resistência* leaders, wrote in 1973 that "today all confirm what was said without contradiction at the time: the Law School of the University of São Paulo was the most active, most combative, and most conscientious democratic redoubt of Brazil during the whole period of the 'Estado Novo.'"[1]

Reasons for this role of the São Paulo Law School, long the chief training center for Brazil's political leaders, are mentioned in some of the chapters that follow and include the school's deeply ingrained liberal tradition and the frequently acrimonious relations, prior to November 1937, between São Paulo's leaders and Getúlio Vargas, creator of the Estado Novo. Neither the reasons for the school's *resistência* movement, nor the charge that it was "romantic," nor the differences of opinion among students about methods to be used detract from the idealism and courage of the participants, nor from the ultimate effectiveness of the movement, which, after a slow start, contributed mightily to the fall of the Estado Novo.

During the *resistência* movement, the authorities exiled political opponents, invaded homes and places of business, seized papers and personal mail (such as correspondence of student José Bonifácio

Coutinho Nogueira addressed to his father in Buenos Aires), dismissed and arrested professors, wrecked printing presses, carried out frequent imprisonments (student Germinal Feijó was jailed twenty-nine times), and made use of an assortment of favors in an effort to influence students (who were in many cases short of funds). Without doubt, popular backing for the *resistência* movement was greatly enhanced by the barbaric nature of its repression by the Special Police of São Paulo in November 1943. As Arrobas Martins wrote thirty years later, "the blood of the young people, shed in a public square," stirred the entire nation.[2]

After the authorities drafted some of the *resistência* students to serve as soldiers in the Brazilian Expeditionary Force in Italy, one of them wrote from the Apennines to try to express how much the São Paulo Law School "means to me." He said that his "friends there and the struggles in which we participated are probably the most important part of my life."[3] For the *resistência* students, the classroom work was far less important than the political struggles, the friendships that were formed, and the inspiration received from professors who defied the dictatorship.

The scrapbooks and collections of papers that have been preserved for forty years, and the accounts of incidents written by the participants in the early 1940s and later, seem to have been waiting to be assembled into a story of the effort to extend to the nation the democratic principles praised and practiced in "the free territory of the Largo de São Francisco" (the São Paulo Law School). It is the story of a group of young people (not all of them actively anti-Vargas) who engaged in hard-fought student elections and who, after 1945, held prominent positions in Brazilian politics, business, and professions. When Jânio Quadros, a law student during the early years of the Estado Novo, was elected president of Brazil in 1960, São Paulo Agriculture Secretary José Bonifácio Coutinho Nogueira hailed "the triumph of the renovating message for which our generation has struggled since school days."[4]

It is to be regretted that the papers of Roberto Victor Cordeiro, who was deeply involved in the story, were destroyed following his death in 1979. It is also to be regretted that the scholarly João Nery Guimarães, one of the prominent participants, desisted from the intention he once had of writing the story, because a foreigner to all that happened, such as myself, is bound to fail in many ways. My failures would have been even more numerous and serious than they are—the task, in fact, would have been impossible—without the warm and invaluable cooperation of scores of the participants. The help of one of them, Flávio Galvão, deserves special mention. I am grateful also to the Andrew W. Mellon Foundation and the Institute of Latin American Studies of the University of Texas at Austin for a fellowship that provided financial assistance to help me carry out research in São Paulo.

J.W.F.D.

Austin, Texas

The São Paulo Law School and the Anti-Vargas Resistance (1938–1945)

I

Pre-1930 Résumé (1827–1930)

1. The First Days (1827–1831)

The São Paulo Law School, the oldest institution of higher learning in Brazil, is known for the lasting personal relationships and ideas that were developed there, in and outside the classrooms, by a veritable Who's Who of Brazilian history. It is known also as the cradle of movements that affected that history.

The imposing law school building, which stands four stories high in the heart of a metropolis of skyscrapers, has a history that is much older than that of the law school. It goes back to an authorization, issued in 1624 by the Franciscan Order (the Ordem Seráfica de São Francisco de Assis), for the establishment of a monastery in the country-side area then known as the Vila de São Paulo. The original construction, undertaken fifteen years later, was soon abandoned in favor of a new location, where the members of the order started in 1643 to build their spacious monastery and an adjoining church. The two-story monastery, of simplest baroque design and built firmly of wood and a durable material made from the local soil, was inaugurated on September 17, 1647. The building has occasionally undergone remodeling, such as that which followed a fire in 1880. Widespread modifications, carried out between 1932 and 1941 (chiefly in 1934), increased the height to four floors and gave the structure its present handsome façade.[1]

In 1823, when São Paulo's population of almost ten thousand made it Brazil's tenth-largest city, educational matters were discussed in Rio de Janeiro at the constitutional assembly of the recently formed Brazilian Empire. José Feliciano Fernandes Pinheiro's proposal for a university in São Paulo was followed by other proposals, favorable to Olinda (in the northeast), Rio de Janeiro, Bahia, Minas Gerais, and elsewhere. Concern about São Paulo's lack of accessibility and housing, and the alleged bad pronunciation of the Paulistas, was apparently overcome by consideration of the town's good climate and low cost of living, and on November 4, 1823, the constitutional assembly sanctioned a law to establish universities in São Paulo and Olinda. The dissolution of the constitutional assembly by Emperor Pedro I on November 12, 1823, was a setback for São Paulo, as was a decree to start a course in law provisionally in Rio de Janeiro. But the decree was not executed and in mid-1826 the representatives to the nation's Chamber of Deputies reviewed the decision of the constitutional assembly.

Bernardo Pereira de Vasconcelos, congressman from Minas Gerais, felt that the law courses should be given in the national capital, Rio de Janeiro, in order to assure the prevalence of loyalty to the imperial government. He feared a revival in the provinces of the autonomist and liberal spirit, such as the *bandeirantes* (Paulistas) had displayed in the past. It might well become necessary, he said, for the presidents of the provinces to send professors and students in chains to be held in the Rio fortresses as "republicans and firebrands."[2]

Despite this warning, the Chamber of Deputies, on August 11, 1826, enacted legislation for establishing institutions in São Paulo and Olinda to provide five-year courses of legal instruction. The legislation, which also outlined preparatory studies, or *cursos anexos*, was slightly altered by subsequent amendments and was promulgated by Emperor Pedro I on August 11, 1827—a date that has long been remembered.[3]

Seventy-one-year-old José Arouche de Toledo Rendon, a wealthy Brazilian general with legal training and experience, was named director of the São Paulo Law School in October 1827, and at the same time the first teaching appointment went to José Maria de Avellar Brotero, a 29-year-old Portuguese doctor of law whose involvement in a political conspiracy had forced him to leave Lisbon.[4] Brotero, a vociferous liberal with good connections in the Brazilian royal court, was an eloquent orator, and his lectures to students resembled speeches of a political campaigner. He was so combative that he soon alienated Law School Director Rendon and terrified the second instructor to be appointed, Dr. Baltasar da Silva Lisboa, a 67-year-old Baiano who reached São Paulo in 1828.[5]

In November 1827, before the teaching had started, Rendon advised José Feliciano Fernandes Pinheiro, then serving as imperial minister with the title of Visconde de São Leopoldo, that he wanted to hold classes in the run-down São Francisco monastery, which by then was being used by only six friars. Rendon wrote that it would be possible to have "three law classes on the upper floor, and four preparatory classes on the ground floor, without demolishing anything and without annoying the friars," and he added that the monastery contained a "good library" of about five thousand volumes. Although the monastery was not turned over to the law school until late in 1828, the teaching of the thirty-three students who first enrolled was begun early in March of that year. This was two and one-half months before classes began at the Olinda Law School (which was moved to Recife in 1854).[6]

The number of students enrolling each year at the São Paulo Law School would have averaged a little over thirty during its first eight years except that ninety-nine entered in 1830. Most of the early students came from provinces other than São Paulo.[7] Due to the scarcity of housing in São Paulo, some of them lived in cells of the monastery. When groups of students found accommodations in houses, they called their groups *repúblicas*, perhaps because, as one writer has pointed out, they adopted a democratic method of choosing the officers of their groups.[8]

In the early days of the law school, the monastery's patio, or inner courtyard, was known as the *gerais* in accordance with the custom at Coimbra University in Portugal. In 1885 it was referred to as the *arcadas do antigo convento* by Lúcio de Mendonça, the author and Supreme Court justice who graduated in 1877. Thereafter, the expression *as arcadas* was used in reference to the law school itself.[9]

The *arcadas*, or law school, came to be regarded as off bounds for the police. This sentiment was reflected in 1850 when Law School Director Manoel Joaquim do Amaral Gurgel refused to allow the police to assist him in quelling a riot by students engaged in the *trote* (the annual hazing of new students). On August 11, 1930, students were moved by the same sentiment when they adopted a resolution proposed by Adriano Marrey, son of Paulista political leader José Adriano Marrey Júnior. The resolution, in a reference to the public square where the school is located, proclaimed "the free state of the Largo de São Francisco" (São Francisco Square).[10]

Neither the square nor the school building entrance opening onto it existed when the first students attended their classes. They had to enter the school through the church because the extensive agricultural property of the friars was bounded by a wall that was right in front of the school. Rendon asked the authorities of the province of São Paulo to cut two streets through the agricultural land. Senator Rafael Tobias de Aguiar, delighted with this idea, also insisted that the wall come down so that the public could have access to a square and make use of a well that had formerly furnished water exclusively to the friars.[11]

Before Rendon finally persuaded the authorities in Rio to accept his resignation from his law school post in 1833, he became engaged in a controversy with the São Francisco Church about the ringing of the bell, which was used in common for church and educational activities. The bell ringer of the church was enthusiastic about his profession, much to the annoyance of the professors whose lectures he interrupted. Rendon also found himself involved in tiring and acrimonious disputes with Professor Brotero.[12]

Brotero pleased the students, who, in the words of Antônio de Toledo Piza, were "eminently Brazilian and liberal in a society of backward Portuguese and indifferent French" and who were "considered a dangerous element."[13] The students, forming a small, homogeneous, intellectual group not adverse to such pranks as stealing the clapper from the bell at the *arcadas*, found an advocate and friend in João Baptista Badaró, whose offer to teach geometry at the Curso Anexo without pay was accepted by Rendon in 1828 because the contracted professor failed to show up. Líbero Badaró, as the young new instructor called himself, was a liberal-minded medical doctor who came to Brazil from Italy in 1826 and moved two years later from Rio to São Paulo, where he took the lead in distributing smallpox vaccine. In 1829 he founded the *Observador Constitucional*, which defended students, accused of breaking laws, and viciously attacked representatives of Pedro I, who was becoming autocratic. Badaró's assassination in November 1830 and the subsequent trial, which acquitted a judge who had been the object of Badaró's scathing remarks, stirred up much animosity against Pedro I in Minas Gerais and other provinces. When the emperor abdicated in April 1831 in favor of his 5-year-old son, the São Paulo law students rejoiced.[14]

2. The Bucha (founded in 1831)

General Rendon has been described by Spencer Vampré, in his history of the São Paulo Law School, as more interested in military matters than letters. He was also interested in the cultivation of tea and, in using some of his large landownings for this purpose, was the first to grow tea in São Paulo. Relaxing in retirement in 1834 at his home on the Morro do Chá (Hill of Tea), he said to Júlio Frank, history teacher at the Curso Anexo: "Within a century São Paulo will be the world's largest exporter of tea!"[1]

Several years earlier Rendon had come to know Frank, a liberal Protestant born in Germany in 1808, because students had spoken of him with admiration. Frank had reached Brazil in 1828, but he might not have become a resident of the city of São Paulo had not some boys, taught by him in Sorocaba, west of the city, persuaded him to accompany them after they had passed the exams necessary for entering the Curso Anexo. In São Paulo, Frank gave classes at the

"República da Rua São José," shared in the lives of the students, and enjoyed the friendship of Rafael Tobias de Aguiar, a liberal who became president of the province following the abdication of Pedro I.[2] In 1833 Frank accepted the students' idea that he be a candidate for a history and geography teaching position at the "Curral dos Bichos" (the students' name for the Curso Anexo), and he therefore presented himself to Carlos Carneiro de Campos, successor of General Rendon. It is reported that the celebration that followed Frank's passing the test lasted for seven days and nights.[3]

Júlio Frank is considered Líbero Badaró's successor in spreading liberal ideas in Brazil. A single suggestion, which Frank advanced in 1831, has brought him the reputation of having contributed more than anyone else to the advancement of liberal ideas in Brazil in the nineteenth and early twentieth centuries. The suggestion was made when students were discussing, at one of the *repúblicas* one night, the financial problems of their less fortunate schoolmates. Frank spoke of the Burschenschaften, secret student associations in Germany that assisted needy students and that had "a moral code and type of ritual that attracted students to the esoteric." Thus the liberal-minded Burschenschaft, or Bucha as it is usually called, came into existence at the *arcadas* in 1831, with Frank reportedly explaining: "Those in the Academy will continue the work of assistance; those who complete their courses will have an alumni society, very useful, and will help each other over the years. And, even later, the society will be able to govern the country."[4]

When Júlio Frank died of pneumonia in 1841, at the age of 32, his student friends insisted that he be buried, as he had once suggested, at the law school itself. Frank had not been a religious person, but his Protestant background made burial in a Catholic cemetery impossible. Acting Law School Director Brotero, liberal and aggressive, overcame the objections of the bishop, who is said to have remarked that the grounds of the old monastery contained "the remains of men who had feared God and whose bones would feel badly near those of the heretic."[5] The monument over Júlio Frank's grave, with a four-meter-high obelisk at its top, has continued in its original place at the *arcadas* despite the building's alterations and has weathered depredation attempts made in the 1930s by members of the military and the fascistlike Integralista movement.[6]

Historian Brasil Bandecchi describes the Bucha as a sort of Masonic order of the school, secret, philanthropic, and liberal, and he adds that it supported republican and abolitionist ideas. He writes that "the General Communion of the Bucha, under the leadership of the Chaveiro [Keeper of the Key], had a Council of Apostles and a

Council of Invisibles." Professor Ernesto de Morais Leme, a leading *bucheiro* (Bucha member) has declared that "no poor student,in difficulty about continuing with his course, failed to receive pecuniary assistance from an invisible hand." Afonso Arinos de Melo Franco writes that the membership of the Bucha did not exceed 10 percent of the student body and consisted of the intellectual and moral elite.[7]

The members, at their secret sessions, wore robes and displayed sashes showing either a blue cross (representing Faith), a green anchor (representing Hope), or a red heart (representing Charity).[8] Frank's idea was so successful that similar secret societies, sometimes also called *buchas*, were organized elsewhere: the Tugendbund at the Recife Law School, the Landmanschaft at São Paulo's Escola Politécnica (founded in 1895), and the Jugendschaft at São Paulo's Faculdade de Medicina (founded in 1913).[9]

As the São Paulo Law School provided so many national leaders, among them seven presidents of the Old Republic (1889–1930), it is not surprising that the law school alumni who had been inducted into the Bucha as students were considered to have had "secret society" ties that influenced national events. Although this influence faded in the late 1920s and collapsed in the early 1930s, it has been written that President Getúlio Vargas, shown a partial list of Bucha members by Ademar Pereira de Barros in the late 1930s, told the São Paulo *interventor* that "one cannot govern Brazil without those people." Carlos Lacerda declared that "it is impossible to write the history of the Republic without writing the history of the Bucha."[10]

3. Abolition and the Republic (1888–1889)

One of the *bucheiros* was Rui Barbosa, a transfer from the Recife Law School who became a third-year student at the *arcadas* in 1868. His oratorical career began when he and the young poet Antônio de Castro Alves, also a transfer from Recife, joined their new classmates, among them Joaquim Nabuco and Afonso Pena, at a banquet honoring popular Professor José Bonifácio de Andrada e Silva, who had called for political regeneration in an eloquent speech in the Chamber of Deputies in July 1868. The professor, known as José Bonifácio, o Moço (because his uncle, "The Patriarch of Brazil's Independence," bore the same name), had already distinguished himself as a liberal legislator, imperial cabinet minister, journalist, and teacher of civil law. After he died in 1886, a statue of José Bonifácio, o Moço, the first statue to be placed in a public square in São Paulo, was set up in the Largo de São Francisco. Today it stands inside the law school building.[1]

Rui Barbosa, leader in the prodemocracy political oratory of the Clube Radical and Ateneu Paulistano in 1869 and 1870, joined such classmates as Joaquim Nabuco and Castro Alves in directing an abolitionist offensive. He was active in the work of Fraternidade Primeira, a public version of the secret *fraternidade* group that had for several years sought to promote the freedom of slaves. In that work in 1870, Rui was joined by his conservative classmate Francisco de Paula Rodrigues Alves. Rui and Rodrigues Alves both defended blacks who were held in slavery illegally or who had been abandoned by their owners.[2]

The abolitionist offensive and the campaign for giving Brazil a republican regime became vigorous in the 1870s and 1880s. At the São Paulo Law School the Clube Republicano Acadêmico was founded in 1876, together with its organ, *A República*. In the next year law students established the Clube Liberal Acadêmico, which advocated abolition and a republic; among those who wrote for its organ, *O Liberal*, were *bucheiros* Pedro Lessa and Júlio Mesquita (both associated also with *A República*). The students' Centro Abolicionista Acadêmico came into existence in 1883 and started publishing *A Onda*.[3]

In the words of Afonso de Carvalho, a law student in the late 1880s, the voices of antislavery students, at the law school and elsewhere, became "the predominant factor of popular emotion" during the months before complete emancipation was achieved by a royal decree in May 1888. On the more practical side, history Professor Joseph L. Love points out that "repeated slave uprisings . . . interfered with" São Paulo's successful program of using widespread immigration to provide good and cheap labor, and he adds that the role of Antônio Prado, a São Paulo Conservative Party leader and minister of agriculture in 1888, was critical "in bringing about nationwide abolition."[4]

This abolition without indemnification deprived the throne of much of its former support. And on November 15, 1889, the republic, which had been a vision of a good many law student publications, became a reality. When it did, commercial law Professor Antônio Carlos Ribeiro de Andrada Machado e Silva, son of the statesman with the same name, presided over a faculty meeting of thirteen professors to decide how the law school should react. After a suggestion was made to offer the faculty's backing to the new government, João Mendes de Almeida Júnior, a new professor who was a monarchist and devout Catholic, suggested that the republican government be recognized simply because it existed. Others, including recently appointed Professor Pedro Lessa, agreed that it was not up to the faculty to take a position although the members might do so as individuals, and this view prevailed. It was further decided that exams, scheduled for November, be suspended for three days to allow the students to participate in the celebrations that greeted the new republic. Elsewhere in the city of São Paulo, Prudente José de Morais Barros and Francisco Rangel Pestana took over the state government and appointed a state cabinet that included Júlio Mesquita as secretary of the cabinet and Bernardino de Campos as police chief. All these men, São Paulo law school graduates, were associated with *A Província de S. Paulo*, the newspaper that was later renamed *O Estado de S. Paulo*.[5]

For five years military leaders occupied the Brazilian presidency, and then civilians took over. Brazil's first four civilian presidents were members of the Burschenschaft, as was the Barão do Rio Branco, whose achievements as foreign minister were accomplished soon after the turn of the century. According to Afonso Arinos de Melo Franco, in 1906 the baron made indiscreet references to the Bucha when speaking with old friends and was therefore admonished severely by the head of the General Communion of the secret society.[6]

4. The Centro Onze de Agosto (founded in 1903)

The so-called *ensino livre* (liberated instruction), which made class attendance optional so that students could acquire knowledge where they pleased, was decreed in 1879 and was in effect at the São Paulo Law School in the 1880s and early 1890s. Classes were poorly attended, the students saw little of each other, and the number of student publications and organizations declined. The *repúblicas* practically went out of existence.[1]

The influence of *ensino livre* was predominant in 1891 and 1892 when the government of the new republic issued regulations for the institutions of higher learning that were under the jurisdiction of the Justice Ministry: the law schools in São Paulo and Recife, the medical schools in Bahia and the federal capital, the Politécnica in the federal capital, and the School of Mines in Minas Gerais. These regulations made it possible, Pedro Dória writes, for the law students to graduate in "as little as two years, which they frequently did, almost without getting to know the Academia or their classmates." He adds that the revolts during the unsettled times of the republic's early years also contributed to the dispersion of the São Paulo law students.[2]

Law 314 of October 30, 1895, contained stricter provisions for students of social and juridical sciences who wished to graduate. Law students found that they had to devote five years to the courses and attend classes quite regularly. As the new law applied only to those students who entered school after it was enacted, it was not until 1900 that the law schools began to have students in all five years subject to the provisions of Law 314.[3]

At the *arcadas* the associative spirit reappeared as early as 1899 when some second-year students formed an association for their class. It published a magazine that lasted for two or three years. Successors, who were second-year students in 1900, created a short-lived Clube Acadêmico for their class. The organizers, among them Plínio Barreto and Pedro Dória, published one number of *A Luta* and elected Dória president of the Clube. In 1902 the second- and third-year students founded the Círculo Jurídico Acadêmico; it published *A Época*, to which José Carlos de Macedo Soares, José Joaquim Cardoso de Melo Neto, José de Paula Rodrigues Alves, and others contributed. More and more student publications appeared but they were of short duration.[4]

The time seemed ripe for the organization of an association that would be for the members of all five classes. Thus plans for the establishment of the Centro Acadêmico Onze de Agosto were advanced by a rather large group, which included Luís Pereira de Campos Vergueiro, José Carlos de Macedo Soares, Joaquim de Souza Pinheiro, César Lacerda de Vergueiro, Cardoso de Melo Neto, José de Paula Rodrigues Alves, Pedro Dória, and Júlio Prestes de Albuquerque. At assemblies at the *arcadas*, statutes were approved and a slate of officers was elected. Pedro Dória became the Centro Onze de Agosto's first president, in part because he was in his fifth year, one of the requirements of the organization's presidents. José de Paula Rodrigues Alves was elected first orator, and Professor Pedro Lessa was chosen lawyer of the Centro. To produce the Centro's organ, *O Onze de Agosto*, a five-man editorial board was elected. Among the five were Pedro Dória and José Bento Monteiro Lobato.[5]

Law School Director João Pereira Monteiro was so cooperative that electric lighting was installed in the *salão nobre* of the school so that the official installation meeting of the Centro could be held at night on August 11, 1903. Until then gas lights had been used exclusively at the school and no large meeting had been held there at night.[6]

For the occasion, the first number of *O Onze de Agosto* was distributed. It contained a tribute to the Barão de Ramalho, who had been director of the law school at the time of his death at the age of 93 in August 1902. During his career of politics, teaching, and hospital and Masonic Order work, Joaquim Ignacio Ramalho had resided for only two years outside the city of São Paulo—during his governorship of the province of Goiás.[7]

The first number of *O Onze de Agosto* recalled the times when "the voice of the academic tribune, in the public square, incited the people to revolt against social institutions that enshrined injustice." It expressed the hope that the new Centro would "initiate the complete revival of the old splendor of academic life, form true combatants for the struggle in favor of the interests of Brazilian society," break down barriers between students in different years of study, and strengthen relations between professors and students.[8]

While Pedro Dória was president of the Centro, a campaign was begun to raise funds for a new law school banner, the old one being in decrepit condition. Before the banner was purchased, in 1904, Dória turned over the presidency to Luís Campos Vergueiro, the winner of an election that was uncontested because the rival candidate withdrew.[9] The withdrawal, a step taken to preserve harmony, was not typical of what was to follow. With the passage of years, campaigns for the Centro officerships, often involving several student parties and their newspapers, developed into contests that were usually heated. The Centro officers, elected each November, became, in effect, the student body officers.

As the younger founders of the Centro reached their last school year they became eligible for the presidency. José Carlos de Macedo Soares was president from March 1905 (when the school year began) until March 1906, and Joaquim de Souza Pinheiro was elected to succeed him. Among the others who started serving in March 1906 were Vice President César Lacerda de Vergueiro, First Orator Victor Konder, and Second Orator Waldemar Ferreira.[10]

César Lacerda de Vergueiro, a Centro founder during his first year at school, was responsible for establishing the Centro's inalienable fund (*patrimônio inalienável*).[11] The fund helped keep the Centro Onze de Agosto flourishing, unlike most of the student associations, and eventually the Centro became known as the oldest student association in Brazil—as Pedro Dória pointed out in 1939. In accordance with the Centro's statutes of 1913 (which were still in effect in 1946), the *patrimônio inalienável* was to receive the income from subscriptions to *O Onze de Agosto* and was to invest it and its other revenues in shares of two railroad companies: the Paulista and the Mogiana.[12]

As vice-president, César Lacerda de Vergueiro took over the presidency on May 9, 1906, and was acting president until he became a fifth-year student, when he served as elected president in a term that ended in March 1908. The first orator, on the victorious slate he headed, was author Monteiro Lobato's close friend Ricardo Gonçalves, the poet who committed suicide.[13]

Throughout his life César Vergueiro, an unmarried man, continued to have a deep interest in the Centro Onze de Agosto. Like José Carlos de Macedo Soares, he became a benefactor of the Centro and exercised the right, given to all former Centro presidents, to vote in the elections for officers. César Vergueiro's other great interest was in the Partido Republicano Paulista (PRP), which dominated the state during the Old Republic, which lasted until 1930.[14]

During the 1909–1910 contest for the Brazilian presidency, César Vergueiro participated, with the PRP majority, in the unsuccessful *civilista* campaign for the election of Rui Barbosa. Rui's opponent, Marshal Hermes da Fonseca, was not popular in São Paulo but did have the support of influential Paulista Congressman Pedro de Toledo and a few law students (including Aureliano Leite).[15] Following the marshal's election, César Vergueiro was at the forefront in organizing *centros antiintervencionistas*, a part of the PRP program to prevent federal intervention in the state. The program, which brought a French military mission to build the state police (Força Pública) into a small army, succeeded in part because of negotiations of the marshal's brother and because the PRP adroitly picked a new governor, former Brazilian President Francisco de Paula Rodrigues Alves, who was well regarded by the marshal.[16]

César Vergueiro served as federal congressman almost continually from 1914 until Congress was closed as an aftermath of the 1930 revolution. He was a director of *Correio Paulistano*, organ of the PRP, and in the late 1930s was state justice secretary. A founder of the PSD (Partido Social Democrático) in 1945, César Vergueiro was elected federal senator in the early 1950s, thus following in the footsteps of his grandfather, Senator and Imperial Regent Nicolau Pereira dos Campos Vergueiro.[17]

5. The Liga Nacionalista (founded in 1917)

By 1915, an *O Estado de S. Paulo* article explains, the student body at the São Paulo Law School had become divided between a conservative wing and an activist one, which wanted to have the students "assume the same responsibilities as in other historic moments, such as those of the Abolition and the Republic." Among the leaders of the activist wing were the sons of Júlio Mesquita, the director of *O Estado de S. Paulo*: Júlio de Mesquita Filho ("Julinho") and his more athletic brother, one year younger, Francisco Mesquita ("Chiquinho").[1]

The activist wing found its opportunity when the 50-year-old poet Olavo Bilac returned from war-torn Europe in 1915 with ideas for revitalizing Brazil. Bilac, after getting in touch with law school Chaveiro Júlio de Mesquita Filho, expressed his ideas in a speech at the *arcadas* on October 9, 1915.[2] "The fervent appeal to youth by the great poet and patriot" was made in "words of magic," according to *O Estadinho*, the afternoon paper on which Júlio de Mesquita Filho was getting his training in journalism. Bilac called for a renewal of faith in Brazil and argued for obligatory military service as "the first step for convalescence." Denying that he was a militarist, he said that his recommendation was "the best way to combat the possible supremacy of the military caste."[3]

Olavo Bilac's appeal to students to "close ranks around the national banner" was the start of a nationalist campaign in São Paulo that was led by the law school and assisted by other colleges and *O Estado de S. Paulo*. An inscription was begun for volunteers, who would train at the army's Gericinó Camp near Rio de Janeiro. The forty places allotted to volunteers from São Paulo had to be increased to three hundred to accommodate the volunteers from the law shool, the Escola Politécnica, and the Faculdade de Medicina.[4]

Bilac continued giving speeches calling for a stronger Brazil. Similar calls were made by Afonso Arinos de Melo Franco, the writer in Minas, and Miguel Calmon, a young former federal cabinet minister from Bahia who had recently visited Europe. Miguel Calmon, with help from Supreme Court Justice Pedro Lessa (a *bucheiro*), established the Liga de Defesa Nacional in Rio on Independence Day (September 7) in 1916.[5] Brazilian President Wenceslau Brás (another *bucheiro*) was named president of the Liga, and on November 10, 1916, the army took steps to implement obligatory military service.[6] When Olavo Bilac was in São Paulo again in March 1917, the state directorship of the Liga de Defesa Nacional was set up with Governor Altino Arantes (a *bucheiro*) as president. In April, Arantes named Antônio Prado, PRP leader Carlos de Campos, and Júlio Mesquita to direct the work.[7]

In the meantime a more dynamic movement, the Liga Nacionalista, was being developed among students by São Paulo law instructor Frederico Vergueiro Steidel after Olavo Bilac advanced the idea in a letter written to Júlio de Mesquita Filho on October 25,

1915.[8] Steidel, 50 years old, was a grave and severe instructor, thin and often stooped, whose education had been achieved with outside financial help due to the poverty of his family. He was a Freemason and a Bucha leader and considered the Liga Nacionalista a project whereby the Bucha could bring outstanding students together to carry out a large-scale patriotic and humanitarian movement of liberal views.[9] When the Liga Nacionalista was launched, early in 1917, Steidel became its president. The vice-presidencies went to leaders of the Landmanschaft (of the Escola Politécnica) and the Jugendschaft (of the Faculdade de Medicina). Bucheiro José Carlos de Macedo Soares was named treasurer, and law student Abelardo Vergueiro César, also a *bucheiro*, was named secretary. The Liga Nacionalista's large directive board included Conselheiro Antônio Prado; law Professor Luís Barbosa da Gama Cerqueira; lawyers Waldemar Ferreira, Antônio de Sampaio Dória, Spencer Vampré, Roberto Moreira, and Prudente de Morais Neto; *O Estado de S. Paulo*'s Júlio de Mesquita Filho and Plínio Barreto; law student Joaquim Sampaio Vidal; and Arnaldo Vieira de Carvalho Filho, founder of the Faculdade de Medicina and the Jugendschaft. It also included the Centro Onze de Agosto president, tall, handsome Antônio Pereira Lima, who made ends meet during his law school days by working at *O Estado de S. Paulo.*[10] Paulo Duarte, a law student during the early and mid-1920s, describes the Liga Nacionalista as the "official organ" of the Bucha.[11]

Like the Liga de Defesa Nacional, the Liga Nacionalista advocated military preparation, but it showed more interest in political reform and in dealing with Brazil's widespread illiteracy and disease. Its program for ending electoral fraud contained the suggestion that voting be secret and obligatory, as proposed by Waldemar Ferreira at a July 1917 Liga Nacionalista meeting and as frequently advocated by Liga board member Mário Pinto Serva. As a part of its *campanha do voto secreto*, which continued with vigor into the early 1920s, the Liga released many publications, among them speeches by PRP politicians Roberto Moreira and João Sampaio. It also persuaded citizens to register for voting in elections.[12]

The Liga Nacionalista gave extensive assistance to Paulistas struck down by the devastating epidemic of grippe in 1918, and it expressed the hope that the teaching of Brazilian history and the Portuguese language would be required of foreign private schools in Brazil.[13] A night school at which law students taught reading and writing to the less fortunate had already been set up by the law school's recently established Grêmio Literário Álvares de Azevedo, and this educational project, the idea of student Paulo Nogueira Filho, became such a successful part of the program of the Liga Nacionalista that it was later described by Pedro Lessa as "the most precious jewel of the Liga Nacionalista."[14]

To promote civic education, in 1919 the Liga Nacionalista published (with a preface by Steidel) a manual, *O que o cidadão deve saber*, by Antônio de Sampaio Dória, an important *bucheiro* who had graduated from the *arcadas* in 1908 after coming from the northeastern state of Alagoas. Sampaio Dória began teaching at the law school in 1919, and in 1920 he was appointed state director of public education by the new governor, *bucheiro* Washington Luís Pereira de Souza. In this post Sampaio Dória was able to increase considerably the enrollment in public schools, thus achieving a goal of the Liga Nacionalista.[15]

With Brazil's declaration of war against Germany in October 1917, following the sinking of Brazilian ships by the Germans, the students belonging to the Liga Nacionalista were critical of PRP federal Congressman José Valois de Castro, who had abstained from voting for war and whom they considered pro-German. When the PRP nominated him in 1918 to fill a vacancy in the state senate, the Liga Nacionalista embarked on a political campaign by presenting an opposition candidate: erudite medical doctor Luís Pereira Barreto, who had presided at the Congress of Brazilian Youth (held in 1917 at the suggestion of Centro Onze de Agosto President Antônio Pereira Lima and Liga Nacionalista Secretary Abelardo Vergueiro César). The Pereira Barreto election campaign, solidly backed by *O Estado de S. Paulo*, was notable for the enthusiastic work of young Liga Nacionalista members. But the candidate of the PRP's dominant political machine was declared the victor.[16]

6. Student Opposition to the Liga Nacionalista and the Bucha (1918–1927)

Law student Paulo Nogueira Filho, member of a wealthy family well known in sugar-producing and PRP circles, participated actively in the Liga Nacionalista's unsuccessful campaign for Pereira Barreto. Although Nogueira Filho belonged to the Bucha,[1] he became a leader of a movement at the *arcadas* to protest the domination of the Liga Nacionalista by Steidel and his group of *bucheiros*. Discussing the Liga's directorship at the *arcadas*, and the way it was chosen, Nogueira Filho has written that the *oniscientes* (omniscients) of the Liga, considering themselves omnipotent and "possessors of all the virtues," advocated the secret vote "for external use only" and gave no attention to the social question despite the workers' general strike in São Paulo in 1917.[2]

The Steidel group represented only a minority of the students. This became clear late in 1917 with the selection of a successor to Centro President Antônio Pereira Lima, who was about to graduate and become a *promotor público* (prosecuting attorney) in the northeast of the state.[3] The slate of the Steidel group, headed by Joaquim Sampaio Vidal, was defeated by the so-called *plebeus* (who described the losers as "the aristocrats").[4]

The election of the next year occurred after the federal government decreed that, in view of the widespread grippe of 1918, students would be promoted without having to pass examinations. The Steidel group did not make itself popular when it ruled that students associated with the Liga Nacionalista should nevertheless take the exams. While dissidents complained that the ruling had been reached undemocratically, the Centro presidency was won late in 1918 by Antônio Carlos de Abreu Sodré, who had reservations about the Steidel group.

In January 1919, after the Steidel group took steps to expel from the Liga Nacionalista all students who had refused to take the examinations, Abreu Sodré was one of five newly elected Centro officers who joined Nogueira Filho, Cândido Mota Filho, and Osvald de Andrade in signing a manifesto in which sixty young men who had worked for the Liga attacked Steidel and left the Liga. Steidel was quickly defended by *O Estado de S. Paulo* and in a manifesto signed by such Liga stalwarts as Antônio Pereira Lima, Abelardo Vergueiro César, Antônio de Sampaio Dória, Armando de Sales Oliveira, Plínio Barreto, Waldemar Ferreira, Luís de Toledo Piza Sobrinho, Nestor Rangel Pestana, Roberto Moreira, Mário Pinto Serva, João Sampaio, Arnaldo Vieira de Carvalho Filho, Júlio Mesquita, Francisco Mesquita, and 50-year-old law Professor Reynaldo Porchat.[5]

Antônio Carlos de Abreu Sodré was a successful "president of conciliation."[6] When he reviewed the work over which he presided in 1919, he spoke of the campaign of the Centro and the Liga Nacionalista to raise funds for a monument to honor Olavo Bilac, who had died in December 1918, and a campaign of the Centro against alcoholic drinks.[7] Unlike Pereira Lima, Abreu Sodré was not in robust health; he suffered from tuberculosis. Some felt that his decision, upon graduation, to take the posts of *promotor público* in Olímpia and Botucatu, in the state's interior, was influenced by his hope that the altitude there would provide a healthy climate.

Abreu Sodré's successor as Centro de Agosto president, Alcides de

Araujo Sampaio, was chosen in a divisive election, which revived the squabbles between the *partido de cima* (ruling party) and the *partido de baixo*. But starting with the election of Rafael Corrêa de Sampaio Filho in 1920, student politics became calm for several years because they were so completely dominated by Antônio Gontijo de Carvalho. *Bucheiro* Gontijo de Carvalho, a defender of Steidel and the Liga Nacionalista, was a short, thin student from Minas who never sought office himself and who ran a machine that presided over the distribution of favors, such as railroad passes. In his pockets he carried lists of students and copies of speeches of Rui Barbosa.[8]

In 1923 Gontijo de Carvalho helped organize the law students in a movement of support for Joaquim Francisco de Assis Brasil, who was combating the questionable reelection of Antônio Augusto Borges de Medeiros to a fifth term as governor of Rio Grande do Sul. Late in that year Gontijo de Carvalho became the law school *chaveiro*, receiving the famous key from his predecessor (Frederico Martins da Costa Carvalho) at the traditional annual Festa da Chave (Key Celebration), sponsored by the Bucha. He has been described as wise and honorable, and as an unselfish young Machiavelli, deeply "devoted to the cause of his friends."[9]

In 1923, as in 1918–1919, a group of students directed attacks against Steidel. The professor, who had received tenure in 1919 (becoming a *professor catedrático*), was accused of playing a role in Centro Onze de Agosto politics and of contributing to the 1922 election of Centro President Aguinaldo de Melo Junqueira (candidate of Gontijo de Carvalho and the Liga) by using a political machine, which, like the PRP, promised positions in government departments controlled by its friends. In 1923, after Aguinaldo de Melo Junqueira was criticized for ignoring the opposition's complaints, a Centro assembly was called to discuss Steidel and the Liga. Fist fights broke out.[10]

Anti-Bucha law student Paulo Duarte, who considered Gontijo de Carvalho "spiteful, despotic, insolent, and not intelligent,"[11] directed the opposition newspaper at the *arcadas*, *A Chave*, from the time of its organization, in November 1923, until his graduation, late in 1926. *A Chave* wrote that the Liga Nacionalista had failed to raise its voice against Brazilian President Artur Bernardes' authoritarian acts, such as the extension of the state of siege.[12] *A Chave* also complained that Aguinaldo de Melo Junqueira had telegraphed his support to Bernardes, a *bucheiro*, on the ground that the Centro owed him favors.[13] When federal Congressman César Lacerda de Vergueiro obtained contributions from politicians for the Centro's *patrimônio inalienável*, Paulo Duarte, writing in *A Chave*, argued that this made it impossible for the Centro to censure reprehensible acts that might be committed by those politicians.[14]

According to the irreverent Paulo Duarte, Odecio Bueno de Camargo, Aguinaldo's successor in the Centro presidency, was a perfumed youth, unable to utter two words without committing three grammatical mistakes, who owed his election to his father being state finance secretary. On December 17, 1923, Duarte and his friends, seeking to reduce the prestige of the Bucha and its "Pharisees," held the first of a series of annual *festas* in opposition to the Festa da Chave. At the new *festa*, the Festa da Banana, a decorated specimen of "the national fruit, symbol of academic eminence," was passed from an outstanding fifth-year student, the *bananeiro*, to his successor.[15]

The Oposição Acadêmica, defended by *A Chave*, was unable to dislodge the candidates of the Situação Acadêmica until after October 26, 1925, when Centro members, by a 79-to-19 vote, adopted the *voto secreto* for Centro elections.[16] In the election of November 22, 1925, the Oposição's Afonso Martins Ribeiro (having been chosen democratically at a *prévia*, or nominating meeting, of Oposição members) won the Centro presidency by defeating the Situação's Paulo Mesquita (the vote was 118 to 115), and Paulo Duarte was elected first orator.[17] The Bucha lost again a year later when the Oposição, now calling itself the Antigo Oposição (Former Opposition), elected track star Joviro Gonçalves Foz to the Centro presidency in a victory over the Partido Acadêmico (which the winners described as the "*antigo situacionismo*").[18] During a somewhat heated assembly, at which Foz took over the Centro presidency, outgoing President Afonso Martins Ribeiro, in a reference to the Bucha, replied to a question by stating that no member of his party, the Antigo Oposição, was affiliated with a certain secret society that had "exercised an evil influence among the students."[19]

7. The End of the Liga Nacionalista (1924)

In 1924 the Liga Nacionalista ran into more serious trouble than that given by law students. The trouble developed during an uprising in São Paulo by military rebels, known as *tenentes*, who sought to reform political and electoral ways and depose Brazilian President Artur Bernardes (1922–1926), a native of Minas Gerais.

During three weeks in July 1924 the rebels controlled the city of São Paulo. Despite the reformist program of the rebels, Júlio de Mesquita Filho informed their chief, Isidoro Dias Lopes, that "my father cannot agree with a movement that is based simply on the force of arms; he is a *civilista*" (civilian-minded person).[1] Both Júlio Mesquita and São Paulo Commercial Association President José Carlos de Macedo Soares (first treasurer of the Liga Nacionalista) rejected suggestions of the revolutionaries that they serve on a three-member board to govern the state in the absence of Governor Carlos de Campos, who had fled from the state's capital.[2]

Led by Professor Steidel, the Liga Nacionalista issued declarations condemning shootings by the rebels and the subsequent bombardments of the city, by forces loyal to Bernardes, that were "killing women and children and others unconnected with the political struggle." The Liga and Macedo Soares were among those who set to work to relieve the suffering of the Paulistas by keeping hospitals operating, providing shelter, evacuating civilians, handling traffic problems, and working with the rebel leaders about such matters. Student Paulo Duarte, at the request of Macedo Soares, organized a Brigada Acadêmica, of about two hundred students, to help supply police protection during the emergency. Like Duarte, the Liga's Abelardo Vergueiro César assisted Macedo Soares.[3]

After rebel chief Isidoro agreed that his cannons would not be used to cause damage in the city, a discussion by Liga leaders (including Steidel, Macedo Soares, João Sampaio, Roberto Moreira, Professor Reynaldo Porchat, and Joaquim Sampaio Vidal) resulted in the formation of a commission to negotiate with the federal government. For the commission (made up of Archbishop Duarte Leopoldo e Silva, Mayor Firmiano Pinto, Steidel, Júlio Mesquita, and Macedo Soares), Steidel drew up a telegram that asked President Bernardes to call off the federal bombardment, but the response from Rio was unfavorable. Rebel chief Isidoro, cooperating with Macedo Soares, agreed to release imprisoned fire fighters following a devastating blaze at the Crespi textile plant caused by the federal bombardment.[4]

Federal planes, which had been dropping bombs on São Paulo, dropped leaflets in which the war minister called on the Paulistas to save themselves from a new, intense artillery bombardment by withdrawing from the city. This withdrawal of the remaining 400,000 people (the normal population was over 700,000) was impossible, and so Macedo Soares, after negotiating with Isidoro, appealed on July 27 to the federals to accept Isidoro's offer to seek a peaceful settlement under which the rebels of 1922 and 1924 would receive complete amnesty. After the federals ignored the offer, Isidoro and his revolutionaries departed from the city.[5]

The negotiations of Paulistas with the rebels were regarded with disfavor by the Bernardes government and it was irked further because, after the rebels fled, *O Estado de S. Paulo* and other São Paulo dailies criticized the behavior of the victorious Bernardes troops in the city. Early in August, Júlio Mesquita and Macedo Soares were arrested and transferred to Rio for questioning. *O Estado de S. Paulo,* like the more recently founded *Folha de S. Paulo,* was forced to suspend publication. On August 7 President Bernardes issued a decree that closed the Liga Nacionalista of São Paulo for six months for having carried out "acts harmful to the public good."[6]

With these events, the law students separated into three groups. One group favored the *tenente* rebels (who had gone west to the Paraná River), and a second group called for profound, but nonviolent, changes in Brazil. A small third group, made up of friends and relatives of members of the Bernardes administration, joined like-minded students at the Escola Politécnica, Faculdade de Medicina, and Escola de Engenharia Mackenzie in publishing a message to express the students' satisfaction at "the reestablishment of order" carried out by Governor Carlos de Campos. As the message bore the signature of the Diretoria do Centro XI de Agosto, a group of law students issued a manifesto repudiating the message.[7]

Macedo Soares, accused of various "crimes," including the effort to negotiate an amnesty for rebels,[8] was finally set at liberty in Rio on September 22, 1924. The 71 São Paulo law students who signed a telegram, to tell him of their pleasure, represented a large part of the student body of 293 since about 100 students seldom frequented the *arcadas.* But the Centro Onze de Agosto *diretoria,* at that time still in the hands of the Situação Acadêmica, was cautious. It had not protested the arrests of Mesquita, of Macedo Soares (its former president), or of a law student who had signed a prorebel bulletin, nor had it protested the closing of the Liga Nacionalista. When Centro President-elect Odecio Bueno de Camargo (chosen in November 1924 to succeed Mário Tavares Filho) withdrew from a law student commission headed by Paulo Duarte, which was preparing to welcome Macedo Soares on his return to São Paulo, *A Chave* found one more reason to attack the Situação Acadêmica.[9]

The São Paulo state government called for a prolegality rally at the same hour and place scheduled for the Macedo Soares reception. Then Macedo Soares advised Paulo Duarte that he was revising his plans, leaving them indefinite, so that no welcoming meeting could be held for him. But, even so, he was rearrested in Rio before he could leave for São Paulo and was forced to depart for Europe.[10]

In Congress *bucheiro* César Lacerda de Vergueiro sought to defend the government of Bernardes, who, as one of the Bucha's Council of

According to Paulo Duarte, the PD "inaugurated political *caravanas* [caravans] and placards in Brazil."[11] *Caravanas* of a nonpolitical nature had for years been a part of the law school life, with their *embaixadas* (embassies) of student envoys making speaking trips to Brazilian cities and towns, and in 1927 a particularly elaborate law school Caravana Acadêmica do Centenário was organized to spread the word about the one-hundredth anniversary of the school.[12] Political *caravanas* had been a feature of the Luís Pereira Barreto campaign undertaken by many São Paulo students in 1918. But the *caravanas democráticas* of the PD, which set out on July 14, 1927, to visit each of the state's 243 municipalities, were the most ambitious that Brazil had ever seen.[13]

In September 1927 the PD turned itself into a national party by forming a new directorship that included some opposition congressmen from the federal district and Rio Grande do Sul, and then, in February 1928, Waldemar Ferreira and Paulo Nogueira Filho participated in a *caravana* that visited Rio Grande do Sul to strengthen ties with the oppositionist Partido Libertador, headed by Joaquim Francisco de Assis Brasil (a law school classmate of Júlio Mesquita). With Assis Brasil, Nogueira Filho went on to Buenos Aires to call on exiled *tenentes*, such as former army Captain Luís Carlos Prestes, who had been involved in uprisings against the government of President Bernardes. But upon returning to São Paulo, Nogueira found the PD leaders in no mood for revolution.[14]

In 1929 Brazilian President Washington Luís Pereira de Souza (1926–1930) picked São Paulo Governor Júlio Prestes de Albuquerque, a fellow *bucheiro* and PRP leader, to be the official candidate for president in the election of March 1930. Rio Grande do Sul Governor Getúlio Vargas, presidential candidate of the Aliança Liberal, offered a program that included points favored by the PD, such as the secret vote, the right of political minorities to have representation, and amnesty for all the rebels of the 1920s. Law Professor Luís Barbosa da Gama Cerqueira, president of the PD, was ill on August 31, 1929, when the party met to decide whether to support the Aliança Liberal, and therefore another law professor, PD Vice President José Joaquim Cardoso de Melo Neto, presided. By a vote of 341 to 3, the PD leaders chose to support the Aliança Liberal.[15]

At the São Paulo Law School, 18-year-old Roberto Victor Cordeiro, a second-year student whose family roots lay in Rio Grande do Sul, helped organize the Partido Liberal Acadêmico to represent those among the law school's 685 students who opposed the PRP's domination of Brazil.[16]

9. Law School Reaction to João Pessoa's Assassination (August 1930)

Professor Waldemar Ferreira has referred with pride to the reaction at the law school to the news of the assassination in July 1930 of João Pessoa, Vargas' running mate in the Aliança Liberal's unsuccessful bid to unseat the establishment at the ballot boxes in March.[1] The reaction was expressed strongly on August 7 and has been recalled vividly by Hermann de Morais Barros, a student who participated in the oft-cited conflicts between students and police on that day.[2]

The protest against the assassination began with speeches in the morning, near the statue of José Bonifácio, o Moço, which stood on an elegant pedestal in the Largo de São Francisco, a few meters from the majestic door of the two-story law school building. By the time of the final, inflaming speech of Centro First Orator Romeu de Andrade Lourenção, the approximately one hundred students had been joined by almost as many applauding bystanders.[3]

The police, lurking in large numbers next to the nearby Empresa Funerária Rodovalho, had persuaded some of the students to agree that no march would follow the rally. Nevertheless, student José Augusto Costa, declaring that he had made no agreement, seized the school's Brazilian flag and started to lead a march. The police, using their billies, battled the students. When the students finally withdrew into the school building, many were aching and in torn clothes. The flag was in tatters and its pole was broken.

Paulo de Almeida Sales and Hermann de Morais Barros were chosen to accept the invitation of two police *delegados* to negotiate in front of the school. Despite a wary attitude, Paulo was grabbed, forced into a police car, and driven away. Hermann, after exchanging blows with the police in a vain effort to save Paulo, reached the shelter of the school, which by then was crowded with students, their teachers, and friends and relatives, many of whom had entered through a basement side door on Riachuelo Street. Colleagues of the politically dominant PRP joined the resistance against the police, represented by a platoon of cavalrymen and a large group of infantrymen near the school.[4]

Early in the afternoon, students broke into the school's *sala do tiro de guerra* (military training room), where they found three hundred rifles, bayonets, and boxes of munitions, but the cartridges turned out to be harmless imitations for use in practice. Nevertheless, while Hermann de Morais Barros and orator Romeu de Andrade Lourenção left the building to throw stones at the cavalry troop, the harmless weapons were brandished threateningly at the windows and central door. When they were discharged, the police retreated in disorganization, and the students and their friends occupied the nearby Largo do Ouvidor and several streets. They were acclaimed by the people.[5] Many rejoiced at the withdrawal of police *delegado* Laudelino de Abreu, a law school graduate of December 1919 who had made a name for himself torturing prisoners in the dungeons of Cambuci prison in 1924.[6]

After the police brought reinforcements to the neighborhood, the students retreated to the *arcadas*, and the law school director, Antônio Januário Pinto Ferraz, telephoned the general barracks of the army's Second Military Region for help. He explained to army First Lieutenant Euryale de Jesus Zerbine that the school, property of the federal government, needed protection.[7]

Half an hour later the students hailed the arrival of a small truck bringing a combat group of well-armed Military Region soldiers. While the soldiers set about guarding the school's main door, students pilfered cartridges from them and loaded the school's rifles. Former student Aureliano Leite, and others who had joined the school's defenders, also supplied arms and munitions.

The impetuous Romeu Lourenção and several schoolmates, making their way toward unpaved Senador Paulo Egídio Street, hurled stones at the police cavalry. Using pistols, the cavalrymen attacked the school. A shot wounded army Second Lieutenant Wallenstein de Mendonça in the hand while he waved his arms and called on the police to suspend the attack. The battle went on, with the students protected behind windows, firing real cartridges. An army sergeant was seriously wounded in the thigh, and a soldier, João Villela, was killed. Student Antônio Grassi Mamana, wounded in the knee, was helped over a high wall (a difficult feat, due to his weight) and driven by colleagues Aloisio Ramalho Foz and Francisco de Morais Barros to a doctor on São Bento Street.

The police, suffering the most wounds, finally retreated down José Bonifácio Street, leaving a few riderless horses behind. Students celebrated at the Praça do Patriarca, where people cheered them with cries of "Viva São Paulo."[8]

During the evening the law school faculty met with state government officials, and then, at night, the students who had been involved were summoned to the school's ornate *salão nobre* to face faculty members, dressed in their robes. Pinto Ferraz, the kindly school director,[9] called on Professor Waldemar Ferreira to speak. The professor, seated next to student Paulo de Almeida Sales (recently released by the authorities), explained with emotion that state officials had "ended up by understanding the legitimate reaction of the students."[10]

During the meeting the students were given the tattered remains of the Brazilian flag, which the police had seized earlier. They decided to place the remains around a pedestal, in the *salão nobre,* that supported a statue of the Barão do Rio Branco. Waldemar Ferreira, resuming his statement, expressed regret for the violence and stressed his admiration for the courage of the students "defending the traditions of our beloved Faculdade de Direito." "Return to your homes," he concluded, "with the certainty that you have fulfilled your duty." His point of view was shared by the other professors.[11]

The August 7 clashes with the police were discussed at a Centro Onze de Agosto meeting on August 11. Centro President José Edgard Pereira Barreto called on João Batista de Arruda Sampaio, one of the speakers on the morning of the seventh, to recount the events of that day. Paulo Marzagão, another who spoke on the seventh, introduced a resolution lamenting the death of soldier João Villela. Paulo Lauro, second orator of the Centro, proposed that a commission visit wounded student Antônio Grassi Mamana. The resolution presented by Paulo de Almeida Sales called on *O Onze de Agosto* to express the students' appreciation of support received from the press and people of São Paulo.

It was during the closing moments of the meeting that the students adopted the resolution of Adriano Marrey proclaiming "the free state of the Largo de São Francisco."[12]

II

São Paulo and Vargas (1930–1938)

1. An Unhappy Partido Democrático (1930–1932)

Aureliano Leite has written that the conflict at the *arcadas* on August 7, 1930, perhaps brought on the revolution of October 1930.[1] That conflict, in fact, was one of many demonstrations stirred up throughout Brazil by Aliança Liberal adherents to protest the assassination of João Pessoa. They built up popular backing for the well-planned revolution of October, which was so successful that in Rio on October 24 President Washington Luís was overthrown.

The PRP, which had been making effective use of the São Paulo police, lost control of the state capital that day. Law students were at the forefront of the invasion of the luxurious PRP headquarters in the Martinelli Building,[2] and they clashed with policemen who sought unsuccessfully to prevent groups from storming PRP-supporting newspapers. Mobs invaded the Empresa Funerária Rodovalho, on the Largo de São Francisco, and made off with coffins and wreaths, appropriate for observing the funeral of the PRP.[3]

On the next morning Professors Vicente Ráo and Braz de Souza Arruda, together with law instructors (*livres-docentes*) Mário Masagão and Honório Fernandes Monteiro, organized law students, delighted with the political turn of events, into a large emergency police contingent. Its members included Romeu Lourenção, Paulo Marzagão, Hermann de Morais Barros, Antônio Grassi Mamana, and Roberto Victor Cordeiro (organizer of the Partido Liberal Acadêmico). Paulo Duarte took the lead in signing a demand that political prisoners be released from the São Paulo prisons, and the commander of the Força Pública complied.[4]

The work of the Partido Democrático, a participant in the Aliança Liberal, would seem to have reached fruition. While law Professor Francisco Morato, head of the PD, awaited a call by victorious Getúlio Vargas to take over the São Paulo state government, his party named a state cabinet that included *O Estado de S. Paulo* Chief Editor Plínio Barreto (Justice), José Carlos de Macedo Soares (Interior),

Mastroleo, Iracema 12-02-87

PLEASE ↓ PRINT

DATE 10-21-87	QUANTITY 1
AUTHOR Dulles, John W.	
TITLE The Sao Paulo Law School & the Anti-Vargas	
PUBLISHER University of Texas Press	
PAP ☐ HB ☑	PRICE 30.00
SPECIAL INSTRUCTIONS	
0-292-77599-7	
BOOK PRICES ARE SUBJECT TO CHANGE WITHOUT NOTICE.	SL 6028
TELEPHONE NUMBER 474-6922	DEPOSIT ~~NONE~~ BALANCE
DEPOSIT NOT REFUNDABLE UNLESS BOOKS CANNOT BE DELIVERED.	

SPECIAL ORDER

WITH

UNIVERSITY CO-OPERATIVE SOCIETY
2246 GUADALUPE STREET
AUSTIN, TEXAS 78705
(512) 476-7211

SPECIAL ORDERS WILL NOT BE HELD AFTER 30 DAYS.

WE WILL CONTACT YOU AS SOON AS YOUR SPECIAL ORDER ARRIVES.

PLEASE ↓ PRINT

NAME IRACEMA MASTROLEO

ADDRESS 1630-B W 6th St.

CITY, STATE, ZIP Austin TX 78703

(THE ABOVE SHOULD BE YOUR COMPLETE MAILING ADDRESS)

F136-20M-684

7296
10/27/87

and banker José Maria Whitaker (Finance). Francisco Mesquita was named secretary of the state government. Law Professor Vicente Ráo, the son of Italian immigrants and president of the influential Institute of Lawyers of São Paulo, became chief of police. Law Professor Cardoso de Melo Neto, son-in-law of former Brazilian President Francisco de Paula Rodrigues Alves, was named mayor of São Paulo.

Although Gastão da Costa Vidigal, another law school graduate, had opposed the 1930 revolution, he was appointed director of the state bank. But Antônio Pereira Lima, a creator of the PRP's reformist Ação Nacional wing, was punished for his opposition to the 1930 revolution. He was dismissed from the command of the Guarda Civil, which he had founded in the state capital in 1926, and for a while was held under house arrest.[5]

The origin of the long struggle between the São Paulo Law School group and Getúlio Vargas had its inception even before Vargas reached Rio de Janeiro at the end of October 1930 to take over the national government. Passing through São Paulo on his way from the south, Vargas revealed plans for having the recently formed state secretariat govern together with João Alberto Lins e Barros, a *tenente* from Pernambuco, who was to have full powers "to consolidate the revolutionary work in São Paulo." Professor Morato, approached about becoming finance minister in the national cabinet, retorted that he was not seeking a job but was upholding the right of São Paulo to govern itself and was defending the position of his party, without whose help, he added, there would have been no successful revolution.[6] Whitaker became finance minister in Rio, and, therefore, the state cabinet chose Plínio Barreto as its presiding officer. But before the end of 1930 the state cabinet of Paulistas resigned in disgust (becoming known as "the secretariat of forty days") because João Alberto, appointed *interventor* in November, was running the state with the backing of the Vargas government and the *tenentes*.

João Alberto tried, without success, to govern a São Paulo agitated by press and politicians who disliked him and by the proletarian Legião Revolucionária of Miguel Costa, a *tenente* hero who headed the Força Pública. When João Alberto resigned in July 1931, Plínio Barreto, disliked by the *tenentes*, seemed to be the choice to succeed him. Students, backing Barreto, became involved in street fights with members of the Legião and the Força Pública.[7] Under these circumstances, law students Miguel Reale and José Augusto Costa, leaders of an independent Marxist movement, signed a manifesto (along with Adriano Marrey and other law students) to back Barreto. It explained that the law students favored the just demands of striking workers but that the students, and also the true Marxists, opposed the exploitation of the proletariat. The manifesto denounced professional agitators, unthinking Communists, and others who sought to stir up the workers against the student class, "the only class that has defended them when necessary."[8]

Unable to convince Rio that Miguel Costa's activities should be curbed, Plínio Barreto stepped aside. Those who did succeed João Alberto as *interventores*, trying to run the state on behalf of the central government, had no success in reducing the manifestations in São Paulo that revealed loathing for the Vargas regime, ruling the country without a Congress or a constitution. The Paulistas' feelings were reflected at the mass demonstrations inspired by such organizations as the Liga Paulista Pro-Constituinte, formed early in 1932 by law students and headed by Roberto Victor Cordeiro. Aureliano Leite has recalled that "the young people of the *academias*, notably those of the law school, played a large role in stimulating the masses in the streets."[9] Such was the hatred of the Vargas regime in São Paulo that in February 1932 the two old enemies, the PD and the PRP, decided to join forces against it.

2. São Paulo's Unsuccessful Constitutionalist Revolution (1932)

Defying the government in Rio, São Paulo politicians in May 1932 formed a state cabinet of their own liking, which included Professor Waldemar Ferreira in the key post of justice secretary and Joaquim Sampaio Vidal as head of the Department of Municipalities. Wealthy Gofredo da Silva Telles was chosen mayor of the state capital.

A multitude, stirred by this show of independence from Rio and by the oratory of Ibrahim Nobre, attacked the headquarters of a pro-*tenente* group and was shot at. Among those who died were some young men who were promptly honored by the use of the initials of their names, MMDC, as the name of a secret *guarda paulista*. The twenty-seven organizers of the MMDC included Joaquim Sampaio Vidal, Aureliano Leite, Paulo Nogueira Filho, Roberto Victor Cordeiro, Antônio Pereira Lima, Francisco Mesquita, Júlio de Mesquita Filho, Prudente de Morais Neto, medical Professor Antônio Carlos Pacheco e Silva, and Hermann de Morais Barros (whose uncle Paulo de Morais Barros was working for a revolution against Vargas).[1]

The secret MMDC, setting up groups in each sector of the city, attracted several thousand members, many of them students who were prepared to use revolvers to protect São Paulo's leaders against supporters of the "oppressors." MMDC military training, directed by Força Pública Captain Antônio Pietscher, was soon coordinated with the anti-Vargas military conspiracy, which Paulista leaders placed in the hands of veteran revolutionary Isidoro Dias Lopes.[2]

The outbreak of São Paulo's Revolução Constitucionalista against the Vargas regime began on July 9, 1932. That evening about fifteen hundred MMDC members, coming from different sectors of the city, met in front of the law school. Professor Waldemar Ferreira, visiting the Largo de São Francisco, was so moved by the acclaim he received, and the "heroic calls for insurrection," that he resolved to transfer his title from secretary of justice to secretary of war.[3]

Many MMDC members spent the night at the school after student Roberto Victor Cordeiro opened the building's doors. On the next morning, Sunday, July 10, MMDC leaders, establishing their headquarters at the *arcadas*, were joined by Força Pública Captain Romão Gomes. Gomes incorporated some of the MMDC groups, such as that led by recent law school graduate Hermann de Morais Barros, into his own volunteer unit, which was headquartered at the Várzea do Campo barracks and was also full of students. Thus the first Batalhão Paulista da Milícia Civil, an auxiliary of the Força Pública, was formed. (Eventually Romão Gomes' *coluna invicta*—unconquered column—marched north and fought the Mineiros in operations that brought distinction to Herbert Levy, a 20-year-old civilian whom Gomes placed in command of five thousand men.)[4]

Immediately following the outbreak of the Revolução Constitucionalista, Roberto Victor Cordeiro, as president of the Liga Paulista Pro-Constituinte, issued a proclamation calling on all able-bodied Paulistas "who truly love São Paulo" to go to the *arcadas* to receive arms and become incorporated into the fighting forces. The *arcadas* became, on July 11, a busy and sometimes confused enlistment headquarters. The teaching of law was suspended.[5]

The congestion at the *arcadas* was so great that the school director, José de Alcântara Machado d'Oliveira, proposed that other locations be used for some of the mobilization work. MMDC groups therefore found housing elsewhere—some at the Clube Comercial. At the suggestion of Dr. Pacheco e Silva, the principal MMDC office was moved from the *arcadas* to the Forum Cível.[6]

One law school instructor, Manuel Francisco Pinto Pereira, became a simple soldier in the Batalhão Voluntários de Piratininga, which former Centro Onze de Agosto President Antônio Pereira Lima helped organize at the *arcadas*. Most of the professors constituted a rear guard, which, on August 11, 1932, sent messages to the fighting students expressing admiration and affection and "complete confidence in the forthcoming victory of the cause of law and liberty."[7]

Francisco Mesquita, 40 years old, fought early as a volunteer in the Valley of Paraíba and then joined the Batalhão Voluntários de Piratininga. Taken prisoner on August 19 by Vargas-supporting Lieutenant Siseno Sarmento, Corporal Mesquita was sent to a prison camp on Ilha Grande. His brother Júlio concerned himself with the revolution's organization and was appointed captain on the staff of Colonel Euclides Figueiredo. Antônio Pereira Lima also fought in the Batalhão Voluntários de Piratininga.[8]

Roberto Victor Cordeiro had been elected vice-president of the Centro Onze de Agosto for 1932 but he became acting president in that eventful year and was elected president for 1933. At the outset of the civil war of 1932 he formed a student battalion, the Batalhão Acadêmico 14 de Julho and it operated in the southern sector. Antônio de Almeida Júnior writes that "the role of the Law School, whose building was immediately transformed into wartime barracks, was brilliant in all phases of the movement; and, to commemorate the bravery of its sons who fought with arms, and some of whom lost their lives in the trenches, there now stands, in the Pátio das Arcadas, the monument to the Constitutionalist Soldier."[9] Waldemar Ferreira has listed seven young men, five of them law students and two of them very recent graduates, who were killed. Most of them belonged to the Batalhão 14 de Julho.[10]

Following the military defeat of the Paulistas early in October 1932, the *Pedro I* took about one hundred of the rebellion's leaders to Recife and from there another ship took them to exile in Portugal. Together with the military leaders of the rebellion, the ship carried such civilians as Waldemar Ferreira, Francisco Morato, Paulo Nogueira Filho, Paulo Duarte, Júlio de Mesquita Filho, Francisco Mesquita, Prudente de Morais Neto, Joaquim Sampaio Vidal, and Antônio Pereira Lima. Professor Vicente Ráo, who was in Europe on a mission for the Constitutionalist Revolution, also took up forced exile in Portugal.[11]

In São Paulo, Carlos de Souza Nazareth, of the São Paulo Commercial Association, coordinated the collection of contributions that were sent to help exiles in financial difficulties. In this way Antônio Pereira Lima, spending time in exile at the temporary residence of Professor Vicente Ráo, received aid from many of his Paulista friends.[12]

3. The Constitutionalization of Brazil (1934)

General Waldomiro Lima, after helping defeat the Revolução Constitucionalista, was named *interventor* of São Paulo. For advice he turned to Plínio Salgado, who had established a Sociedade de Estudos Políticos in São Paulo and was launching his Integralista Green Shirt movement, nationalist and anti-Communist. At Salgado's suggestion the general chose, as secretary-general of the state government, intellectual José Carlos de Ataliba Nogueira, a Sociedade de Estudos Políticos member, law school graduate (1925), and Bucha opponent, who had not participated in the 1932 revolution.[1]

Waldomiro's regime was short-lived due to the outcome of the May 1933 election for representatives to the national constitutional assembly. In this election (relatively honest and with the secret vote) a resounding victory was won by the anti-Vargas Chapa Única por São Paulo Unido, a coalition of the PD and PRP. Vargas, taking this outcome into consideration, named engineer Armando de Sales Oliveira of the PD to be *interventor*. Armando, who had married a daughter of Júlio Mesquita, was president of *O Estado de S. Paulo* at the time.[2] His brothers-in-law were in exile in Portugal.

Despite the forced absence of many of the politically active São Paulo Law School professors and alumni, the school was well represented at the constitutional assembly that gathered in Rio late in 1933. Of the twenty-two members of the São Paulo *bancada* (bloc), fifteen had attended the law school, fourteen of whom had graduated.[3] Four, among them Cardoso de Melo Neto and Law School Director (1931–1935) José de Alcântara Machado d'Oliveira, were on the law school faculty. When Alcântara Machado, a PRP man who was chosen leader of the São Paulo *bancada*, raised his voice before the constitution writers in Rio to declare his pride at being "a Paulista of four hundred years,"[4] he used an expression that would long be repeated.

The São Paulo *bancada* included former Centro Onze de Agosto Presidents José Carlos de Macedo Soares and Antônio Carlos de Abreu Sodré. Abelardo Vergueiro César, another member of the *bancada*, had been *chaveiro* of the class of 1917 and had worked with his exiled classmate Antônio Pereira Lima for the Liga Nacionalista and the PRP's reformist Ação Nacional wing. During the Constitutionalist Revolution he had achieved the rank of lieutenant-colonel in the MMDC. Henrique Bayma, another law school graduate and early Liga Nacionalista supporter who won election to the constitutionalist assembly, had fought as a common soldier in the recent revolution before being held prisoner on Ilha Grande.[5]

The anti-Vargas sentiment in the São Paulo *bancada* did not prevail in the full assembly. After writing the constitution of July 1934, the assembly chose Vargas to serve as president of Brazil until May 1938. Then, with Armando de Sales Oliveira showing a willingness to cooperate with the new federal administration, Vargas picked Professor Vicente Ráo (not a "Paulista of four hundred years") to be justice minister and José Carlos de Macedo Soares to be foreign minister. The exiles returned from Portugal and not a few of them, such as the Mesquitas, Paulo Nogueira Filho, Professor Waldemar Ferreira, and Antônio Pereira Lima, helped organize a new party, the Partido Constitucionalista (PC). The PC, led by Armando de Sales Oliveira and made up largely of the PD wing of the Chapa Única and the Ação Nacional wing of the PRP, acquired *Correio de S. Paulo*, an afternoon newspaper. This PC organ attained a good circulation under the directorship of Pedro Ferraz do Amaral (former chief editor of the Partido Democrático's defunct *Diário Nacional*), Penteado Médici, and Rubens Amaral Filho.[6]

The PRP, retaining its identity, objected to cooperation with Vargas. It was defeated, although not badly, by the PC in the congressional elections of 1934. The PC, in control of the state legislature, picked Henrique Bayma, a former PD man, to be majority leader,[7] and the majority chose *interventor* Armando de Sales Oliveira to be governor of the state.

When the new federal Congress convened in 1935, Professor Cardoso de Melo Neto was chosen to head the *bancada paulista*, which included fellow professors Luís Barbosa da Gama Cerqueira (70 years old) and Waldemar Ferreira, along with Antônio Carlos de Abreu Sodré (the most-voted-for Paulista), Paulo Nogueira Filho (the second-most-voted-for Paulista), Abelardo Vergueiro César, Aureliano Leite, and others.[8] Following the unsuccessful Communist uprising of November 1935, the *bancada paulista* gave full support to the "laws of exception" sought by Vargas, Justice Minister Ráo, and the police in dealing with enemies of the regime. Nogueira Filho and Waldemar Ferreira (chairman of the Chamber of Deputies commission of constitutional matters) spoke in favor of the congressional declaration of a "state of war" that allowed the Vargas regime to imprison four opposition congressmen and one senator considered to be "far leftists."[9] In São Paulo, where the jails were filled with hundreds of "far leftists," Governor Armando de Sales Oliveira set up a Special Police force.[10]

Working as a lawyer of the São Paulo state government was Roberto Victor Cordeiro, Centro Onze de Agosto president during and after the Constitutionalist Revolution of 1932. Cordeiro had not become a member of the Bucha.[11] Although Politécnica graduate Armando de Sales Oliveira, a Landmanschaft member, had wanted him in the Bucha, some old PRP *bucheiros* had opposed Cordeiro because of his PD work and close association with Paulo Duarte, and Cordeiro, no "Paulista of four hundred years," had resented this attitude. In any case, the Bucha, torn by the splits of the late 1920s and unattractive to young PD adherents, was quite inactive in the early 1930s. The Festa da Chave was a thing of the past.[12]

Like *bucheiro* and PRP devotee César Lacerda de Vergueiro, who had also served as acting president and then president of the Centro during an earlier generation, Cordeiro was deeply interested in the law school throughout his life. He was said to have "lived for it." Unmarried (as was César Lacerda de Vergueiro), Cordeiro was considered to have a family of friends—and it was large, especially among members of the law school group. Although he did not drink alcohol, he was known as a bohemian, for he frequently participated in night life. He enjoyed discussing politics and interpreting news items. And he interested students in assuming active roles in the law school electoral parties that contested the Centro posts in November each year.[13]

Armando de Sales Oliveira still had the title of *interventor* in 1933 when his brother-in-law Júlio de Mesquita Filho, back from Portugal, persuaded him to establish the University of São Paulo. Following Armando's decree of January 25, 1934, Mesquita, Fernando de Azevedo, and Teodoro Ramos structured the university. To the already existing Colleges of Law (the largest) and Medicine and the Escola Politécnica, they added a new College of Philosophy, Sciences, and Letters and centralized the university around it. From abroad they brought outstanding professors, such as Claude Lévi-Strauss, Alfred Reginald Radcliffe-Brown, and Emmanuel De Martonne, and for years the University of São Paulo was one of the best in the world. "In a sense," Joseph L. Love writes, it was "Brazil's first real university."[14]

So that it could become a part of the university, the College of Law, formerly a federal institution, was transferred to the state of São Paulo on April 10, 1934. Thus Ernesto Leme, named professor of civil law in February 1934, became the last "federal professor" at the school. Leme, 37 years old, won his post of *professor catedrático* in a competition against Sebastião Soares de Faria and *livre-docente* Honório Fernandes Monteiro. A little later Monteiro became the first law professor named by the state of São Paulo.[15]

A controversy arose as to whether to transfer the law school physically to the location chosen for the university. Júlio de Mesquita Filho, arguing for the transfer, wrote in July 1935 that reforms made recently to the law school building had deprived it of its original "colonial baroque style, so representative of the soul of São Paulo and the students," and had given it "a pure baroque style that does not even remotely resemble our colonial art." He added that, with this remodeling of the building in the 1930s, "everything disappeared and tradition died." But, in the end, the law school remained at the old premises at the Largo de São Francisco. The building was not turned over, as some had proposed, to the municipality's Department of Culture and Recreation.[16]

4. At the *Arcadas* (1935–1937)

In the mid-1930s the law school had approximately one thousand students, compared with about five hundred each at the Politécnica and Faculdade de Medicina. The Faculdade de Filosofia was getting started, and the much respected university-level engineering school of the Mackenzie College was at a temporary low point of about twenty five students, due to the federal government's withdrawal of recognition.[1] In a typical law school class of about two hundred, perhaps six young women and one or two blacks might be found. (The first black professor, Antônio Ferreira Cesarino Júnior, was a mulatto who specialized in social legislation and started teaching at the school in 1939.)[2]

Students from the same regions, such as those from São José do Rio Preto or Ribeirão Preto in the state's interior, often remained close to each other while at law school. Those from Ribeirão Preto even had their own law school student newspaper, *Terra Vermelha*.[3]

Although very few law students came from what might be called "working-class" families, more than half of the students held jobs in order to help cover expenses and the 200 milreis (200$000) annual tuition. Many worked for newspapers or the state government, and some taught at secondary schools. Roberto Victor Cordeiro found jobs for several students at the United States consulate.[4]

The state and federal governments had good reasons to seek the support of students, and both of them gained some good will by financing trips, or *caravanas*, of student groups. São Paulo state government officials, in a position to offer favors and jobs, were often accused of influencing the outcome of elections at Centro Onze de Agosto. One of the most effective means the state had for doing this was to provide free railroad passages for students who lived outside São Paulo city and who made up about 30 percent of the law school student body. These students came from the state's interior and from other states, especially the south of Minas Gerais.[5]

Three law school student parties, one backed by Roberto Victor Cordeiro, offered candidates for the November 1935 election of Centro officerships. But the presidency was won that year by an independent, Roberto Whately, son of a Vargas-hating PRP leader of Ribeirão Preto. Independents customarily lost, and Whately's election can be attributed to the popularity that stemmed from his fame as an athlete—he was Brazil's tennis champion in the mid-1930s. One of the *cabos eleitorais* who worked for Whately's election was first-year law student Jânio Quadros.[6]

The year 1936 saw the formation of a new law school student party, the Partido Acadêmico Conservador. Its presidential candidate, Cícero Augusto Vieira, wrote the *Folha da Manhã*'s column about university life and belonged to the Bucha, which its members were trying to revive but was merely an exclusive secret organization without importance.[7] Campaigning for the Centro presidency, Cícero Augusto Vieira adopted a platform calling for the realization of an old dream, the construction of a building for housing students without much money.[8]

The Conservadores, victorious in the election, assumed their Centro posts in March 1937 and promptly examined the prospects of constructing a Casa do Estudante do Centro Acadêmico Onze de Agosto. Funds were unavailable due to the need to pay off the Centro's debts, including back rent (5:000$000 monthly) for its headquarters in the Martinelli Building (São Paulo's tallest at the time). But after months of negotiation and some assistance from 68-year-old Law School Director Francisco Morato, the city councilmen and Mayor Fábio Prado agreed to the municipality's donating a plot of land on recently opened Avenida São João to be used as the site of the Casa do Estudante. Its value was estimated at 180:000$000 (180 contos de réis, or 180 thousand milreis).[9]

In another development during the presidency of Cícero Augusto Vieira, the Centro Onze de Agosto obtained quarters of its own at the remodeled law school and moved out of the Martinelli Building. The new space, in which a bar, billiard room, and barber shop were installed, was not large, and most of the students' time was spent, as formerly, in the ample patio, which survived the remodeling of the 1930s along with the Júlio Frank mausoleum.

In the patio the students engaged in heated discussions about the extremist ideologies prominent in the mid-1930s. Plínio Salgado's anti-Communist Ação Integralista Brasileira, whose members marched in green shirts and were generally regarded as pro-fascist, had its share of advocates. They included former Marxist Miguel Reale (a prolific writer before and after he graduated in 1934), Damiano Gullo (who later directed the excellent student law school newspaper *A Balança*), and Gofredo da Silva Telles Júnior (known as "Gofredinho" to distinguish him from his father, "Gofredão," the mayor of São Paulo in 1932). Among the supporters of the Communist Party of Brazil (PCB) in 1937 were law students Antônio Costa Corrêa (who came from a working-class family and entered the school in 1937) and José Zacarias Sá Carvalho.

As the national campaign developed in 1937 for the election of a successor to Vargas, Communist law student Iturbides Almeida Serra launched a university newspaper, *Frente Democrática*. Its initial number, that of June 1937, printed a list of complaints that the regional committee of the PCB had against Armando de Sales Oliveira, a candidate for the Brazilian presidency. A couple of months later *Frente Democrática* became the organ of the Frente Nacional Democrática de São Paulo, a Communist front.[10]

The venerable *Revista "XI de Agosto"* (established in 1903 as *O Onze de Agosto*) deplored, in November 1937, "the infiltration of exotic doctrines which desire, at all costs, to set themselves up here to the detriment of our traditional characteristics of an essentially liberal nation."[11] But for the most part the *Revista "XI de Agosto"* limited itself to carrying on the strong literary tradition at the *arcadas*. It tried to appear annually in August but did not appear at all some years. In two numbers in 1937 (May and November) it presented fiction by Auro Soares de Moura Andrade, Antônio Calvo, and Germinal Feijó and the poetry of José Malanga, Jânio Quadros, and Luís Swarztman (director of *Terra Vermelha*). Ulisses Guimarães contributed a piece about author Euclides da Cunha, and André Franco Montoro discussed the "ideal man." Second-year student Antônio Sylvio Cunha Bueno reported on the law student *caravana* to Ubatuba, a São Paulo coastal town, and two pages in Spanish reminded readers that a Brazilian student delegation had attended the meeting of the Federación Universitária held in Buenos Aires in September 1937.[12]

Aspiring student writers could join the Associação Álvares de Azevedo and hope to win its prose and poetry contests, which were judged by members of the august Academia Paulista de Letras.[13] The students, too, had an *academia de letras*. Unlike the Brazilian and São Paulo *academias de letras*, each limited to forty "immortals," the Academia de Letras da Faculdade de Direito da Universidade de São Paulo (with a large turnover due to graduations) was limited to twenty-five.

Student newspapers were abundant in the weeks preceding the Centro elections, for it was then that the organs of the political parties appeared frequently. *O Conservador*, early in November 1937, pointed out that the *patrimônio inalienável* of the Centro had long remained stationary but that, while Cícero Augusto Vieira served as president, it had come to consist of the municipality's land donation as well as 1,007 shares of Paulista Railway Company stock.[14] Conservador propaganda was spread also by party workers, such as Ulisses Guimarães, Trajano Pupo Netto, and Jânio Quadros.

Two law school parties opposed the powerful Partido Acadêmico Conservador in 1937. One was the Arcadas, whose presidential candidate, André Franco Montoro, belonged to Juventude Universitária Católica (JUC)—more conservative than the JUC of the 1960s.[15] Despite propaganda published in *Arcadas*, the Arcadas candidates were all defeated.

Reação Acadêmica, the other contesting party, captured the Centro presidency. Its candidate, Joaquim Augusto Ribeiro do Valle Neto, received 316 votes compared with 293 given to the Conservadores' Nelson Fortunato de Almeida and 225 given to André Franco Montoro. Most of the posts, however, went to Conservador candidates, such as Francisco de Paula Quintanilha Ribeiro, who became second secretary, and Auro de Moura Andrade, who became first orator. Before the election, Professor Spencer Vampré described Moura Andrade as "the leader of academic oratory." *Terra Vermelha* quoted this remark and recommended that votes be split between the Reação Acadêmica and the Partido Conservador in a manner that corresponded closely to the outcome.[16]

Soon after the election, ceremonies were held at the school's João Mendes Júnior Room to honor Mayor Fábio Prado and the erect and formal Francisco Morato. The deed transferring the Avenida São João plot, signed on that occasion, called for a "permanent commission" to supervise the construction of the Casa do Estudante.

At commission meetings, Cícero Augusto Vieira argued forcefully that the railroad shares in the *patrimônio inalienável* (worth about 200:000$000) should be sold and the proceeds applied to construction of the Casa. This proposal was not adopted because commission members César Lacerda de Vergueiro and José Carlos de Macedo Soares (donors of some of the railroad shares)[17] insisted that the *patrimônio inalienável* remain intact.[18]

5. November 10, 1937

In December 1936, when Armando de Sales Oliveira decided to become the Partido Constitucionalista candidate for the Brazilian presidency, he incurred the ill will of Vargas. After he stepped aside as governor late in the month, the state was run for a week by Henrique Bayma, president of the state legislature, and then the legislature selected a new governor: law Professor José Joaquim Cardoso de Melo Neto, who had been leader of the Paulista bloc in the federal Congress.

Professor Vicente Ráo, closely associated with Armando de Sales Oliveira, left the federal Justice Ministry. José Carlos de Macedo Soares, who had resigned as foreign minister in the vain hope of becoming a strong presidential candidate with PRP support, took over the Justice post that Ráo had vacated.

A large part of the elite of São Paulo had high hopes that São Paulo would regain its national influence, lost in 1930, by the election of Armando de Sales Oliveira. Rio Grande do Sul Governor José Antônio Flores da Cunha threw his support to Armando; and so did Rio de Janeiro's popular ex-mayor, Pedro Ernesto Batista, thus disappointing Armando's chief opponent in the presidential race, northeasterner José Américo de Almeida. Congressman Paulo Nogueira Filho became head of the São Paulo propaganda organization of the União Democrática Brasileira (UDB), a new national party formed to take Armando to the presidency.[1]

By the end of the first week of November 1937 it seemed evident that Vargas, backed by the military and many state governors, planned to cancel the election. While Armando de Sales Oliveira appealed to the military to protect the ballot boxes, Waldemar Ferreira delivered a vehement speech in the Chamber of Deputies on behalf of the maintenance of democracy.[2] But on November 10 the Vargas regime called off the election and closed the federal and local legislatures. Under a new authoritarian constitution, promulgated by Vargas and his cabinet that day, the states were to be run once more (as from 1930 to 1934) by *interventores*, chosen by the national government and responsible to it.

At the law school on the morning of November 10 a *concurso* (competition) was under way to determine which of four candidates would become *professor catedrático* of judiciary penal law, and which ones would become *livres-docentes* in that discipline. During the *concurso*, one of the judges of the candidates, São Paulo law Professor Rafael Correia Sampaio, suddenly died.[3] Governor Cardoso de Melo Neto came quickly to the school. While speaking to the mourning professors and students, he gave the news, which he had just received, of the establishment of the Estado Novo—the new regime headed by Vargas.[4]

Cory Porto Fernandes, who was completing the two-year preparatory course, recalls that one person started the law school resistance movement by placing, as a protest to the news from Rio, some black cloth across a part of the school building where all could see it. He was third-year law student Francisco Morato de Oliveira, a dedicated supporter of Armando de Sales and a veteran of the anti-Vargas warfare of 1932.[5] The cloth, whether considered a sign of mourning for the loss of democracy or a professor, could not have remained in place very long. It was not there when preparatory student Antônio Cândido de Mello e Souza, shocked by the coup of November 10, went to the *arcadas* to see what the reaction was there. He found no reaction—no activity.[6] Luís Gonzaga Bandeira de Melo Arrobas Martins, who was also taking the two-year Curso Pré-Jurídico, has written that on the afternoon of November 10 one could hear "in the patio of the *arcadas* and in the corridors of the school, the first manifestations of protest, vague and imprecise because no one knew exactly what was going to happen."[7] One could hear also expressions of belief that the new strong government might be just what was needed to change Brazil for the better, and they were not limited to the Integralistas.[8]

Antônio de Almeida Júnior, who was then the state director of education, has written about the law school's "perplexed" reaction to November 10. Explaining that the school "gave the impression of a political Babel at that time of national disturbance," he also reminds us of the existence of an "amorphous mass of those who were indifferent—the neutrals of all times."[9]

The most sensational student protest occurred not at any of the University of São Paulo colleges but at the Escola Livre de Sociologia e Política, located at the Largo de São Francisco. As the Escola Livre had been founded only in 1933 by businessman and senator Roberto Simonsen, its graduation exercises held late in 1937 were its first. In the presence of Simonsen and the federal ministers of war and education (invited by Simonsen), graduating student Herbert Levy, the *coluna invicta* hero of 1932, gave a speech that called clearly for liberty and democracy and warned against statesmen "who become the instruments of their own ambitions." He received a standing ovation by his Constitucionalista Party companions and most of the other people present. *O Estado de S. Paulo*, defying the censorship recently imposed by the Estado Novo, printed the speech in full. As a result of this incident, Levy spent several days in jail immediately; his name was placed on a "black list" so that, on five other occasions, when anti–Estado Novo activity was rumored, he was among those rounded up by the police.[10]

The law school's graduating ceremonies were held on January 18, 1938. Law Professor Jorge Americano—chosen by the graduating class to be its *paraninfo*, or spokesman—was careful but suggestive in his speech. "More than ever before," he said, "it is difficult now to speak to young people. . . . Whoever utters a word cannot know what reaction it will produce in those who hear it."[11]

By this time the law school students were on their summer vacation, which began in December and lasted until early March. And more had been learned about the Estado Novo. A decree issued on December 2 banned all political parties, including Ação Integralista Brasileira (the Green Shirts). In response to another ruling of the Estado Novo, forbidding law school professors to serve concurrently as judges, Professor Mário Masagão left his post on the São Paulo state court of appeals, to which he had been appointed seven years earlier.[12]

6. Reactions of Some Paulistas (1938)

Armando de Sales Oliveira was arrested and "exiled" to a mining camp in Minas Gerais. Professor Cardoso de Melo Neto, who had favored a PC faction not led by Armando, was allowed to remain as chief executive of São Paulo (now as *interventor*) and was accused by Armando's supporters of cooperating with Vargas. Cardoso de Melo Neto's friend Gastão da Costa Vidigal, who had been a federal congressman, became state secretary of finance.[1]

Among the furious professors was Antônio de Sampaio Dória, who had served as state director of public education in the early 1920s. Defying the Vargas government, he refused to consider the 1937 Constitution worthy of study in the classroom, and, therefore, in December 1937 he gave up teaching constitutional law, choosing instead private international law. He also became vice-director of the school for the 1938 school year, at which time Spencer Vampré served as director. Whenever he could, Sampaio Dória attacked the "*carta constitucional*," as the anti-Vargas professors called the new constitution. He declared that the Estado Novo was offensive to human decency as well as to constitutional law.[2]

Antônio Carlos de Abreu Sodré, having lost his mandate when Congress was closed, opened a small law office at the Largo do Café in the center of the city of São Paulo. The office became the headquarters of the "democratic resistance in São Paulo" and a center from which recommendations went to resistance groups in other states. Resistance-minded São Paulo law students were in almost continuous contact with Abreu Sodré.[3]

Francisco Mesquita, who had been a state legislator since 1934, returned to *O Estado de S. Paulo*. He handled commercial and administrative matters of the newspaper. Júlio de Mesquita Filho (known as "the captain" by his followers) ran the newspaper, was rude to censors, and coordinated plans for Paulistas to cooperate with discontented groups elsewhere in overthrowing the Vargas regime. Outside São Paulo, plots were being developed by a circle close to Flores da Cunha (in exile in Uruguay), a few politicians of the pre-1930 regime (such as Otávio Mangabeira), disappointed Integralistas (with whom Mesquita was not very friendly), and dissatisfied military officers (especially in the navy, where Integralismo was strong). Júlio de Mesquita Filho's arrest on January 1, 1938, for hatching subversive plots, was one of seventeen times that he was arrested in the year following November 10, 1937.[4]

Júlio de Mesquita Filho found time to collaborate with his friend Paulo Duarte (a state legislator before November 10) in publishing a clandestine journal, *Brasil.* Its first number bore the dateline of Terra de Ninguém (no-man's-land), January 3, 1938, and carried a front-page photograph of the flag of São Paulo followed by a note saying that when the Estado Novo, in a symbolic flag day ceremony, burned the state flags, the first to be burned was São Paulo's flag—which had been raised in 1932 to bring "order and liberty to the entire country." Writing about Vargas, the "third-class dictator," *Brasil* asserted that treason was his only principle, and administrative, political, and intellectual dishonesty his only program. Paulo Duarte, although arrested several times, was only once in prison at the same time as Mesquita, and so during most of 1938 *Brasil* kept on making appearances—and kept on being seized by the police.[5]

Among those who lost their seats in Congress on November 10, 1937, was the Mesquitas' close friend Antônio Pereira Lima. He engaged in newspaper work and became involved in the anti–Estado Novo resistance, especially with Antônio Carlos de Abreu Sodré, Professor Waldemar Ferreira, and the law students. He also developed contacts with anti-Vargas military officers in Rio de Janeiro and elsewhere.[6]

This conspiratorial work with military plotters like former Colonel Euclides Figueiredo, hard-fighting veteran of the 1932 revolution, was also carried out by João Batista Silva Azevedo of São Paulo. Azevedo, known to resistance-minded students and others as Joca, had been highly regarded for his prowess at sports, especially rowing. After his brother was killed in the 1932 revolution, Joca got in touch with Paulo Nogueira Filho and Antônio Carlos de Abreu Sodré and became president of the Partido Constitucionalista committee in the Cambuci district. Following the establishment of the Estado Novo, Joca served as a link between civilian and military plotters.[7] He was a man of action.

On the intellectual front, journalist Pedro Ferraz do Amaral ("Pedrinho") distributed anti–Estado Novo tracts while directing the *O Estado de S. Paulo Suplemento de Rotogravura.* He was a friend of the law students and an inseparable companion of leading conspirator Paulo Nogueira Filho.[8] Nogueira Filho was occasionally confined to the *pavilhão político* (political section) of São Paulo's Tiradentes Prison, sometimes together with Júlio de Mesquita Filho, Roberto Victor Cordeiro, Antônio Pereira Lima, and Antônio Carlos de Abreu Sodré.[9]

Although ex-Colonel Euclides Figueiredo and Otávio Mangabeira remained under arrest in Rio following a plot uncovered there by the authorities in March 1938, the work went forward. Joca (João Batista Silva Azevedo) took two machine guns from Santos to Rio to strengthen an attack on Guanabara Palace, the presidential residence, to be led by Lieutenant Severo Fournier, a subordinate of Euclides Figueiredo in the 1932 revolution.[10] General José Maria Castro Júnior, who was assumed to be in charge of the insurrectional plans in Rio, told Mesquita to wait, and so the uprisings in Rio on the night of May 10–11, 1938, were not seconded in São Paulo.[11] They were unsuccessful and were followed by the arrest in Rio of over fifteen hundred individuals, many of them Integralistas. The National Security Tribunal, established in 1936 after the unsuccessful Communist uprising of 1935, had its hands full judging the new cases along with a backlog of cases against Communists.

Armando de Sales Oliveira, who had been released from his Minas internment early in May, was placed under arrest in the interior of São Paulo. The arrests of Mesquita and his followers were stepped up in order to encourage them to go abroad.

III

Early Anti–Estado Novo Manifestations (1938–1939)

1. The União Cultural Brasil–Estados Unidos (established in 1938)

Late in April 1938 Vargas replaced São Paulo Interventor Cardoso de Melo Neto with Ademar de Barros, an obscure former PRP legislator and holder of a medical degree from Rio de Janeiro. The new *interventor* quickly suspended the publication of *Diário da Noite* because it printed the facsimile of a messy note in his handwriting in order to demonstrate his "mental backwardness." Soon the city was flooded with copies of the facsimile and propaganda against the "almost illiterate" *interventor*.[1]

The administrative changes, which brought César Lacerda de Vergueiro to the post of state secretary of justice, did not augur well for the Armando de Sales Oliveira backers who had managed to retain their state government jobs under Cardoso de Melo Neto. Some of Armando's young admirers held minor jobs, which helped them get through school. Such was the case of Francisco Morato de Oliveira, the courteous fourth-year law student who became known as "Chico Boletim" because of his proclivity to issue strongly worded anti–Estado Novo leaflets. Francisco Morato de Oliveira was a conscientious government clerk. But the new regime was not concerned whether the students to whom it assigned jobs earned their pay; it did, however, expect their loyalty.[2]

Another whose position was in jeopardy was Roberto Victor Cordeiro, lawyer in the state labor department. Cordeiro, sometimes called the "Alemão" (German) because his mother, a widow in Rio de Janeiro, was of German background, had campaigned for Armando de Sales Oliveira in 1937 in Rio Grande do Sul and São Paulo. He was disliked by Ademar de Barros. As reported later by *O Estado de S. Paulo*, he continued with his "tireless struggle against the dictatorship" even after Ademar became *interventor* and César Lacerda de Vergueiro became justice secretary.[3]

In June 1938 Roberto Victor Cordeiro was among those involved in the movement to found the União Cultural Brasil–Estados Unidos (UCBEU; the Brazil–United States Cultural Union)[4]—a movement inspired in part by some professors and students who wanted to demonstrate close relations with a "champion of democracy" at a time when Vargas appeared attracted to the Axis nations. Cordeiro's close friend Horácio Cherkaski, a first-year law student brought into the União Cultural work by Cordeiro, has described the União as "our trench" and added that participation in its affairs "was a sign of opposition to the Estado Novo."[5]

The initiative for the UCBEU came from the Faculdade de Medicina, and the principal organizational work was carried out by medical Professor Antônio Carlos Pacheco e Silva, with valuable assistance from law Professor Jorge Americano. The first meetings of the organizing group took place at the Sanatório Esperança because the directors of the Faculdade de Medicina opposed having their school used for a purpose that aroused suspicion in the authorities.[6] The participating law professors were Spencer Vampré, Antônio de Sampaio Dória, Noé Azevedo, and *livre-docente* Cândido Mota Filho.

The early work was supported by the presidents of the São Paulo university students' *centros acadêmicos*.[7] And a role was played by sports enthusiast José Gomes Talarico, who, it turned out, was a personal friend of Vargas and an advocate of "reconciliation" between the Vargas regime and the nation. Talarico, although not a university student, was influential at the Faculdade de Medicina Centro Acadêmico Osvaldo Cruz, where he served as secretary (a paid job).[8] He acted for awhile as secretary general of the UCBEU, but for the most part that post was held by law school graduate Rone Amorim, a United States Consulate employee who was the UCBEU's driving force and who disliked Talarico.[9]

Following the UCBEU installation meeting at the Clube Piratininga on October 22, 1938, Pacheco e Silva, the first president of the UCBEU, was warned by the police to be careful lest "extremists take advantage of" the new organization.[10]

2. Hydrosulphuric Gas for the Dictator (July 23–24, 1938)

Throughout Brazil, Getúlio Vargas enjoyed considerable popularity among the masses, perhaps in part because he seemed to have a pleasant personality and in part because the regime established in 1930 issued decrees intended to assist the urban workers. The forced silence of the opposition to the Estado Novo, along with the work of the government's Department of Press and Propaganda (DIP), contributed to strengthening the image of the regime in the minds of many.

When Vargas left Rio in July 1938 on a trip to make speeches extolling the Estado Novo, he was still benefiting from the feeling of indignation that had followed the news of the shots fired against him and his family at Guanabara Palace during the "putsch" on the night of May 10–11, 1938. After the fiasco, the controlled press and the DIP worked overtime at applauding the outcome and downgrading the plotters.

Vargas and his speeches were well received in Minas Gerais. He went on to visit São Paulo state for the first time since he had assumed the leadership of the Brazilian government in 1930. After addressing workers in the state's interior, he traveled to the state's capital on July 23, 1938, to inaugurate the July 9 Tunnel, named in honor of São Paulo's outbreak of 1932 against Vargas.

When the Centro Onze de Agosto learned in mid-July of Vargas' forthcoming visit to the city, some of its Partido Conservador members saw an opportunity to have the Centro declare him persona non grata. This was not the wish of the Centro leadership, controlled by the Reação Acadêmica party. However, Centro President Joaquim Ribeiro do Valle Neto was sick. The anti-Vargas Conservadores kidnapped Vice President Lúcio Seabra Leal and, thus, First Orator Auro Soares de Moura Andrade, a Conservador and *bucheiro*, became acting president. With Moura Andrade's help a motion was passed declaring Vargas persona non grata.[1]

Moura Andrade and about thirty other activist anti-Vargas students, mostly from the law school, resolved to instigate several antidictatorship demonstrations in São Paulo on July 23. With assistance from Paulo Duarte and Joca (João Batista Silva Azevedo) they also made plans to disrupt the banquet and dance scheduled to be given in Vargas' honor at the Municipal Theater by Interventor Ademar de Barros. Paulo Duarte was especially helpful. With the aid of a chemist he was able to furnish the students dozens of glass capsules containing hydrosulphuric gas to be used to fill the Teatro Municipal with a foul smell.[2]

Five students were chosen by the thirty to dress in formal attire and carry out the mission. They were Ciro Savoy (president of the Grêmio Politécnico) and law students Moura Andrade, Vergniaud Gonçalves, Nelson Perroud, and Germinal Feijó.[3] Feijó had entered the law school in March 1937, not with the idea of attending classes but to agitate against the Vargas regime. His father, Roberto Feijó, an immigrant from Portugal, was a lawyer who had graduated from the São Paulo Law School in 1911. The author of *Dicionário da Questão*

Social, Roberto Feijó had been attracted first to anarchist ideas and then to the ideas of Astrojildo Pereira, founder of the Brazilian Communist Party (PCB) in 1922.[4]

The planned daytime disturbances against Vargas on July 23 did not materialize.[5] But the five students, with the capsules of *gás sulfídrico* in their pockets, succeeded in gaining admittance to the Teatro Municipal around midnight, when the elaborate champagne dinner had been consumed and the speechmaking completed. The students found themselves in a ballroom bedecked with flowers and filled with three hundred distinguished guests, including Vargas and his wife and daughter, three state *interventores*, and two federal cabinet ministers.[6]

The capsules were released and trampled under foot. Antônio de Almeida Júnior describes the scene (not mentioned in the newspapers of the day): ". . . the foul-smelling gas rapidly filled the . . . place. The guests were dumbfounded. Confusion increased and became general. Seized by fear, ladies made their departure, taking their husbands with them. After a short while the dictator himself felt it prudent to leave and breathe the fresh air in cold . . . Ramos de Azevedo Square."[7]

Germinal Feijó, the leader in carrying out the release of the capsules, recalls that men in formal dress, who turned out to be police agents, were soon at his side. They frisked him and put him in jail. The arrest, which lasted for two days, was the first of Feijó's twenty-nine arrests (totalling about six months of time served) during the Estado Novo. The police began a surveillance of the Feijós' house, which lasted for months.[8]

3. A Conservador Victory (November 1938)

In October and November 1938, deportation orders, threats, and harassments forced the exile of Armando de Sales Oliveira and others considered most dangerous to the Estado Novo: Otávio Mangabeira, Júlio de Mesquita Filho, Paulo Nogueira Filho, Paulo Duarte, and Luís de Toledo Piza Sobrinho (who had been the secretary of agriculture under Governor Armando de Sales Oliveira). With the exile of Júlio de Mesquita Filho, *O Estado de S. Paulo* was run by Carlos Vieira de Carvalho, brother-in-law of Júlio de Mesquita Filho and son of the founder of the São Paulo School of Medicine.[1]

By the time Armando de Sales Oliveira and Júlio de Mesquita Filho left for France on the *Lipari* early in November, the annual contest for Centro Onze de Agosto officerships was under way. It was an exciting election, of interest beyond the law school, and proved that electoral democracy, eliminated from national and local politics, remained alive at the *arcadas*.

The Reação Acadêmica, which had won the Centro presidency a year earlier, joined with the Arcadas party in putting up a slate headed by wealthy Francisco Eumene Machado. *O Momento Acadêmico*, organ of the Reação Acadêmica, said that if Machado were elected he would arrange for the construction of a sports stadium for the law students, "an old aspiration of all of us."[2]

Pressure in favor of the Reação Acadêmica–Arcadas joint slate was exerted by Justice Secretary César Lacerda de Vergueiro. Some of the students, due to return home soon for the holidays, received free railroad passes from the state government.[3] Others learned from Ademar de Barros, in September 1938, that the state government was financing their trip to Chile, where they were to attend, with students from Rio, a Congresso Internacional de Criminologia.[4]

Lúcio Seabra Leal, the Centro vice-president who had been kidnapped by anti-Vargas Conservadores in July, headed a ticket offered by the União Acadêmica. But the strongest opposition to the Reação Acadêmica–Arcadas slate was that put up by the Partido Conservador. The Conservador's Directive Commission, which selected the candidates, included Francisco Morato de Oliveira, Centro First Secretary Quintanilha Ribeiro, and Centro First Orator Auro de Moura Andrade.

Following the suggestion of Moura Andrade, the Conservador directorship picked Trajano Pupo Netto to run for the Centro presidency. Handsome Pupo Netto had been a founding member of the União Cultural Brasil–Estados Unidos, and his candidacy was supported by Roberto Victor Cordeiro. Professor Antônio de Sampaio Dória, admired by many for his advocacy of individual rights and condemnation of the 1937 "*carta constitucional*," also backed Pupo Netto.[5]

Among the other Conservador candidates were Salim Arida for vice-president, poet Jânio Quadros for first secretary, Ulisses Guimarães for first orator, Américo Marco Antônio for second orator, and first-year student Oscar Augusto de Barros Bressane for *procurador*. The Conservador candidates for the editorial commission were poet José Malanga, agitator Germinal Feijó, Roberto Teixeiro Pinto Filho, and Rui Homem de Melo Lacerda.

The Conservador ticket was the richest in literary talent. Ulisses Guimarães continued to fill the press of the *arcadas* with his essays on Brazilian literary figures. (His piece in the November number of *O Conservador* discussed José de Alencar, the esteemed author of *Iracema* and a graduate of the law school class of 1850.)[6] Jânio

Quadros, working his way through law school by teaching Portuguese and geography at the Colégio Cante Alighieri (an excellent secondary school),[7] was first secretary of the Associação Acadêmica Álvares de Azevedo. José Malanga had published a book of poetry, *Coração Proibido*, and had recently been elected a member of the Academia de Letras da Faculdade de Direito.

The Conservadores pledged that, if they were returned to office, they would give a needed renewal of attention to the Centro's Casa do Estudante, which they had initiated. During the administration of the Reação Acadêmica, the state government of Ademar de Barros had contributed 50:000$000, but the appeals of Centro President Joaquim Ribeiro do Valle Neto to the federal government for 500:000$000 had received a negative response from Education Minister Gustavo Capanema.[8]

Voting began at 8:00 A.M. on November 17 and lasted until 6:00 P.M. The counting continued until after midnight amid the shouts of partisans. When the Conservadores appeared to be winning, the lights went out. But if the supporters of the Reação Acadêmica–Arcadas ticket were hoping to seize the ballot boxes they were foiled by the Conservadores, who had been expecting such a move. After gaining control of the ballot boxes, Conservadores called on Law School Director Spencer Vampré to assure an honest count. At about 1:00 A.M. Vampré announced the final results, a victory for most of the Conservador candidates. Of the ten officership posts, the Conservadores lost only that of archivist. However, José Malanga was the only Conservador elected to the editorial commission.[9]

At about 2:00 A.M. the victors were celebrating at the Confeitaria Formosa, on Formosa Street, when a group arrived with the intention of beating up Pupo Netto and his friends. Auro de Moura Andrade helped hold off this attack by some of the losers, who were accompanied by aggressive members of the state police and Javert de Andrade, an assistant to Justice Secretary César Lacerda de Vergueiro.

Despite this incident, Vergueiro sent a message to Pupo Netto offering peaceful relations between himself and the newly elected Centro directorship. Pupo Netto simply replied that, as he had become the representative of the students, he would do what was best for them.[10]

At the insistence of Ademar de Barros, Roberto Victor Cordeiro was dismissed from his post in the state labor department. He obtained a job as lawyer of *O Estado de S. Paulo*.[11] He continued in the company of antidictatorship law students, giving suggestions about practical politics. Using his connections with foreign firms, he found jobs for students. Not infrequently he obtained free donations of paper (from a Swedish firm, T. Janer) for the publication of *O Onze de Agosto*.[12]

4. The Birth of the UNE (Rio de Janeiro, December 1938)

Following the Centro election, the December 1938 number of *O Onze de Agosto* announced that Spencer Vampré was leaving the law school directorship, which he had exercised since early in the year. On another page of the same number, Antônio Sylvio Cunha Bueno, Ulisses Guimarães, and three others wrote of their gratitude to Ademar de Barros and Pedro Ludovico Teixeira, the *interventores* of São Paulo and Goiás, for contributions to the students' campaign to pay for a monument to the Bandeirantes in the recently built city of Goiânia. The five students, interested in the development of central Brazil, had made a goodwill trip to Goiás.[1]

An article by João Paulo Bittencourt in *O Onze de Agosto* stressed the need of universities to concern themselves with politics. Bittencourt attacked regimes that "asphyxiate moral and intellectual values" by insisting on "absolute obedience to the regimes' interests and propaganda," and he elucidated on the "sad aspect" of the universities in Italy, Germany, and Russia. In a different vein, José Barbosa, a preparatory student, praised the Estado Novo in a front-page article in *O Universitário*, organ of the pre–law school students. Under the Estado Novo, Barbosa wrote, Brazil was awakening "from the romantic lethargy that had dominated it from colonial times" and was entering "a new life" that was "freeing it from the old and once-celebrated individual liberalism."[2]

João Paulo Bittencourt, opponent of authoritarianism, was one of the two São Paulo law students who spent a part of their December-February vacation in Rio de Janeiro as the school's representatives to the Second National Congress of Students. The Congress was the result of a call, made in April 1938 by the Casa do Estudante do Brasil (founded in 1929) and the Conselho Nacional de Estudantes (founded in August 1937), and was expected to continue with work done earlier to form a strong national student organization.[3] When the Congress met, from December 5 to 21, 1938, the representatives of the Centro Onze de Agosto (Bittencourt and César Barbosa Filho) found themselves with representatives of about eighty colleges and secondary schools. Antônio Franca, an anti-Vargas Rio law student from Pernambuco, proposed the creation of the União Nacional dos Estudantes (UNE), which was to be for university students and separate from the Casa do Estudante do Brasil. On December 22, 1938, the Conselho Nacional de Estudantes held its second assembly (the first having taken place in August 1937), approved the UNE statutes, and chose UNE officers. Valdir Ramos Borges, a Gaúcho, became UNE president; Antônio Franca became secretary general; and the Centro Onze de Agosto's César Barbosa Filho became second vice-president.

The UNE was provided a small office at the quarters of the Casa do Estudante do Brasil but quarreled bitterly with the Casa and its dominating figure, Ana Amélia de Queiroz Carneiro de Mendonça, the pretty daughter of wealthy parents and wife of a soccer star.[4] Ana Amélia, who had done much to make the Casa do Estudante a place of recreation and inexpensive meals for students in Rio, considered the UNE as one of the sections of the Casa, and the UNE complained that the Casa sought to belittle and control it. Besides, Arthur José Poerner writes, the character of the Casa do Estudante do Brasil was "profoundly governmental" and it restricted its activities to student aid and therefore was in conflict with the anti-fascist ideological tone of the theses of the Second National Congress of Students.[5]

Future UNE congresses could expect somewhat more unity among the University of São Paulo delegations as a result of Pupo Netto's successful effort to form the Conselho de Presidentes dos Centros Acadêmicos de São Paulo. The Conselho came into existence on May 8, 1939, at a meeting attended by the presidents of the Centro Acadêmico Onze de Agosto (law), Centro Acadêmico Osvaldo Cruz (medicine), Grêmio da Faculdade de Filosofia, Ciencias e Letras, Grêmio Politécnico, Centro Acadêmico 25 de Janeiro (pharmacy and odontology), and Centro Acadêmico de Medicina Veterinária.[6] The first act of the Conselho, headed by Pupo Netto, was to address a petition to Ademar de Barros, objecting to the proposed doubling of the 200 milreis annual student fee. In reply, the *interventor* agreed that the fee would not be increased in 1939.[7]

5. The Dismissal of Some Law Professors (January 1939)

The anti-Vargas resistance at the *arcadas* gained some determined members with the entry of the class that began the five-year course in March 1939. Nevertheless, the activists—those who had the time and resolution to keep up an attack against the Brazilian dictatorship—numbered only several dozen.[1] They were joined from time to time by others, particularly when the authorities engaged in acts of hostility to the school, as was the case in 1939.

When Vargas and Ademar de Barros discussed the São Paulo Law

School professors late in 1938, Vargas suggested that five of them, considered most unfriendly to the regime, be dismissed in accordance with an amendment to the 1937 Constitution that had been decreed on May 16, 1938, after the putsch of May 10–11. The amendment reactivated constitutional Article 177 allowing the government to dismiss civilian and military personnel "in the interest of public service or for the convenience of the regime."

The list of five professors was reduced to three after it was decided that Cardoso de Melo Neto had already been punished by being removed from the interventorship and after Ademar de Barros made favorable remarks about Ernesto Leme. Leme, a Bucha leader, had participated as a soldier in the Batalhão Piratininga in 1932 and been elected to the state legislature on the PD ticket in 1934. As majority leader of the legislature, Leme had often given assistance to the PRP minority, which had included Ademar de Barros.[2]

The dismissal orders were issued on January 13, 1939, while the school was on vacation, and affected Waldemar Ferreira, Vicente Ráo, and Antônio de Sampaio Dória. It was Ernesto Leme who proposed, at a faculty meeting on February 2, that the faculty express its objection to the rulings. Waldemar Ferreira, upon being advised of the faculty's adoption of the proposal, exclaimed: "The irregular act of my forced resignation—and it was to be expected!—has not hurt my moral and intellectual patrimony. Rather, it has given me honor, in which I can take great pride."[3]

A committee of ten students issued a printed invitation to a dinner to be given by the Centro Onze de Agosto in honor of the three dismissed professors on the evening of August 11, 1939, at the Brasserie Paulista Restaurant. The commission members were Antônio Sobral Júnior, Domingos Luz de Faria ("Domingão"), Fernando Pereira da Rocha Filho (son of a São Paulo police *delegado*), Francisco Morato de Oliveira, Germinal Feijó, Haroldo Bueno Magano, Roberto Costa de Abreu Sodré, Roberto Heladio Azevedo Sodré, Wilfrido Cid Valério, and Wilson Barbosa Martins.[4]

When commission members called on Sampaio Dória, whose health was poor, they pointed out that the police might make trouble, which the professor should perhaps avoid. Rising from his chair, Sampaio Dória retorted: "I shall certainly go. But I shall take a cane with me!"[5]

The dinner, noisy and successful, was not disturbed by the police. But the police took to arresting members of the dinner commission in the weeks that followed. Wilfrido Cid Valério and Antônio Sobral Júnior, two commission members who were good friends of Pupo Netto, were picked up by police agents at a railroad station. Pupo

Netto phoned the new law school director, civil law Professor Sebastião Soares de Faria, who answered the call although he had retired for the night. Soares de Faria was always eager to help the students, and from his bed he immediately phoned Ademar de Barros to say that he would resign the school directorship if the students were not released. Ademar ordered the release.[6]

João Nery Guimarães, a student then and now a distinguished lawyer and scholar, has revealed that Ademar de Barros took steps to close down the Bucha and that Professor Jorge Americano, who was directing the secret organization, therefore ordered that the Bucha's files be burned. Whatever the fate of the files, which may have been hidden rather than burned, the move against the Bucha, Guimarães asserts, "radicalized even further the position of the Faculdade de Direito against the Estado Novo and its so-called *gauleiter* in São Paulo, Ademar de Barros."[7]

6. *"folha dobrada"* (May 23, 1939)

In France in February 1939, Armando de Sales Oliveira wrote a long epistle to Army Chief of Staff Pedro Aurélio de Gois Monteiro, supporter of the Estado Novo. "Brazil," Armando wrote, "must be removed from the nightmare in which it has been living since November 10."[1]

Copies of the epistle, printed in Paris, were given to Alcides Procópio, a Brazilian tennis star who had been participating in an international tournament in Paris; it seemed unlikely that the Brazilian police would bother the hero upon his return to his homeland. After reaching Brazil he flew to São Paulo, where his greeters included Pedro Ferraz do Amaral, director of the *O Estado de S. Paulo Suplemento de Rotogravura*. With the aid of students and other friends, Ferraz do Amaral arranged to have Armando's subversive letter given wide distribution.[2]

Ferraz do Amaral and Joca (João Batista Silva Azevedo) helped law students publish six numbers of *"folha dobrada,"* whose name was derived from four lines of verse written by Tobias Barreto in 1865 and later etched in bronze at the *arcadas*:

Quando se sente bater
No peito heróica pancada,
Deixa-se a folha dobrada
Enquanto se vai morrer.[3]

Joca collected the articles prepared by students for *"folha dobrada"* and turned them over to Ferraz do Amaral. Ferraz do Amaral, serving informally as *secretário* of the subversive publication, edited the articles and then gave them to his friend, printer Neptuno Gasparini. Gasparini, who had been tortured by the police in Rio de Janeiro in May 1938 after helping Joca take machine guns there, handled the paging, layouts, and illustrations of *"folha dobrada."* He printed the little newspaper on the small press of a friend in the Bom Retiro district. When the fifth number was being printed, the police arrested the owner of the press and closed down his plant. The last number of *"folha dobrada"* was printed in the city of São Roque.[4]

The first number of *"folha dobrada"* was dated May 23, 1939, seventh anniversary of the killing of the young Paulistas whose names furnished the initials MMDC. Among the ten student editors of the eight-page number were four members of the commission that organized, a little later, the dinner for the dismissed professors: Roberto de Abreu Sodré (younger brother of Antônio Carlos), Wilfrido Cid Valério, Fernando Pereira da Rocha Filho, and Roberto Heladio Azevedo Sodré. The other six were Fausto Geraldo Barbosa, José A. Furquim Fonseca, Péricles Rolim, Otávio Augusto Machado de Barros, José Maria Ribeiro de Barros, and José Gomes Filho.[5]

A front-page illustration, representing the verse of Tobias Barreto, showed a sword and helmet on an open book with one of its pages partly doubled over. The accompanying editorial, in large type, called for popular representation, universal suffrage, freedom of expression, and a "Constitution of the People." In a fighting tone it concluded: "The books remain on the table, perhaps never again to be opened."

Preparatory student Paulo Nogueira Neto, elder son of exiled Paulo Nogueira Filho, wrote that the Paulista banner, unfurled on May 23, 1932, "is a symbol of liberty and autonomy; it continues, proud and lofty, dominating the spirit of millions of *bandeirantes*!" According to an article by Francisco Geraldo Barbosa, the new generation of the law school felt an even greater desire for liberty than did that of 1932.

First-year law student Haroldo Bueno Magano wrote, "We want liberty!," and second-year student Roberto de Abreu Sodré wrote that the young people of Brazil "do not support what goes on." Antônio Costa Corrêa, who had left the Communist Party during its 1937–1938 schism, predicted that many sacrifices would be demanded of the youth of the Americas. "Our generation will be unhappy but heroic," he wrote, and he added that the ultimate result would be an America "that is free and grandiose on account of the liberty and well-being of its sons."[6]

7. The "Friends of Rui Barbosa" Denounce Vargas (May 23, 1939)

The first number of "*folha dobrada*" called attention to the Sociedade Acadêmica Amigos de Rui Barbosa, which was organized early in May 1939. Whereas the União Cultural Brasil–Estados Unidos was rather circumspect, developing cultural relations and obtaining U.S. government funds for trips, the new *sociedade*, limited to law students, was a hard-hitting arm of the anti-Vargas activists. Formally, it was a student literary society that attracted some non-activists, but its organizers and directors used it to protest the dictatorship in an aggressive manner.[1]

Fifth-year student Francisco Morato de Oliveira became president of the Sociedade Acadêmica Amigos de Rui Barbosa, and fourth-year student José Maria Ribeiro de Barros became vice-president. Germinal Feijó (hard to classify as he was not in school to study) was chosen an orator. Feijó, soft-spoken in conversation, coordinated the agitation at the *arcadas* and kept in touch with Antônio Carlos de Abreu Sodré, who was regarded as chief of São Paulo's anti-Vargas movement following the exile of Júlio de Mesquita Filho.[2]

The "*folha dobrada*" article concerned the session held by the Sociedade Acadêmica Amigos de Rui Barbosa on May 13 to commemorate the abolition of slavery in Brazil. For the occasion a crowd filled the João Mendes Júnior Room, a ground-floor classroom (with seats for about 150 students) that was customarily used for the meetings of student associations. With Francisco Morato de Oliveira presiding, two accomplished student orators, Germinal Feijó and Américo Marco Antônio, spoke before Professor José Soares de Melo delivered the main address. The article in "*folha dobrada*" was mostly a transcription of the speech of Feijó, which stressed, in dramatic words and with many references to Rui Barbosa, that the purpose of the new Sociedade was to struggle for liberty. "Liberty, your name is sacred!" Feijó concluded.[3]

At the Largo de São Francisco on the afternoon of May 23, 1939, the Sociedade Amigos de Rui Barbosa observed the killings of seven years earlier (MMDC). Feijó opened the speechmaking by condemning "the wrongs and humiliations that irresponsible men have thrust upon this much-sacrificed land." He shouted that "the people want order! The people want law! The people want a constitution!"[4]

Feijó's oratory was followed by that of Centro First Orator Ulisses Guimarães (not a *resistência* activist), Romeu de Andrade Lourenção (who had orated and hurled stones during the reaction to João Pessoa's assassination), and Américo Marco Antônio. Américo Marco Antônio suggested that the meeting was a trial for judging a criminal known to everyone. He called for a formal accusation by a competent authority, and then *promotor público* Ibrahim Nobre spoke up. Nobre, a mature orator who had stirred the Paulistas in 1932, listed crimes of the Estado Novo and closed by exclaiming, "The present moment is similar to May 23, 1932; therefore, the men responsible for the Brazilian political situation should not be surprised by a repetition of those bloody events."

After the close of the meeting late in the evening, law students went around the city gathering up pictures of Vargas, which a government regulation required that bars, restaurants, and places of business display. They used the pictures to make bonfires, one on Líbero Badaró Street and the other at the Largo de São Francisco.

On the next day the Sociedade's president, Francisco Morato de Oliveira, was dismissed from the clerical job he had held in the state government. Furthermore, he was arrested, together with other leaders of the Sociedade. Professor Antônio de Almeida Júnior writes that the authorities also arrested some of the older enemies of the Estado Novo, such as Waldemar Ferreira, Aureliano Leite, Antônio Pereira Lima, and Francisco Mesquita. These arrests, the professor says, were carried out in accordance with the custom of the São Paulo police and without any reasons being given.[5]

8. Pupo Netto, UNE President (1939–1940)

Among the student associations that kept the João Mendes Júnior Room in frequent use were the Grêmio Universitário Alberto Torres, the Liga Estudantil Nipo-Brasileira, the Sociedade Universitária Amigos da Itália, and the recently formed Sociedade Universitária de Cultura. (The considerable number of associations of "amigos"—friends of this country and that—led student Pedro Brasil Bandecchi to propose humorously an association of "the friends of Brazil.") The associations frequently called on First Orator Ulisses Guimarães to participate in programs that offered talks on cultural matters.

The faculty at the start of the 1939 school year consisted of sixteen *professores catedráticos* and seven *livres-docentes*. José Carlos de Ataliba Nogueira, who had helped Waldomiro Lima run the state after the Constitutionalist Revolution, was a *livre-docente* of penal law. In the field of judiciary penal law, new titles were conferred in July 1939 as a result of the *concurso* of November 10, 1937, which had been interrupted by the death of an examining professor. Thus, a full professorship (*catedrático*) was conferred on Joaquim Canuto Mendes de Almeida, the only pro-Vargas professor and a nephew of monarchist João Mendes de Almeida Júnior (known as João Mendes Júnior). Two other participants in that *concurso* became *livres-docentes*. The youngest of the four contestants, former Integralista Gofredo da Silva Telles Júnior, was judged to have made a brilliant presentation but, as a member of the December 1937 graduating class, he had lacked time to build up a reputation in the profession.[1]

The Partido Acadêmico Conservador, in control of the Centro Onze de Agosto, undertook a fund-raising drive for the Centro's Casa do Estudante. To every newspaper in the state's interior (whose young people might benefit from the construction) letters were written asking for backing and emphasizing "the practical results that could come from a perfect understanding between journalists and students."[2] Pupo Netto found an enthusiastic benefactor of the *arcadas* in Vicente Amato Sobrinho, an Italian who had come to Brazil in the early 1930s and set up a laboratory that made him rich. Amato, full of affection for Brazil and fond of the São Paulo law students, became a Brazilian citizen and usually responded cheerfully to the students' requests for donations.[3]

The chief impetus for proceeding with the construction of the Casa do Estudante of the Centro came late in the administration of Pupo Netto. The law school, represented by Director Soares de Faria, agreed to make the Centro a twenty-year loan of 700 contos de reis (700:000$000) at 5 percent annual interest. Engineer and builder Alfredo Mathias, who had been engaged during the Centro administration of Joaquim Ribeiro do Valle Neto, went ahead with his plans for an eleven-story building. "He did not charge for his work because he liked the students," Pupo Netto recalls.[4]

In Rio in August 1939, Pupo Netto, Ulisses Guimarães, and four other university students from São Paulo attended the third Conselho Nacional de Estudantes. By an almost unanimous vote, Pupo Netto was chosen president of the UNE to serve until July 1940. Antônio Franca, president of the Centro Acadêmico Cândido de Oliveira of the Federal District's Faculdade Nacional de Direito, was reelected secretary general. Of the three new vice-presidents, one was from Belém and another from Bahia. The third vice-president, Celso Peçanha, belonged to the Centro Acadêmico Evaristo de Veiga of the Faculdade de Direito de Niterói, in the state of Rio de Janeiro, and was in a position to serve as acting president if Pupo Netto was unable to attend meetings in Rio.[5]

While the third Conselho Nacional de Estudantes was taking place, war clouds gathered in Europe. Shortly before World War II broke out in September 1939, the exiles from São Paulo, such as Armando de Sales Oliveira, Júlio de Mesquita Filho, Paulo Nogueira Filho, and

Paulo Duarte, made their way to the United States and Argentina. The UNE, after the war broke out, took a strong position in favor of neutrality. In March 1940 it issued a message "to the youth of Brazil and the Americas" in which it argued that it was a mistake to believe anyone who said that the war was being fought in the name of civilization. "Such a statement, paradoxical and demagogic, is used by those who want to spread the conflict, hurling the whole world into the flames."[6] (This point of view, supported by the Brazilian Communists after the Stalin-Hitler Pact, appealed to Communists in the UNE, such as Secretary General Antônio Franca.)

The chief attention of the new UNE directorship was devoted to the conflict with Ana Amélia de Queiroz Carneiro de Mendonça and the Casa do Estudante do Brasil. While the third Conselho was holding its sessions in August 1939 and passing resolutions demonstrating independence from the Casa do Estudante do Brasil (CEB), the *Bulletin* of the CEB published a note considered offensive to the UNE. The squabble about the note was followed by disagreements concerning representatives to be sent from Brazil to international student gatherings. The UNE argued that the statutes of the International Confederation of Students required that the UNE choose the athletes to be sent to the biennial International University Games in Monaco. But Ana Amélia pointed out that she had obtained the necessary financial assistance from the Brazilian government; and, in the words of the UNE, she "organized the delegation in her own way, by means of one of her satellites" (such as the Federação Atlética de Estudantes). The Casa do Estudante do Brasil and its "queen," or *rainha* (as the UNE called Ana Amélia), refused to recognize the Confederação Universitária Brasileira de Esportes (CUBE), which, in accordance with the resolutions of the third Conselho Nacional de Estudantes, was established in São Paulo in September 1939 with José Gomes Talarico as president.

The UNE asserted that student matters should be handled by the students themselves. It objected to the arrangement whereby the president of the Casa do Estudante de Pernambuco was chosen by the state *interventor*, Agamenon Magalhães. For a while, both the Casa do Estudante de Pernambuco and the president of the Diretório Acadêmico da Faculdade de Direito do Recife, an official in Agamenon Magalhães' state government, supported Ana Amélia and attacked the UNE. After the Pernambuco students decided to cooperate with the UNE, the *rainha* resolved that the Casa do Estudante do Brasil should break completely with the UNE.

The correspondence leading up to the break began in November 1939 when the UNE wrote Ana Amélia asking for the opinion of the

Casa do Estudante do Brasil about the resolutions adopted at the third Conselho Nacional de Estudantes. According to the reply, sent in April 1940, the Conselho had perverted its purposes and, therefore, the Casa do Estudante do Brasil had no interest in its activities. Further correspondence, signed in May 1940 by UNE Secretary General Antônio Franca, brought a reply asking the UNE to get out of its small office at the Casa within three days.

When the UNE directorship reported in July 1940 to the fourth Conselho Nacional de Estudantes, it pointed out that "we are without material resources, we are without any support or guarantee beyond the cohesion formed around the UNE. But that cohesion is sufficient backing and guarantee for us to continue."[7]

IV

The Libertadores' First Year (1940)

1. *Resistência* Activists Promote Party Schisms (August–November 1939)

In August 1939, when campaigning began for the November Centro Onze de Agosto election, the directorship of the dominant Partido Acadêmico Conservador named a slate headed by Francisco de Paula Quintanilha Ribeiro. Quintanilha Ribeiro, a party founder, had shown electoral strength in 1937 and 1938, but his nomination provoked a revolt by a minority of Conservadores, who felt that the party leadership was anything but dynamic in demonstrating resistance to the Vargas dictatorship. Many of these disenchanted Conservadores belonged to the Sociedade Acadêmico Amigos de Rui Barbosa, and some of them had published "*folha dobrada*" and burned pictures of Vargas.

The Conservador dissidents released a bitter manifesto to say that "within the Partido Acadêmico Conservador, of splendid democratic traditions, a group took over the Comissão Diretora by assault and imposed its candidate for the presidency."[1] The manifesto proclaimed that the legitimate representatives of the party were unanimous in nominating, for the Centro presidency, José Maria Ribeiro de Barros. "Zé" Maria Ribeiro de Barros was vice-president of the Sociedade Acadêmica Amigos de Rui Barbosa, a "*folha dobrada*" editor, and a close friend of Roberto Victor Cordeiro.

The forty signers of the manifesto did not present candidates for posts other than the presidency; they called themselves the Comissão Coordenadora to work for the victory of Ribeiro de Barros and wave again the "glorious banner" that had been abandoned by the Conservador directors. Among the forty were Francisco Morato de Oliveira, Germinal Feijó, Antônio Costa Corrêa, Roberto de Abreu Sodré, Wilson Cury Rahal, Luís Leite Ribeiro, Wilson Martins, Haroldo Bueno Magano, Fernando Pereira da Rocha Filho, José Gomes Filho, Otávio Augusto Machado de Barros, and Roberto Heladio Azevedo Sodré.

Comissão Coordenadora member Antônio Costa Corrêa, a calm and able leftist, was a nephew and admirer of Miguel Costa, and he admired also Communist prisoner Luís Carlos Prestes, who had been chief of staff of the rebellious column headed by Miguel Costa in the 1920s. Costa Corrêa, the son of a São Paulo Gas Company worker, did not feel altogether comfortable among the wealthier anti-Vargas students, who conspired often in the house of Paulo Nogueira Filho on Avenida Brasil. He did feel comfortable in the company of Wilson Cury Rahal, another student with poor parents.[2] And he had reason to admire Rahal. When the government tried to bribe Rahal, by offering him a post of *inspetor de ensino* (inspector of schools), Rahal, although poor and trying to help his brothers and sisters, refused to compromise his ideals by accepting the position.[3] Costa Corrêa was also very close to Germinal Feijó, whose leftist attitude was sometimes labeled Communist by dominant members of the Partido Acadêmico Conservador (and by Estado Novo administrators).

After leftist and liberal activists created the schism in the Conservative Party, a schism developed in the Reação Acadêmica, which had won the Centro presidency in 1937. In 1939 the Reação Acadêmica nominated a slate headed by Luís Swarztman, a good orator and writer who was not known for political activity. Thereupon thirty-two founders of the Reação Acadêmica, including former party President Celso Augusto Assumpção, issued a declaration supporting José Maria Ribeiro de Barros, favorite of the Conservative dissidents. The dissidents of the Reação Acadêmica affirmed that the new directors of the Reação Acadêmica were politically inexperienced and had yielded to "injunctions from outside."[4]

A new law school party, the Partido Reformador, offered a slate headed by Paulo Penteado de Faria, member of the school's Academia de Letras. The Partido Reformador, close to the conservative Catholic JUC,[5] attracted Vargas supporter José Barbosa, who belonged to the working class. It also attracted *A Balança* Director Damiano Gullo, the former Integralista, and he became one of the party's candidates for an editorial commission post. The manifesto of the new party, bearing almost 270 names, preached law student unity and promised to maintain the Centro "separate from any outside connection."[6]

A fifth presidential candidate, jovial Hélio Rubens Junqueira Caldas, headed a slate proposed by a Movimento Acadêmico Independente. Two of the Conservador candidates were included on the Movimento Independente slate: Domingos Luz de Faria, candidate for the vice-presidency, and Afrânio de Oliveira, candidate to serve on the Comissão de Sindicância (financial accounts).[7]

The first number of *O Libertador,* "official newspaper of the Frente Única Pró Candidatura José Maria Ribeiro de Barros," stated that the São Paulo law students should participate in the November 15 Day of the Republic celebrations in a manner that would demonstrate that they were not moved by the "false democracy of the speeches" but demanded "concrete and positive acts of respect for the freedom of citizens." The newspaper carried a letter from Ribeiro de Barros that accused the Conservador Party of employing totalitarian tactics and of having displayed the banner of democracy only to mislead people.[8]

The writers for *O Libertador,* admirers of Franklin D. Roosevelt, were mostly Conservador and Reação Acadêmica dissidents who had been involved in earlier election campaigns. But a few were first-year students, such as Astolfo Pio Monteiro da Silva. He wrote in *O Libertador* that the greatest responsibility for the destiny of the Centro, and "for the reputation of . . . all the university student class of Brazil, is without doubt in the hands of those of us who are the first-year students in this law school, due to our position of having no ties to any existing political faction and to our large number, which is able alone to win an election."[9]

Another first-year student who helped publish *O Libertador* was Luís Gonzaga Bandeira de Melo Arrobas Martins, a dedicated liberal, proficient linguist, and superb extemporaneous orator. Arrobas Martins, a practicing Catholic with a high moral code, kept himself in good physical condition by rowing and swimming. He inherited many of the characteristics of his father, Aurélio Arrobas Martins, who had come to Brazil from Portugal and directed the Ginásio São Luís, in Jaboticabal, São Paulo, between 1917 and 1933. Aurélio was a Latin scholar, devout Catholic, and foremost educator, whose use of discipline helped develop character and culture in his pupils.[10] When Aurélio moved to São Paulo city in 1933 to direct the eight-hundred-student Liceu Franco-Brasileiro, many of the Ginásio's pupils, such as Luís' classmate Paulo Henrique Meinberg, also moved from Jaboticabal.[11] Aurélio died in June 1936.

Despite difficulty with mathematics, Luís Arrobas Martins received the prize awarded to the Liceu's best student in each of the three years he attended the Liceu.[12] In 1937 and 1938 he took the law school's *curso pré-jurídico.* An avid reader, Luís inherited a good library, devoted chiefly to the humanities. It filled two rooms of the modest home where he lived with his mother (cousin of newspaper publisher Francisco de Assis Chateaubriand Bandeira de Melo) and one of his sisters. At the law school Luís was a gifted leader of the anti-Vargas movement, intense, often stubborn, severe on himself and others. His loyal following included law school classmate Antônio Cândido de Mello e Souza, who was at the same time a student at the new College of Philosophy, Sciences, and Letters.

2. A Defeat for the *Resistência* Activists (November 18, 1939)

The Ribeiro de Barros movement, into which Arrobas Martins threw himself, had only about six weeks in which to try to upset a well-entrenched party. Arguing that the Centro Onze de Agosto should not limit its attention to matters of immediate concern to the law students, it sponsored (in the words of Arrobas) "a contest about the theory of 'vital space' in order to discredit the doctrine of that name invented by Hitler." Contestants, asked to reply to the question of whether the theory was justifiable, submitted papers.[1]

Like the other electoral groups, the Frente Única Pró José Maria Ribeiro de Barros attracted student interest by holding *chopadas* (beer sessions) and used São Paulo theaters and radio stations for cultural and propaganda purposes. Law student Maria Amélia Figueiredo Rosa, the "Queen of the Students of São Paulo," spoke on a Ribeiro de Barros radio program. So did Conservador leader Ulisses Guimarães, who said that he did not mind speaking on a program that did not represent his own party because the movement was a "stupendous indication" of the democratic spirit at the *arcadas*. He referred to the hundreds of campaign posters (some enormous) that covered the inside and outside walls of the school building. "The young people," he declared, "are never compatible with the stagnation of a single directive nor with the paralyzing effect of a single opinion."[2] Waldomiro Alves Junqueira, who had won a Comissão de Sindicância position as a Conservative candidate a year earlier, told the radio audience that the victors of 1938 had betrayed the principles for which they had campaigned.[3]

Germinal Feijó, speaking to a reporter from *O Estado de S. Paulo*, declared that "the forces of the Partido Acadêmico Conservador, to which I belonged, were disgusted with the orientation provided by a certain group that took steps without consulting the electorate of the party." Giving the closing speech at a *chopada*, Feijó said that the law students had always participated in the nation's great civic campaigns and should play "a preponderant role in the present historic moment."[4]

However, on November 18, 1939, Conservador Quintanilha Ribeiro defeated his four opponents for the presidency. The Conservadores did well, winning also the vice-presidency and several other posts. A painful reverse for the Amigos de Rui Barbosa was the defeat of

Américo Marco Antônio, Conservador candidate for first orator. Among the first-year students winning places on the Comissão de Redação (editorial commission) were Damiano Gullo, of the Reformadores, and poet Péricles Eugênio da Silva Ramos (a Conservador with many friends in the Frente Única Pró José Maria Ribeiro de Barros).[5]

Reviewing the outcome, the campaigners for Ribeiro de Barros concluded that "we no longer have before us the time-honored and glorious Faculdade [College], so rich in traditions and which provided so many epic achievements to the Brazilian Nation. . . . It is sad to have to confess that the heritage bequeathed by past generations is almost destroyed. Outside commitments, forced apathy, successive blows against the Arcadas' autonomy place in risk more than the name and traditions of the Arcadas—the very life of the Faculdade."[6] The "outside commitments," Arrobas wrote later, resulted from the work of the "federal and state governments" to prevent the victory of the group most clearly opposed to them. In particular the state government exerted pressure by offering jobs.[7]

José Maria Ribeiro de Barros maintained his habitual calm in the face of defeat. On January 4, 1940, he joined his recent backers in giving a lunch at the Brasserie Paulista to honor seven members of their group who were graduating, such as Francisco Morato de Oliveira and Wilson Martins. Américo Marco Antônio opened the speechmaking by paying tribute to the seven new graduates. After José Tavares de Miranda, a graduating student, responded, further speeches were given by José Maria Ribeiro de Barros, Francisco Morato de Oliveira, Germinal Feijó, and Paulo Goulart Tormin. Then graduating student Osvaldo Cruz de Souza Dias proposed the creation of a new law school party, necessary on account of "the perversion" of the other parties.

Following the unanimous approval of this idea, Germinal Feijó suggested that the new party be named the Partido Acadêmico Libertador because its mission would be to achieve liberation "from the arrogant and impudent wave that has been seeking to invade the *arcadas*." After this suggestion was accepted enthusiastically, Osvaldo Cruz de Souza Dias recommended the organization of a provisional directorship. His nomination of José Maria Ribeiro de Barros to be honorary president was adopted. In turn Ribeiro de Barros presented a suggested list of provisional directors, which was approved by acclamation. Paulo Biroli Neto (a Reação Acadêmica dissident) became president; Luís Leite Ribeiro, first vice-president; and Salomão Izar Filho, second vice-president. Fernando Pereira da Rocha Filho was named secretary general; José Augusto Pádua de Araujo (a Reação Acadêmica dissident), first secretary; and Luís Arrobas Martins, second secretary. Américo Marco Antônio became first orator; Theodureto de Carvalho, first treasurer; and Astolfo Pio Monteiro da Silva, second treasurer.[8]

3. The Woes of *O Estado de S. Paulo* and *Revista Universitária* (March–April 1940)

The federal and state authorities believed that subversive plots were hatched at *O Estado de S. Paulo* and, therefore, the state police constantly invaded the newspaper's plant and offices, located on Boa Vista Street. Unsuccessful searches were made for radio transmitters and incriminating documents. *O Estado de S. Paulo*, hoping to "avoid useless complications," withdrew the name of Júlio de Mesquita Filho from the masthead and showed, instead, the name of Leo Vaz, alongside that of Plínio Barreto. Vaz had been with the newspaper since 1918.

But the invasions continued. And, although Júlio de Mesquita Filho and Paulo Duarte were in Buenos Aires, the diligent police carried out investigations at Duarte's home after hearing a rumor that Júlio de Mesquita Filho had been meeting there with Antônio Pereira Lima and others (including Reynaldo Saldanha da Gama, who was hospitalized in Campos do Jordão at the time he was said to be conspiring in Duarte's home).[1]

Finally, on March 25, 1940, a troop of the state Polícia Militar claimed the discovery of weapons hidden in the attic above the editorial offices of *O Estado de S. Paulo*. Directors were arrested and documents seized. The newspaper remained closed until April 7, 1940, when it began to circulate once more—but this time under the management of Abner Mourão, who was chosen by the Estado Novo's Conselho Nacional da Imprensa to take over *O Estado*'s management in the place of the Mesquita group. Plínio Barreto and some others belonging to that group were dismissed. Writers, such as Mário de Andrade, refused to collaborate any longer with the newspaper, but Roberto Victor Cordeiro, in need of an income, continued as lawyer of the daily. The government, undertaking an investigation in Rio of *O Estado de S. Paulo*, condemned the exiled Armando de Sales Oliveira to two years in prison.[2]

Francisco Mesquita was held in Rio's Casa de Detenção and then at the barracks of the Cavalry Regiment, also in Rio. After he returned to São Paulo, he devoted his attention, with remarkable success, to turning a long-neglected fazenda into one of the best run fazendas in Brazil. When he was in São Paulo city, he made use of a small office on the Largo do Café. It adjoined the small office of Antônio Carlos de Abreu Sodré.[3]

In March and April 1940, when the Mesquita group lost control of *O Estado de S. Paulo*, the anti–Estado Novo activists at the *arcadas* were preparing for a busy new school year. While they worked at organizing the Partido Acadêmico Libertador, they directed their fire at the *Revista Universitária*, a magazine published on nearby São Bento Street by supporters of the Estado Novo. They could make a good case because, as they pointed out to the Centro Onze de Agosto, the *Revista Universitária* people, unconnected with students, were going around soliciting funds, which they falsely declared would benefit student causes, such as the construction of the Casa do Estudante do Centro Onze de Agosto.

One of the *Revista Universitária* people, explaining to a São Paulo businessman that he was raising funds to help the Centro Onze de Agosto and was a nephew of a Vargas cabinet minister, obtained 6 contos (6 thousand milreis). Thereupon the Conselho de Presidentes dos Centros Acadêmicos de São Paulo issued a notice advising the business community to donate only to authorized students and threatening strong measures against the *Revista Universitária* if it continued to "usurp the name of the Centro Onze de Agosto."

Without the knowledge of Centro President Quintanilha Ribeiro, dozens of law students invaded the upstairs office of *Revista Universitária* on São Bento street on the morning of April 11. Alleging that the magazine's directors had persisted in their dishonest ways despite the warning, the invaders wrecked the office. Students used razors to shave the heads of the directors of *Revista Universitária*. By the time guards arrived, the students had left.

Quintanilha Ribeiro, learning about the event, called an emergency meeting of the Centro Onze de Agosto in the Barão de Ramalho Room, a classroom across the hall from the João Mendes Júnior Room. During the discussion, a first-year student complained that the head shaving was an insult to the first-year students, whose head shaving constituted one of the milder practices of the rough annual hazing (*trote*). First-year students, he said, objected to being put on the same footing as the directors of *Revista Universitária*. When Quintanilha Ribeiro spoke to the press, after the meeting, he defended the sacking of *Revista Universitária*.

Arrobas Martins has written that the "official reason" for the sacking was *Revista Universitária*'s use of the Centro name to solicit funds for the Casa do Estudante do Centro Onze de Agosto. "For us," he added, "the principal objective was to destroy a magazine that was at the service of fascist ideas and the Estado Novo."[4]

4. Launching the Partido Acadêmico Libertador (April–June 1940)

The provisional directorship of the Partido Acadêmico Libertador, named at lunch on January 4, 1940, met for the first time on April 15. It chose Antônio Costa Corrêa to draw up a manifesto of the new party and chose Roberto de Abreu Sodré and Rubens Lessa Vergueiro to draft the party statutes. Five days later it picked a provisional directorship of the party organ, *O Libertador*: Antônio Costa Corrêa, Astolfo Pio Monteiro da Silva, and Israel Dias Novaes.[1]

Israel Dias Novaes, a very intelligent second-year student whose writings revealed an interest in cultural and political matters, was almost always in a good humor. He joked with his friends, sometimes sarcastically, and often gave them nicknames that lasted. Thanks to Israel Dias Novaes, Astolfo Pio Monteiro da Silva became known as "Biquinho" because his hair came down to a point in the middle of his forehead.[2]

Recalling recently the struggles between the Libertadores and Conservadores, Israel Dias Novaes has written that "all the population—our ardent and liberal population—followed closely the student events; the Centro president became at once a national name, because the result came from a free, direct, and secret vote, essential characteristics of legitimacy. Also the men-of-letters and sub-men-of-letters became divided and argued, affiliated as they were obligatorily with one or the other of the two fundamental currents: Libertadores and Conservadores. The first-mentioned were responsible for the democratic agitation at the Arcadas: the strikes, manifestos, street riots. . . . For the conservatives, smug young men, we used the description of reactionaries."[3]

The purpose of the new party has been described clearly by Arrobas Martins. He writes that "we founded the Partido Acadêmico Libertador, an organ through which we sought to dominate the Centro XI de Agosto in order to use the traditional university organization in the combat against the dictatorship."[4]

At the official launching of the Partido Acadêmico Libertador, held on April 23 at the Clube Piratininga, a large gathering of students heard Germinal Feijó read the manifesto written by his good friend Antônio Costa Corrêa. By the time the manifesto was distributed in printed form on May 28, it bore 216 signatures, a fact that its backers hailed (inaccurately) as "without precedence in the politics of the school."[5]

The manifesto spoke of the need to rekindle the enthusiasm of the law students and to demonstrate the existence of an intellectual and moral reaction against "the regressive and antihuman forces" that were "increasing in the world at an appalling rate." It expressed the desire to preserve those virtues "which are great and eternal, good and true, and which should never disappear, lest man disappear: love of liberty, devotion to law and justice, the consecration of human values, honesty, sincerity, pride, and respect for man and his ideas." The manifesto promised that the organization of the new party would be guided by a strict adherence to democracy. And it contained the party's offer to spread the fame of the law school, "upholding itself in all situations, as a force, as a conglomerate of stimulating ideas, as an assemblage of dynamic and active desires, acting in defense of its glorious traditions."[6]

The first draft of the statutes of the party was revised by Arrobas Martins, Paulo Goulart Tormin, and Astolfo Pio Monteiro da Silva and presented in printed form to the party members a few days before the party held its first general assembly. The approval of the statutes by the assembly on June 18 followed much discussion and the adoption of several amendments. In their final form they adhered to the manifesto's pledge of internal democracy. Unlike the other law school parties, the Libertador Party planned to allow all its members to participate in the selection of its candidates (as had been done by the Oposição Acadêmica in the 1920s). The *eleições prévias*, or internal party elections, were to be carried out by registered party members late in August or early in September. The statutes also called for the assembly to elect a fifteen-man directive commission and this was done immediately following the adoption of the statutes. The commission bore a close resemblance to the list of names chosen at the lunch in January.[7]

5. The *Arcadas* during the Presidency of Quintanilha Ribeiro (1940)

The Centro Onze de Agosto, run by Conservador Francisco de Paula Quintanilha Ribeiro, singled out its Casa do Estudante for special attention in 1940. Meanwhile, the Libertadores, often making use of the Sociedade Acadêmica Amigos de Rui Barbosa, attacked dictatorship at home and abroad. "We Conservadores," Antônio Sylvio Cunha Bueno once remarked, "were neutral, and the Libertadores were strongly anti-Vargas."[1]

Following a banquet given by São Paulo business and civic leaders to honor the new director of the pro-Italy *Fanfulla*, Libertadores visited *Diário da Noite* to complain that the foreign press (they had *Fanfulla* in mind) was abusing Brazilian tolerance by attacking nations that maintained a traditional friendship with Brazil. *Diário da Noite* printed the complaint and added that the law students had expressed their repulsion "for certain methods carried out today in international relations."[2] After gaining this publicity, Libertadores proceeded to exterminate the pro-Vargas Frente Nacional de Estudantes, an association that the government had set up in São Paulo, with offices in the Martinelli Building, in an effort to combat student foes of the Estado Novo. The decisive blow was struck when Libertadores and their allies filled a Frente Nacional de Estudantes assembly at which Interventor Ademar de Barros, a Frente sponsor, made an appearance.[3]

The demise of the Frente Nacional de Estudantes was not a serious blow to the government and its agents for they were able to carry on their work among São Paulo university students by using the Movimento Universitário Nacional (MUN). The MUN, which has been described by Vargas' friend José Gomes Talarico as pro-Vargas, had splendid headquarters, on São Paulo's D. José de Barros Street, and apparently the headquarters, together with banquets and cocktail parties, were financed from the funds (tuitions collected from first-year university students) that were supposed to be used to support the *centros acadêmicos*. Following the increase in annual university tuitions (from 300 to 600 milreis) in February 1940, and the refusal of the government of Ademar de Barros to heed the protests of the *centros acadêmicos*, a group of students issued a scathing condemnation of the MUN, which had supported the increase and been given 80 thousand milreis (80:000$000; i.e., 80 contos) to pay the tuitions of fifteen students in each college. The MUN was accused of distributing the tuition money to students who would "undermine the campaign against the tuition increase." It was branded an incubator of spies because it had obtained the power to assign jobs to poor students and grant railroad passes.[4]

Centro President Quintanilha Ribeiro, campaigning against the tuition increase, was described as "ridiculous and impertinent" by the MUN. In this campaign he had the support of *O Libertador*. But the principal objective of *O Libertador*, making its second appearance in June 1940, was to get an early start at defeating the Conservadores in November. Articles by Luís Leite Ribeiro, Paulo Goulart Tormin, and Hélio Rubens Junqueira Caldas repeated the call of the Libertador manifesto for a movement of renovation at the *arcadas*.[5]

Libertadores joined Conservadores as representatives of the *arcadas* at the fourth Conselho Nacional de Estudantes, held in Rio in the latter part of July. Although the Libertador directorship named five official representatives (including *diretoria* members Luís Leite

Ribeiro, Fernando Pereira da Rocha Filho, and Alberto de Almeida Lima),[6] still other Libertadores went to the Conselho in Rio. Germinal Feijó and Antônio Costa Corrêa showed up as representatives of the Sociedade Amigos de Rui Barbosa and the União Nacional Acadêmica de São Paulo. São Paulo sent thirty-four delegates to the fourth Conselho and they brought credentials from almost as many organizations, especially since José Gomes Talarico arrived in Rio as the representative of six organizations.[7]

The Libertadores persuaded the Conselho to adopt a resolution proclaiming the students' "unshakeable faith in Democracy" and their inability to remain silent about the use of force in Europe to overcome liberty and law.[8] But the most influential Paulista at the Conselho was Conservador Quintanilha Ribeiro. He proposed, in the name of the student associations of São Paulo, a slate of UNE officers that was elected by a vote of 248 to 4. The slate, headed by Luís Pinheiro Paes Leme of the Faculdade Nacional de Direito (in the Federal District), brought the secretary generalship to Antônio Franca for the third time and the first vice-presidency to Ulisses Guimarães.[9]

Germinal Feijó returned to São Paulo in time to act as secretary of a meeting at which the leaders of the Sociedade Amigos de Rui Barbosa allotted the Sociedade's officerships for the coming year. With recent graduate Francisco Morato de Oliveira presiding for the last time, Américo Marco Antônio was named to succeed him. The new officers were almost entirely signers of the manifesto launching the Partido Libertador. Feijó was again designated first orator. Roberto de Abreu Sodré became secretary general and Rubens Lessa Vergueiro first secretary.[10]

In August 1940 anti-Vargas activists, such as Arrobas Martins, distributed reproductions of a lengthy letter about petroleum written earlier that month to Vargas by author Monteiro Lobato, a member of the first board of editors of *O Onze de Agosto* (in 1903). The letter, considered by the authorities to be insulting to Vargas, the Conselho Nacional do Petróleo, and the Departamento Nacional de Produção Mineral, resulted in a six-month jail sentence for Monteiro Lobato. Law students protested the jail sentence. Although Vargas ordered the release of Monteiro Lobato after he had served two months, the author never forgave "that monster, called Getúlio," for the prison sentence.[11]

The Conservadores devoted themselves faithfully to raising funds for the Centro's Casa do Estudante. The drive was quite successful, thanks to a donation by the class that graduated in 1909 and a 50:000$000 donation solicited by Law School Director Soares de Faria. Money was also raised by the sale of copies of *Poesia sob as*

Arcadas, edited by Ulisses Guimarães. Many copies of the book, containing poems written by law students between 1935 and 1940, were purchased by José Carlos de Macedo Soares, the Bucha's top man, and Cásper Líbero, the politically ambitious director of *A Gazeta* (who had joined the Bucha around 1906). Plans were made to offer books of the writings of Ulisses Guimarães and his fellow Conservador José Malanga after judges named them the school's best prose and poetry writers of 1939.[12]

Quintanilha Ribeiro's best known step on behalf of the Casa do Estudante was the organization of the Baile das Américas, a formal ball, held on October 12 (Columbus Day) at the Municipal Stadium (Estádio do Pacaembu). Tickets for admission and table reservations were sold at São Paulo's most respectable clubs and at the consulates of some of the American republics. They were bought by members of São Paulo high society and yielded 52:000$000. After deducting expenses, the Casa do Estudante received 28:700$000.[13]

6. Kidnapping of Chico Elefante (September 1940)

Francisco Ramos, the little man who served drinks at the Centro Onze de Agosto bar and took care of the billiard tables, was liked by the students. He liked them well enough but wished they would not keep calling him Chico Elefante. He really did not have a large nose that could be compared with an elephant's trunk (*tromba*).

The idea of kidnapping Chico Elefante occurred to Germinal Feijó and some other members of the Partido Libertador in September 1940 when they were having difficulty getting publicity in the controlled daily press. Israel Dias Novaes has written of the Libertadores: "In order to make their activities known, they reached the point of kidnapping, but on a modest scale."[1]

Chico was at the bar on Thursday, September 19, when a few students invited him to what they promised would be a "formidable banquet" on Saturday night, with champagne and delicious food. When the appointed time rolled around, it was a surprise to Chico to be driven to an unpretentious place for a meal and told that the banquet in São Paulo's Penha district would follow. Chico was even more surprised by what did follow. He was driven at "90 kilometers per hour" for "hour after hour." When he finally suggested that perhaps the students had taken the wrong road to the Penha district, Germinal Feijó and Paulo Biroli Neto (head of the Libertador *diretoria*) explained: "Chico, you have just been kidnapped by us. We are going to take you to a country place in Guararema, where you can rest. You work a lot, never take a vacation, and are emaciated."

Chico became frightened. He recalled (he said later) the fruitless and publicized search for a capybara that had once disappeared from the Jardim da Luz zoo. The capybara had never been found because law students had killed it and, after presenting it to an Italian restaurant as something shot in a hunt, had eaten it.[2] When Chico protested mildly about his own abduction, his captors paid no attention, and therefore he screamed. But upon reaching the country place, a very simple property of Germinal Feijó's family, Chico discovered that he rather liked being kidnapped. He went horseback riding and fished.[3]

In the meantime, in the state capital the fate of Chico Elefante became a matter of concern to his family, to students, and to the public. Students called on the police and press for help. The press published a photograph of the missing "barman," together with a physical description and an account of the clothing he wore when last seen. "If anyone knows about his whereabouts," the story concluded, "would he please communicate with the Centro Acadêmico XI de Agosto."[4]

On Thursday, September 26, "generally well-informed circles" let it be known that Chico had been kidnapped and would be set free at 11:00 A.M. the next day. The return of the captive, at the scheduled hour, took place with great fanfare at São Paulo's Praça da República. A crowd witnessed a celebration for which students had provided a band and a large placard reading "Ordem da Tromba" (Order of the Elephant's Trunk). The unshaven barman was driven through the streets in a noisy parade. When a *Diário da Noite* reporter approached the modest hero, he was told: "Please don't call me Chico Elefante in the newspaper. My name is Francisco Ramos and I don't like the nickname. It's too big for me."

Despite the plea, *Diário da Noite*'s page-one headline announced that "Chico Elefante Appeared!" A long story about the festive reception, illustrated with photographs of crowds beneath the Ordem da Tromba placard, reported Chico as saying that his abductors had treated him like a "lord." Thus the students gained their publicity alongside the accounts of a "furious blitzkrieg" over London in which ninety-eight Nazi planes were shot down. A picture showed Chico Elefante in the company of Libertador leader Luís Leite Ribeiro and Ordem da Tromba President Hélio Rubens Junqueira Caldas.[5]

Chico Elefante received his long-promised banquet around midday on October 12. The printed announcement invited students to join the Ordem da Tromba and attend the "formidable lunch" in the Green Room of the Brasserie Paulista "because it is necessary to glorify the historic personality of Chico Elefante, the greatest figure of the *arcadas* in modern times." The signers of the invitation, all Libertadores, included Luís Leite Ribeiro, Hélio Rubens Junqueira Caldas, Germinal Feijó, Fernando Pereira da Rocha Filho, Renato Pintaudi Macedo, Hiram Mayr Cerqueira, Roberto Heladio Azevedo Sodré, Salomão Izar Filho, Haroldo Bueno Magano, Astolfo Pio Monteiro da Silva, and Lenício Pacheco Ferreira.[6]

"The impossibility of using the press to reveal certain facts that occur within this college"—a reason given for the kidnapping—was one of many complaints listed in an anonymous mimeographed broadside released at the *arcadas* on October 30, 1940. The broadside took aim at law school Director Sebastião Soares de Faria. This was surprising because the director, known affectionately as "O Velhinho" (the Old Man), enjoyed enormous popularity among the students. He was regarded by most of them as neutral in politics, but even the extreme Vargas haters, who classified him as a government supporter, considered him an intelligent and able director. His only interest seemed to be the law school. He personally helped poor students pay their tuitions.[7]

According to the broadside, the director "managed to find, among the students who were short of funds, two or three without character and he maintains them as paid spies to inform him about what goes on in student circles in order to organize his 'black list' of persons to be persecuted." The writers of the broadside added: "Everyone knows that during his directorship he carried out the greatest fraud ever known in the history of the law school—the case of Sr. Casemiro Pinto Neto, nicknamed 'Bauru,' who obtained his degree in the class of 1939, which he never entered, . . . after a clandestine examination."[8] (Casemiro Pinto Neto, a radio news broadcaster and supporter of the Estado Novo, was well known as the inventor of the "Bauru sandwich," enjoyed by law students at the Ponto Chic Bar at the Largo do Paissandu.)[9]

7. An Anti-Vargas Victory, Thanks to Pavan and Cherkaski (November 1940)

The Libertador Party in 1940, unlike the Pro Ribeiro de Barros movement of a year earlier, had plenty of time to organize for a big battle against the Conservadores. The objective of the battle, as seen by dozens of Libertador leaders, was to place the *arcadas* openly and actively on the side of democracy in Brazil and the liberal traditions of the Western world. They viewed the struggle against the Vargas dictatorship as the patriotic duty of true democrats.[1]

The issue in 1940 was clear-cut despite the vagueness of the position of the Partido Acadêmico Conservador, or perhaps because of that vagueness. Should the Centro Onze de Agosto boldly bury vagueness and "neutralism"? Or should its primary concern be the affairs of the school (such as the Casa do Estudante) and the enjoyment of the benefits accruing from an understanding with government officials—which these officials and the Centro recognized could never go so far as to appear to be an outright rejection of the liberal tradition of the *arcadas* and the spirit of 1932?

It was far easier to live with some such understanding than to burn pictures of Vargas and otherwise defy the regime. The strong-arm methods of the Estado Novo had sent its principal political opponents into exile. Jails were filled with people whom the regime regarded as troublemakers. At the same time, the events in much of the world seemed to confirm the thesis that strong, undemocratic governments, such as the Estado Novo, were the most efficient. The "liberal democracy of the past" was having a bad time when the Libertador group at the *arcadas*, having become Brazil's most active opponent to the Estado Novo, tried to take over the renowned Centro Acadêmico Onze de Agosto.

The Libertadores, practicing democracy, held an *eleição prévia*, or meeting to nominate candidates, on August 30 and were pleased when 304 "party members" showed up. It was a peaceful affair. Most of the candidates (who had been required to inscribe their names thirty days before the *prévia*) were unopposed. Thus, without contest Luís Leite Ribeiro became candidate for president, Wilson Rahal for first orator, Rodrigo Barjas Filho for first secretary, João Sanchez Postigo for second secretary, Vítor Tieghi for *procurador*, Renato Pintaudi Macedo for *bibliotecário* (librarian), and Geraldo Mâncio de Toledo for archivist. In the only contests, vice-presidential hopeful Rui de Azevedo Marques swamped his opponent while second-orator candidate Lenício Pacheco Ferreira was nominated without trouble and treasurer candidate Horácio Cherkaski narrowly defeated Paulo Henrique Meinberg. The selections for the editorial commission were Antônio Costa Corrêa, Astolfo Pio Monteiro da Silva, poet Péricles Eugênio da Silva Ramos, and Rui do Amaral.[2]

Luís Leite Ribeiro, nephew of diplomat Orlando Leite Ribeiro (who had worked for revolution with Luís Carlos Prestes in the 1920s), belonged to a prominent and wealthy family.[3] His campaign for the Centro presidency was articulated by Roberto Victor Cordeiro, who had helped create the Libertador Party[4] (and who was in love with a sister of Luís Leite Ribeiro).

To oppose the Libertadores, the Partido Conservador's fifteen-man *comissão diretora* (which included Ulisses Guimarães, José Malanga, and Oscar Bressane) chose a strong slate in September. Presidential candidate Antônio Sylvio Cunha Bueno, nicknamed "Boi d'agua" because of his above-average weight, was intelligent, considerate, and very popular. A past vice-president of the Associação Acadêmica Álvares de Azevedo, he had been one of eighteen students awarded government scholarships for a trip to Japan in the middle of 1940.[5]

Two minor parties were important only because they could give the Libertadores much needed help by attracting votes from the Conservadores. One of them was the Partido Acadêmico Reformador, the conservative Catholic group that had won a few posts in 1939. Its 1940 slate, headed by Osvaldo Pinheiro Dória, included Jarbas Teixeira de Carvalho, candidate for treasurer, and the openly pro-Vargas José Barbosa, candidate for *procurador*. Jarbas and José Barbosa, like most of the Reformador candidates, were also listed by the Chapa Independente, headed by Alcides Prudente Pavan.[6] Pavan, a former Conservador, had prestige, and the schism he brought about in the Partido Conservador damaged Cunha Bueno.[7]

The Partido Conservador was nevertheless expected to win. Its four years of successful life may have given it an edge over a new party since the choice of a party by a new student was often determined by friendships developed with older students.

Like the Libertador Party, the Conservadores named *comissões de representantes* in each of the five classes to work on their classmates. And, like the Libertadores, the Conservadores set up a large radio broadcasting commission (it included Nelson Coutinho, president of the Academia de Letras da Faculdade de Direito) and a strong propaganda commission.[8] Second-year student Rivaldo Assis Cintra, an effective member of the propaganda commission, had joined the Conservadores in his first year because of the friendship of Cunha Bueno.[9]

O Conservador published a picture of the uncompleted eleven-floor Casa do Estudante, which, it wrote, "is the fruit of our activity, of our orientation, and one of the reasons of our electoral campaign." "Three victories in four years," it added, "represent the confidence of the electorate in the candidacies indicated by the Partido Acadêmico Conservador."[10]

The Libertadores released an appeal for votes written by Luís Swarztman, former Reação Acadêmica presidential candidate and recent winner of a Rui Barbosa Oratory Prize awarded by the Sociedade Universitária de Cultura. They gave publicity also to backing received from third-year student Rui Homem de Melo Lacerda, president and organizer of the Sociedade Universitária de Cultura, and third-year student Fernando José Fernandes, first orator of that society.[11]

"Basta!," a mimeographed broadside that appeared on October 31, asserted that one of the candidates (Cunha Bueno), "always divorced from the student class," devoted all his time to "using and abusing the good name of our school in order to make excursions, for his own profit and with his notorious clique, within Brazil and abroad." The broadside accused the candidate of seeking "to deceive the student conscience with illusory and ridiculous promises: trips to Japan and Chile, stays at Poços de Caldas and Lindoia, and other extravagances!" Then Cunha Bueno delivered a statement denying that he was presenting "a pompous program, full of sonorous loquacity and impossible promises."[12]

The Libertadores' Luís Leite Ribeiro released a booklet containing his platform. In the introduction he quoted Olavo Bilac's words, delivered at the *arcadas* twenty-five years earlier, calling on the young people of São Paulo to start a new campaign and to remember the campaigns for abolition and the Republic that "originated here . . . in an impetus of enthusiasm." Leite Ribeiro's *plataforma* echoed Bilac's concern about national defense and therefore recommended aviation instruction for law students and the provision of uniforms for the school's reserve officer training program (CPOR). He also suggested that the Centro membership dues, being paid by only about four hundred, be reduced in order to induce more people to pay them: "Considering the law students, the *pré-jurídico* students, and the graduates, all of whom could be Centro members, there should be about 1,500 yearly contributors."[13]

The electorate was invited to be present at entertainments on the night before the voting. The Partido Libertador called on the law students to attend a "festival" at the Casino Antártica, where the actress Alda Garrido was performing. During an intermission, the party promised, Alda Garrido would be greeted by one of the Libertador leaders.[14]

At the Largo de São Francisco, the walls of the school building were completely covered with electoral posters, the largest one proclaiming the candidacy of Cunha Bueno. The Largo itself was bedlam. The loud speakers used by competing parties made such a din that a passerby told a journalist: "I don't understand why the police allow such an uproar." Local store owners said that the "hullabaloo" was bad for business and painful to the nerves. But the journalist concluded that the electoral activity had "an importance that extends beyond the famous 'Território Livre.'"[15]

Candidates and *cabos eleitorais* were described by the journalist as busy with "intensive intrigue." The most effective bit of intrigue was an understanding reached by two candidates for treasurer, Cherkaski of the Libertadores and Jarbas Teixeira de Carvalho of the Partido Reformador. Both were close to Roberto Victor Cordeiro. Cherkaski agreed that his friends would vote for Jarbas, and, in return, Jarbas' friends would vote for Luís Leite Ribeiro.[16]

This understanding and the Pavan schism brought defeat to the hard-campaigning Cunha Bueno. The following votes were cast for president:[17]

Luís Leite Ribeiro (Libertador)	382
Antônio Sylvio Cunha Bueno (Conservador)	377
Osvaldo Pinheiro Dória (Reformador)	75
Alcides Prudente Pavan (Independente)	65

The minor parties elected only one officer, Jarbas Teixeira de Carvalho (who had made the deal with Cherkaski). Conservador candidates won the positions of first orator (Péricles Rolim), first secretary, *procurador*, and archivist. Libertadores, besides gaining the presidency, won the posts of vice-president, second orator, second secretary, and *bibliotecário* (Renato Macedo). Two of the four editorial commission posts went to Libertadores (Astolfo Pio Monteiro da Silva and Péricles Eugênio Silva Ramos), and they gained one of three places on the *comissão de sindicância* (Nelson Speers).[18]

O Libertador, managed by Antônio Costa Corrêa, Israel Dias Novaes, and Rômulo Fonseca, hailed the "great triumph" of Luís Leite Ribeiro in its December issue. "We found it necessary," a first-page editorial said, "to strike down last-minute collusions, long-established situations, outside protectionism, and many other obstacles." The editorial expressed particular pleasure at the "ideological point of view" assumed by the Libertador Party and added that, while the party had put its ideas into practice "in the daily and persistent struggle . . . to remove . . . apathy . . . , our opponents sought to exaggerate and falsify that aspect of our campaign, using it for electoral intrigue."

In conclusion, *O Libertador* said that the possession of an ideology at the law school "means to want to maintain it as a tutelary haven for a handful of young people . . . who are always ready to assume the post that history bequeathed them of being the leading defenders of the traditions of liberty and culture. It means to want to have the young people of the Arcadas maintain themselves as a great force, as they always have been, conscious of their rights and also of their duties to the people of Brazil, who for a long time have been accustomed to seeing in this youth the pioneer of great achievements!"[19]

V

The Centro in Libertador Hands (1941)

1. *Trote*, *Peruada*, and *Caravanas* (April–July 1941)

Four hundred candidates, having completed *cursos pré-jurídicos*, were given tough written and oral examinations when they sought admission to the 200 available places in the first-year law school class that was to begin its studies in March 1941. Professors Alexandre Correia, Lino de Morais Leme (brother of Ernesto), and Mário Masagão tested their Latin; Professors Honório Monteiro and Antônio Ferreira Cesarino Júnior asked them about philosophical matters; and Professors Noé Azevedo, José Carlos de Ataliba Nogueira, and Cardoso de Melo Neto tested their knowledge of sociology. So difficult were the questions that only 83 applicants were admitted, prompting a São Paulo daily to observe that the 83 ought to look forward to a reception by a band of music at the Largo de São Francisco instead of the customary *trote* (hazing). To increase the number admitted, it became necessary to give further examinations, but they added only 50, to give the new class an enrollment of 133.[1] In future years still others joined the class, some because they had to repeat a year and others by transfer. The many who transferred to the *arcadas* from the Faculdade de Direito de Niterói, where admittance was less difficult, were called *vagabundos* (truants) by their São Paulo schoolmates.

The 133 who passed the entrance exams early in 1941 were greeted by that year's Comitê de Trote, whose director, Vítor Tieghi, had been the Libertadores' unsuccessful candidate for *procurador*. The freshmen's trepidation was understandable because past Comitês de Trote were reportedly responsible for injuries and even a death.[2] Anacleto de Oliveira Faria, historian of the new class, has written:

> For most of the students, who had already been taking courses [*pré-jurídicos*] for two years at the College, the *trote* seemed outlandish and unreasonable. But the veterans did not consider that

> circumstance, and all of us suffered the traditional hardships: heads shaved, flour put all over our bodies, walks practically in the nude in public parks, etc. I recall that one morning we were obliged to dress with trousers and coats on backwards. By means of the coat lapels . . . we were tied up in a long grotesque line! And in that way we went down to São Bento Street, crossed the Viaduto do Chá, and reached the Praça da República, from where we were transported, without shirts or money . . . , to distant Butantã, where we were abandoned.[3]

The *trote*, which usually lasted for about a month, customarily ended with an elaborate parade of floats, known as the *peruada* (flock of turkeys) for the amusement of freshmen and "veterans" and the diversion of spectators—residents of São Paulo who lined the streets. For the *peruada* of 1941, held on Saturday night, June 7, invitations were printed in "Macaroni French" (words bore resemblance to French) and signed by Tieghi "of the red beard" (De La Barbiche Rosé).[4] The event was described in *Tribuna Acadêmica* (directed by João Nery Guimarães and Joaquim Rui Gonçalves): "This year's freshmen should be proud. There was a *peruada* to receive them. . . . It was organized by Tieghi, that heavily bearded veteran who drove us crazy with fear in April and May; that heavily bearded veteran with the air of a revolutionary, the air of one who wanted to drench his beard in the blood of freshmen to make it red; that veteran who refuted all the impressions we had of him by becoming a friend of all of us."[5]

The parade through the city lasted for two hours. The float that paid tribute to Carmen Miranda's success in the United States bore freshmen dressed as Indians, and one as a girl, and was filled with humorous signs set among trees. The Sociedade Acadêmica Amigos das Mulheres (Friends of Women) had a float. Tieghi appeared as Moses bringing tablets with the commandments issued by the Monte Sinai do Largo de São Francisco. A few of the commandments were marked as partly censored.

When the parade was over, freshmen and veterans sang, danced, and stomped at the Largo de São Francisco.[6] The scene prompted *Tribuna Acadêmica* to eulogize the general fraternization.

But there had been, in the first months of the school year, no fraternization between the leaders of the two large parties, Libertador and Conservador. One conflict began in March, after Goiás Interventor Pedro Ludovico Teixeira invited the Centro to send an *embaixada* to visit the Faculdade de Direito de Goiânia and see points of interest in the state. Centro President Luís Leite Ribeiro, drawing up a list of members for this *caravana artística*, included two or three Conservador musicians who had been members of a similar mission to Goiás a year earlier. The Conservador musicians, demanding what Leite Ribeiro called "large and improper concessions" in return for their collaboration, were dropped from the list. As finally constituted, the Centro's "cultural mission," headed by Luís Arrobas Martins, was made up of fifteen members, among them Fernando José Fernandes, Péricles Eugênio da Silva Ramos, Hiram Mayr Cerqueiro, Nelson Speers, and Wilson Rahal (director of the Centro's Departamento Artístico).

Meanwhile some Conservadores secretly organized a Caravana de Goiás, including the musicians dropped from Leite Ribeiro's list. The Caravana de Goiás received financial assistance from the government of Ademar de Barros and money for musical instruments from the law school directorship. Early in April it left for Goiás before the Centro's "official" caravan was scheduled to depart. Centro officers, learning of this development, communicated with Goiás, only to find that the "spurious" caravan was occupying lodgings that the official caravan had expected to use and was visiting points of interest that the official caravan had expected to visit. Leite Ribeiro advised the authorities of Goiás that they were dealing with a group that did not represent the Centro Onze de Agosto. In June *O Libertador* deplored the "intrigue" of the Conservadores and the support given by the law school directorship to the intriguers.[7]

The Libertadores were more successful when the Centro responded to an invitation from Landulfo Alves, *interventor* of Bahia. On the *Pedro I* on July 11, twenty students left Santos for Salvador. Among them were Rui de Azevedo Marques (head of the *embaixada*), Alberto de Almeida Lima (president of the Libertador *comissão diretora*), Paulo Henrique Meinberg (in charge of artistic performances), Renato Macedo, Luís Arrobas Martins, Rui do Amaral, Wilson Rahal, and Heitor Borelli de Alvarenga Freire. Heitor Borelli de Alvarenga Freire's name was unknown to most of the students because he was always called by his nickname "Morango" (Strawberry), a reference to the redness of his nose.

After the disembarkation in Salvador on July 18, the Libertadores' active politician Renato Macedo (known as Renatinho) told the press there of the admiration of the *bandeirantes* for the Bahian students who had visited São Paulo about two months earlier. The São Paulo law students called on the *interventor* and presented, on July 26, two *festivais artísticos*. They were back in São Paulo early in August.[8]

2. Return of the Dismissed Professors and Other Changes (May–June 1941)

From the moment he became law school director in 1939, Sebastião Soares de Faria had his heart set on reversing the decree of January 1939 that had forced the dismissal of Professors Waldemar Ferreira, Sampaio Dória, and Vicente Ráo. First he spoke with Ademar de Barros and learned that the *interventor* would not oppose his wish. Then in February 1940 he and the other faculty members addressed a petition to Vargas. The petition was to be presented to Vargas by a commission made up of Professors José de Alcântara Machado d'Oliveira, Noé Azevedo, and José Soares de Melo, but the commission was unsuccessful in its efforts to see Vargas.

Soares de Faria persuaded Ademar de Barros to forward the petition to the president together with the *interventor*'s favorable recommendation. Next, Soares de Faria spoke with Education Minister Gustavo Capanema during one of Capanema's visits to São Paulo. Capanema promised that the January 1939 ruling would be reversed shortly. A few days later, in the middle of May 1941, Capanema's promise became reality. Alberto de Almeida Lima, president of the Libertador *comissão diretora*, sent congratulatory telegrams, in the name of the party, to Ráo, Sampaio Dória, and Waldemar Ferreira. *O Conservador* also hailed the new development.[1]

As a reporter for *Diário de S. Paulo*, Arrobas Martins described the meetings held at the *arcadas* on the afternoon of May 28 to welcome the returning professors. At the building's entrance, students received the three professors with applause, "vivas," and exploding firecrackers, and then they accompanied them to the desk-filled faculty room. There Soares de Faria, presiding for almost the last time as director of the school, called on Cardoso de Melo Neto to give the welcoming address. Following Cardoso de Melo's remarks, the returning professors pledged themselves to continue to be guided by the principles that had always inspired them. Waldemar Ferreira presented a memorandum, which declared that no step had been taken by any of the three to bring about their return.

The faculty meeting was followed by a crowded *assembléia extraordinária* of the Centro Onze de Agosto in the João Mendes Júnior Room. Rui Homem de Melo Lacerda greeted the returning professors in the name of the Centro, and Germinal Feijó spoke in the name of the Sociedade Acadêmica Amigos de Rui Barbosa. After Waldemar Ferreira, giving a response, recalled his days as a student and Centro orator, the students persuaded Ráo, Sampaio Dória, and Professor Emeritus Francisco Morato also to speak.[2]

The faculty had, two weeks earlier, been expanded as a result of a *concurso* (competition) held in September 1940. The new inductees, both former Integralistas, were Gofredo da Silva Telles Júnior (Gofredinho), new *livre-docente* of the introduction to the science of law, and Miguel Reale, new *professor catedrático* of the philosophy of law.

Reale, by this time the author of nine books (two of them defending Integralismo), had won his September 1940 *concurso* against three rivals by a three-to-two vote in which the negative votes were cast by the two São Paulo law professors on the examining commission (Mário Masagão and Alexandre Correia) and the three favorable votes by the outside professors (two from Bahia and one from the federal capital). Following the *concurso*, São Paulo Law School faculty members had met and voted, fourteen to two, to reject the decision of the commission of the five judges. Reale, objecting to this denial of his professorship, had pointed out that the regulations did not allow Masagão and Correia, examining commissioners, to vote on his case at the faculty meeting and, therefore, the votes against him had been only twelve, which was short of a majority of the full faculty, required for overturning an examining commission decision. Reale's case had gone to the Conselho Nacional de Educação together with supporting opinions of experts, such as Hermes Lima, Francisco San Tiago Dantas, Plínio Barreto, and José Adriano Marrey Júnior. The Conselho had ruled in favor of Reale and in May 1941 he had joined the faculty at the *arcadas*.[3]

Changes in the directorships of student associations were made at meetings held in April 1941. With recent graduate Américo Marco Antônio presiding and Roberto de Abreu Sodré acting as secretary, the Sociedade Acadêmica Amigos de Rui Barbosa met and chose Rubens Lessa Vergueiro president and Antônio Costa Corrêa secretary general. Germinal Feijó was reelected first orator.[4] Israel Dias Novaes and Péricles Eugênio da Silva Ramos were named directors of *Depoimento*, which was to be the organ of the Sociedade but was never published.[5]

José Carlos de Macedo Soares, asked to be present at the installation of officers of the Sociedade Amigos de Rui Barbosa, decided that it would be prudent not to accept.[6] However, as he was president of the Instituto Ítalo-Brasileiro de Alta-Cultura, he agreed to preside at the meeting of the Sociedade Universitária Amigos da Itália where Professor Ataliba Nogueira spoke and where new officers were chosen—among them Antônio Delorenzo Neto (president), Damiano Gullo (vice-president), and Pedro Brasil Bandecchi (Propaganda Department head).[7] Like the Amigos da Itália, the União Cultural Brasil–Estados Unidos met in the João Mendes Júnior Room. It reelected Pacheco e Silva president and Rone Amorim secretary general and congratulated Professors Jorge Americano and Pacheco e Silva for having been chosen to participate in a cultural mission to the United States.[8]

When the São Paulo Italian-language weekly *Corriere degli Italiani* insulted Eleanor Roosevelt and Winston Churchill in a political cartoon in July, groups of law students seized copies of the magazine from the newsstands. Other law students, carrying out a "punitive expedition," invaded the offices of the magazine on the twenty-third floor of the Martinelli Building. They marked the walls with *V*'s (for Victory) and made off with bundles of copies of the magazine. The magazines were piled up and burned in the Largo de São Francisco in a ceremony that attracted the press. After the ceremony, students paraded noisily through the streets shouting vivas for Churchill and Mrs. Roosevelt.[9]

By this time significant changes had taken place in the state administration. Ademar de Barros, on poor terms with Vargas, was replaced early in June 1941 by Fernando Costa, a Paulista who had been serving as minister of agriculture. The new *interventor* was visited by a commission of university students that requested a reduction in the 600-milreis tuition. He explained that Vargas had asked him to show especial kindness to the young people of São Paulo in order that they become completely integrated into the "new spirit of things implanted in Brazil on November 10, 1937." The tuition, he said, would be reduced to what it had been before being doubled by Ademar de Barros in February 1940.[10]

For justice secretary, the new *interventor* chose Abelardo Vergueiro César ("Abelardinho"), the Bucha *chaveiro* who had been secretary of the Liga Nacionalista and an organizer of the PRP's Ação Nacional wing. Fernando Costa also found a new law school director: Professor Cardoso de Melo Neto, the former governor and *interventor* who was widely known by his nickname "Cazuza."[11]

Under Fernando Costa, the State Department of Press and Propaganda (DEIP—Departamento Estadual de Imprensa e Propaganda) was run by law school *livre-docente* Cândido Mota Filho ("Motinha"), former state assemblyman of the Partido Constitucionalista. Antônio Sylvio Cunha Bueno, loser of the Centro election of 1940, was given a post in the office of the new *interventor* in 1941 and was named a state government lawyer in 1942.[12]

Gofredo da Silva Telles ("Gofredão"), the former mayor, headed the Administrative Department (Departamento Administrativo) of the state. One of the members of that department, longtime PRP politician Alexandre Marcondes Filho, became Vargas' minister of labor in January 1942, and Professor Miguel Reale was chosen to replace Marcondes Filho in the Departamento Administrativo. Consequently, Reale's regular teaching schedule, begun in May 1941, was interrupted.[13]

3. Conservadores Infiltrate the Libertadores' Prévia (August 30, 1941)

Centro President Luís Leite Ribeiro was criticized by the Conservadores because he accomplished very little on behalf of the Centro's Casa do Estudante.[1] Some anti-Vargas activists also criticized him. He became, in the opinion of leftist Antônio Costa Corrêa, a government supporter after taking charge of the Centro.[2]

Early in the 1941 school year, Libertador activists looked forward to electing Roberto de Abreu Sodré to the Centro presidency in November. Abreu Sodré ("o Bé"), the Amigos de Rui Barbosa officer who had helped edit *"folha dobrada"* and draft the Libertador statutes, was considered the party's natural presidential candidate. Some Libertadores favored Fernando Pereira da Rocha Filho ("Fernandeta"), the police *delegado*'s son who had been named secretary general of the party in 1940 (at the lunch following the defeat of José Maria Ribeiro de Barros) and who had also edited *"folha dobrada."* But "Fernandeta" stepped aside, leaving the way clear for the Libertadores to launch Abreu Sodré's candidacy (for the August 30 *prévia*) at a *chopada* at the Recreio Molinaro on the evening of May 21.[3]

However, by the time of the *chopada*, the *prévia* candidacy of Abreu Sodré was being contested by Fernando José Fernandes ("Fernandinho"—"o homem dos FF," the man of the FF's). Fernandes was considered a less able orator than Abreu Sodré and his affiliation with the party had been of shorter duration. He was not a signer of the party's April 1940 manifesto. But he and Rui Homem de Melo Lacerda, leaders of the Sociedade Universitária de Cultura, had persuaded friends to vote for Luís Leite Ribeiro in November 1940. "When a young man like Fernando runs for office," an admirer said, "people do not think about parties."[4]

At the *chopada*, Abreu Sodré was praised by Antônio Costa Corrêa, Waldomiro Alves Junqueira, Luís França, José Viegas Muniz Júnior, Vítor Tieghi, and Rui do Amaral. Alberto de Almeida Lima, president of the Libertador's *comissão diretora*, denied that the party was split between two wings.[5]

The 1941 *prévia*, unlike that of 1940, offered voters many choices. The three *prévia* contestants for the vice-presidential nomination were Astolfo Pio Monteiro da Silva, Horácio Cherkaski, and Marino da Costa Terra. The candidates for first orator were Germinal Feijó and Rui Homem de Melo Lacerda (the representative of the university students on the governing Conselho Universitário).[6]

João Nery Guimarães and Joaquim Rui Gonçalves, who were among the many *prévia* candidates, published an issue of *Tribuna Acadêmica* that was filled with Abreu Sodré propaganda. One of its articles was written by *O Libertador* director Antônio Costa Corrêa. No advocate of having people "not think about parties," he lamented that new party members, unfamiliar with the party's initial manifesto, "still do not know what the party signifies." He called the party a renovating and democratic current, "an idea in action," and described Abreu Sodré as unsurpassed in ability "to carry forward the party's ideas, force, and action."[7] When *O Libertador* published pictures of Abreu Sodré and Fernando José Fernandes in June, the picture of Abreu Sodré was the larger and was placed in the more prominent position.

Conservador Cunha Bueno promoted the idea of having Conservadores infiltrate the Libertador *prévia* and vote for "Fernandinho," apparently the weaker candidate. The plan worked.[8] Whereas 304 voters had participated in the 1940 *prévia*, 582 voted on August 30. This was well over half the student body. Fernando José Fernandes received 338 votes and became the Libertador standard bearer, much to the disappointment of Arrobas Martins, an Abreu Sodré backer.[9] (Arrobas customarily became very downcast on suffering setbacks.) Germinal Feijó, regarded by many as the hardest fighter of the anti-Vargas resistance, became the party's candidate for first orator.[10] The vice-presidential nomination was won by Cherkaski, known sometimes as the "Menino de Ouro" (Golden Boy) because of his never failing loyalty to friends and refusal ever to speak poorly of anyone.[11]

4. An Honorary Doctorate for Vargas (September 1941)

Interest in the struggle between Conservadores and Libertadores for Centro posts was diverted in September and early October by a crisis at the law school. The origin of the crisis was a decision, reached by students at some of the São Paulo University colleges late in August, to recommend that Vargas be given an honorary degree (Doutor Honoris Causa) by the university. The idea had been strongly advocated by José Gomes Talarico and two university sports organizations he headed, the Confederação Brasileira dos Desportes Universitários (CBDU, successor of the CUBE) and the Federação Universitária Paulista de Esportes (FUPE). Talarico, close to Education Minister Capanema as well as to Vargas, was pleased with steps taken by the federal administration to recognize the UNE and the CBDU and to finance student trips.[1] Although Talarico spent some time in Rio, he spent more time in São Paulo, where his father, an immigrant from Italy, ran a successful construction business. Besides doing work for university student organizations, the Faculdade de Medicina's Centro Acadêmico Osvaldo Cruz, and the União Cultural Brasil–Estados Unidos, Talarico had attended a course at the Escola de Polícia (Police School) in São Paulo; in 1941 he was studying at São Paulo's Faculdade de Filosofia de São Bento.[2]

With one exception, the presidents of the associations representing the students at the colleges of the University of São Paulo agreed with the idea of the honorary degree for Vargas. The exception was Luís Leite Ribeiro. However, the first orator of the Centro Onze de Agosto, Conservador Péricles Rolim, favored the honorary degree.[3]

Anti-Vargas activists at the law school screamed to protest giving Vargas the same honor that the university had in the past bestowed on such figures as Francisco Morato, Júlio de Mesquita Filho, and Armando de Sales Oliveira. Protests also arose at the Grêmio Politécnico, alma mater of Armando de Sales Oliveira.[4]

In Rio, Capanema conferred with Vargas and then told Benjamim Vargas, the president's brother, that the "Paulistas of four hundred years" resisted Talarico's idea. Benjamim phoned São Paulo Justice Secretary Abelardo Vergueiro César, who went to see Fernando Costa. The *interventor* appeared worried about the idea.[5]

Therefore, Talarico sought the help of DEIP Director Cândido Mota Filho and *A Gazeta* chief Cásper Líbero (both of whom, Talarico felt, hoped to become *interventor* in place of Fernando Costa). Líbero accompanied Talarico and Francisco Eumene Machado (beaten by Pupo Netto for the Centro presidency in 1938) when they took a group of pro-Vargas students to see Fernando Costa and deliver the petition signed by all the *centro acadêmico* presidents save Leite Ribeiro.[6] The visitors asked the *interventor* to recommend to Jorge Americano, university *reitor* (president), that the degree be given, and they said that their idea was supported by a large part of the student body. Costa cautioned them not to present the idea to Vargas until it was clear that they had the full support of the student body and the Conselho Universitário. But Cásper Líbero and some of the students called on Vargas a few days later to explain that the students favored his being awarded the degree.[7]

Immediately after the students made this statement to Vargas, Fernando Costa asked Jorge Americano to take the matter up quickly with the Conselho Universitário. The Conselho met on September 22 and found that only two of its members opposed the honorary degree: Professor Ernesto Leme, representative of the law school, and law student Rui Homem de Melo Lacerda, representative of the university students. A letter from Jorge Americano, dated September 23, advised Vargas that the Conselho Universitário had resolved to confer the honorary degree on him "because Your Excellency has been the institutor of university teaching in Brazil."[8]

An emergency session of the Centro Onze de Agosto was held in the school's patio around midday on September 23. In view of the absence of Leite Ribeiro and the ban against the attendance of Conservador officers of the Centro, Lenício Pacheco Ferreira presided. Renato Macedo served as secretary. Opening the speechmaking, Germinal Feijó called out the names of the law students killed in the 1932 Revolution. As he read each name, the living students shouted "present." Upon the conclusion of Feijó's speech, attacking the "shameful gesture" of the Conselho Universitário, Leite Ribeiro arrived, took over from Lenício Pacheco Ferreira, and called on Rivaldo Assis Cintra. Assis Cintra, a Conservador and an outstanding orator, proclaimed that the Conselho's decision was an attack on the university. His speech drew "vivas" for Rui Homem de Melo Lacerda and Ernesto Leme; and shouts of "down with Vargas" and "down with the Conselho Universitário."

Rodrigo Barjas Filho, the first to have signed the request for the emergency session, proposed a one-day strike and a ban against any appearance of Talarico at the *arcadas*. After the unanimous adoption of these proposals, Wilson Rahal, a good orator with leftist tendencies, said that the moment had come to decide between the death or life of dignity "because the old people have lost dignity whereas the young people have dignity." He expressed surprise that Dr. Benedito Montenegro, "revolutionary of 1932," had voted with the majority of the Conselho. "And," he went on to ask, "what about Dr. Cardoso de Melo Neto, who also belonged to the revolution [of 1932]? These same people, who taught us to carry rifles and kill, now betray us." Rahal agreed that the "scoundrels" who pretended to be university students should be banished, and he made four proposals: (*a*) a student commission would investigate the reasons for granting the honorary degree, (*b*) a strike would take place on September 24, (*c*) black ties would be worn for one week, and (*d*) the Centro would seek the backing of the students at other colleges. These proposals, like the earlier ones, were approved unanimously.[9]

Later in the day, following the emergency session, the idea of draping the law school in black crepe emerged during conversations in which Hiram Mayr Cerqueira, Nelson Speers, Renato Macedo, Fernando Jacob, Arrobas Martins, Paulo Henrique Meinberg, Germinal

Feijó, Roberto de Abreu Sodré, Lenício Pacheco Ferreira, and Centro Second Secretary João Sanchez Postigo participated. By the time some of them went to the Rodovalho Funeral Parlor to buy crepe it was early evening. The proprietor of the parlor, feeling suspicious, turned the students down, and so they made their way up and down Augusta Street although most of its stores had closed for the day. One shop, just about to close, appeared to have what the students wanted. They barged in and practically forced the owner to sell more than ten meters of black crepe. Speers supplied the money. The shop owner refused to furnish an invoice and made a hasty departure lest he be caught cooperating with some nefarious student undertaking.[10]

Renato Macedo, Hiram Mayr Cerqueira, Arrobas Martins, João Sanchez Postigo, and Nelson Speers spent most of the night waiting for an opportunity to use the crepe. Plans to hang it on the front of the building were foiled by guards in the street, stationed around construction work still being done on the building. Early in the morning crepe was placed on the patio monument to students killed in 1932 and on the statue of José Bonifácio, o Moço, in the foyer just within the entrance to the school. A small piece of crepe, thrown at the last minute, hung from the balcony at the front of the building.[11]

The crepe hangers went to advise other students, partisans of their cause, because they wanted a strong group on hand to prevent anyone from removing the crepe after the building opened for the day. One of the first people to enter the school and face the group was Law School Director Cardoso de Melo Neto. He reprimanded the students severely and ordered that the crepe be removed. Near the statue of José Bonifácio, o Moço, Germinal Feijó and Roberto de Abreu Sodré objected strenuously. "Cazuza," shocked by their lack of respect, suspended them both from the school. This step, Arrobas Martins has written, created the necessary climate and reason for the student strike.[12]

5. The Indefinite Suspension of Classes (September 29, 1941)

On September 24, after the altercation with the law school director in the foyer, students followed the advice of Second Orator Lenício Pacheco Ferreira, who had been urging that they make their feelings known beyond the *arcadas*. Carrying the red banner of the Centro, they marched through the Largo do Ouvidor, São Bento Street, Direita Street, the Praça da Sé, José Bonifácio Street, and back to the Largo de São Francisco. In a chorus they chanted, "Down with the Dictatorship! Death to Vargas!" Among the astonished bystanders, Lenício Pacheco Ferreira recalls, was an old Italian who asked, "Who is going to die?" "Getúlio," the students told him. "The President!! Mama mia!!," the wide-eyed old man exclaimed.

The parade ended with a rally in the school's patio, where students declared that their strike would not end until the Conselho Universitário revoked its decision about the honorary degree.[1]

Fernando Costa, explaining the "incident" in a letter to Vargas, wrote that everything about the honorary degree was going well when some contrary-minded students, affiliated with the Armando de Sales Oliveira current, provoked a protest, in the law school patio, against Talarico, "who, without being a student, was always getting involved in matters of interest to students. . . . The protest is not against the granting of the degree by the Conselho Universitário but is against the involvement of Sr. Talarico in student matters." Fernando Costa explained to Vargas that the students themselves had assured him that this was the case. Commenting on the two suspended students, he wrote that Germinal Feijó was "a Communist on the records of the police" and that Abreu Sodré was "a friend and backer of Sr. Armando Sales." The *interventor* recommended that Cardoso de Melo Neto be backed energetically in his disciplinary action, and he added that the commanding general of the region, Maurício Cardoso, was of the same opinion. Furthermore, Fernando Costa made it clear that he and the general were determined that strong action should be taken against any disorder and that any manifestation in the streets should be "categorically prohibited."[2]

When Horácio Cherkaski was asked by a police investigator why he was wearing a black necktie, he said that his grandfather had died. "What did he die of?" the investigator asked. "Of *honoris causa*," Cherkaski replied, apparently satisfying the poorly educated investigator.[3]

To negotiate the withdrawal of the suspension of Feijó and Roberto de Abreu Sodré, the Centro Onze de Agosto named a commission: Fernando Pereira da Rocha Filho and two Conservadores, Arthur Octavio de Camargo Pacheco and Domingos Luz de Faria. Together with Luís Leite Ribeiro, the three commission members signed a letter to Cardoso de Melo Neto arguing that Feijó and Abreu Sodré had simply voiced the feeling of revolt felt by all the students present during the encounter near the statue of José Bonifácio, o Moço, and that neither the two spokesmen nor the other students had intended to show disrespect for the authority of the law school director.[4]

Flávio Mendes, the well-liked administrative secretary of the law school, suggested that the students might do well to seek the help of Professor Emeritus Francisco Morato. Therefore, two commission members—Fernando Pereira da Rocha Filho and Arthur Octavio de Camargo Pacheco—and law school graduate Francisco Morato de Oliveira sought an appointment with the strongly anti-Vargas former president of the Partido Democrático (an important *bucheiro*). Francisco Morato said he would receive them at 7:00 A.M. At this unusually early hour they found him in very formal attire and using a Portuguese they considered suitable for lofty circles in bygone ages. He told them that he had alerted the Armando de Sales Oliveira political wing and that it was threatening to "end the career" of Cardoso de Melo Neto if he failed to act "in a suitable manner."[5]

Cardoso de Melo Neto, who had been the first Estado Novo *interventor* of São Paulo, was not popular with Armando de Sales Oliveira admirers. Writing about these admirers, Arrobas Martins has pointed out that Antônio Carlos de Abreu Sodré, Francisco Mesquita, and Antônio Pereira Lima never failed to give support to the anti-Vargas law students.[6] In the movement to block the honorary degree for Vargas, the law students were supported also by former Centro President Roberto Whately, the physically powerful tennis star who could not forgive Armando de Sales Oliveira for having once cooperated with Vargas.[7]

The movement against the honorary degree spread beyond the law school, and more and more anti-Vargas demonstrations took place in the streets. Meantime, at the law school, clashes occurred when students who wanted to attend classes were forcibly held out of classrooms by pickets of student strikers. The pickets were not always successful. Israel Dias Novaes recalls an unsuccessful struggle that he, Arrobas Martins, and a third picket member had against students who kicked and hit, fighting their way to a classroom.[8]

It began to appear that the continuation of the strike would create such an accumulation of class absences that many students might be dropped and lose a full year. Therefore, Germinal Feijó and Roberto de Abreu Sodré issued an appeal, which expressed appreciation for the support given them but which also urged the students to return to the classrooms. The appeal was ignored.[9]

After pro-Vargas presidents of University of São Paulo student associations ratified their earlier position, conflicts broke out in the city, especially at some of the bars. Efforts to wreck the headquarters of the CBDU, on D. José de Barros Street, brought Talarico, a brave individual, back from Rio to São Paulo. In a fight at the Ponto Chic Bar, he was beaten up by students, and the beating might have been worse had it not been for the intervention of Roberto Whately and other sportsmen. When the police reached the Ponto Chic they found

Talarico suffering from bruises and took him to the police headquarters. While his wounds were treated there, Public Security Secretary Acácio Nogueira tried to learn who had beaten him up, but Talarico gave no names.[10]

The sentiment of the anti-Vargas activists about Talarico is indicated in the notes written by Jarbas Teixeira de Carvalho on the back of a photograph of the Centro's emergency session of September 23. Jarbas refers to the representation, on behalf of the honorary degree, made by "a group of chiselers (*scrocs*) of various colleges, headed by that very ordinary little Italian, Pepino Gomes Talarico."[11]

Anacleto de Oliveira Faria, historian of the class that entered the law school in 1941, has written about a "serious incident" that occurred on September 29 immediately after Cardoso de Melo Neto decided to dismiss the antistrike students in his class rather than lecture under conditions that the prostrike students threatened to make disturbing. Professor Noé Azevedo appeared among the turbulent students and recommended, in courteous words, that they refrain from hostile demonstrations against the government lest the law school be closed, with serious consequences to all. Cardoso de Melo Neto came out of the João Mendes Júnior Room and was expected to add more words intended to calm emotions. "But," Anacleto de Oliveira Faria writes, "the Director limited himself to laying the students low with an Olympic look at them from top to bottom; and then, turning his back on them, he went to the entrance hall. The result of his conduct was what might have been expected: from all sides, boos resounded."[12]

"On that day," Anacleto de Oliveira writes, "the law school was closed." The directive, signed by Cardoso de Melo Neto, said that "at a special session, called by the director and the Conselho Técnico Administrativo, the faculty resolved, because of the need of discipline, to close down the Law school for an indefinite period."[13]

6. Capanema, Tactful Conciliator (early October 1941)

To resolve the crisis in São Paulo, Education Minister Gustavo Capanema arrived from Rio by train on October 2. He and three members of his staff (among them Vítor Nunes Leal) were met at the North Station by a large crowd that included many of the men the minister would be consulting during his visit. The *interventor* was on hand, together with Second Military Region Commander Maurício Cardoso, Justice Secretary Abelardo Vergueiro César, Education Secretary José Rodrigues Alves Sobrinho, Public Security Secretary

Acácio Nogueira, and Finance Secretary Coriolano de Góis. University Reitor Jorge Americano was there and so were Law School Director Cardoso de Melo Neto and DEIP Director Cândido Mota Filho.

Discussions began late in the afternoon, as soon as Capanema and his staff were settled in their rooms at São Paulo's leading hotel, the Esplanada. Among the first to be received by the minister were the university *reitor*, the directors of the university colleges, and Centro Onze de Agosto President Luís Leite Ribeiro. During the evening Abelardo Vergueiro César and State Administrative Department Head Gofredo da Silva Telles paid calls on the minister.[1]

Germinal Feijó and Roberto de Abreu Sodré, hiding from the police, were in a hut in Santo Amaro, then a countryside outskirt of São Paulo. It was a surprise for them to receive from companions the news of Capanema's visit and a greater surprise to receive a letter from Capanema, addressed to Feijó and asking him to confer with the education minister on Friday morning, October 3.[2]

The Esplanada lobby was filled with students. Those who had appointments to see Capanema, such as Feijó, waited in a room that adjoined the minister's. The minister's aides served them whiskey, and thus third-year student Arthur Octavio de Camargo Pacheco (a signer of the petition on behalf of Feijó and Abreu Sodré) drank whiskey for the first time in his life.[3]

The students found Capanema in the company of Jorge Americano and Cardoso de Melo Neto. Quickly they were impressed with Capanema's cordiality. Feijó told him that Vargas had done nothing for the university and that the idea of the degree was simply political. "We are opposed to it," he said.[4]

If the students were pleased with the minister's tact, they were even more pleased with the agreements reached during the conversations with him. Capanema explained to them that Vargas had told him that he was perfectly willing to forego the honor of receiving the degree.[5] Not only were Feijó and Abreu Sodré to be reinstated in the law school but also there were to be no punishments or reprisals for anyone. Absences marked against striking students would be removed from the records.[6]

The letter that Capenema signed on October 3 was addressed to the *reitor* and said that President Vargas was grateful for the decision of the Conselho Universitário but that he had decided to decline because he had no desire to revive the "memory of occurrences happily brought to an end." Capanema told the press, also on October 3, that "everything reached a point of perfect conciliation" in the case of the law school and that he was pleased to have had the opportunity to be with professors and students.[7]

On the afternoon of October 3, the law school directorship announced that the faculty had decided to renew classes on Monday, the sixth. The students, at a Centro assembly, resolved to terminate the strike, and they approved (not for the first time) a motion declaring José Gomes Talarico "persona non grata" and prohibiting his presence at the law school.[8]

Before Capanema left São Paulo on October 4, he completed a heavy schedule of visits, including an inspection of the last phase of the reconstruction being carried out at the law school building.[9] After he left, Fernando Costa commented on the recent victory of the anti-Vargas activists. Speaking to a commission of law students, he said he had been advised that "the young people were acting as an instrument of certain professors who . . . were abusing their influence over the students." A reply to this charge was given a little later in a statement made at a faculty meeting by *bucheiro* Antônio de Almeida Júnior, who had recently won a *concurso* leading to the appointment of *professor catedrático* of medical law. He said that, although the democratic professors agreed with the students in their just desire for the reestablishment of constitutional life, they did not commit the treachery of throwing the students into the fight while they themselves remained in the shadows. Besides, Almeida said, "the young people did not need outside stimulus to react: their own inclinations were enough for that." And Almeida went on to discuss the program of the state's Departamento de Ordem Política e Social (DOPS) as he had learned from the DOPS itself. The program, he said, involved secret enticements for employees and students of the colleges so that they would spy on their superiors, teachers, and colleagues, and it included monetary rewards for spontaneous informers.[10]

As for Talarico, he moved his residence to Rio and found work on newspapers and in the ministry run by Capanema. "I was," he recalls, "the victim of a great deal in São Paulo. There were many brawls. My house was stoned and my brothers suffered. My presence in São Paulo made it difficult for my family and me."[11]

7. Conservadores Overwhelm Dispirited Libertadores (November 1941)

On September 24, after Cardoso de Melo Neto ordered the removal of the black crepe from the law school, copies of an anonymous typewritten bulletin were distributed at the *arcadas* by Libertadores who assailed the head of the Libertador ticket, Fernando José Fernandes. The bulletin, entitled "Where Are Our Ideals?," said that Fernandes "was always associated with, and actively collaborated with, J. G. Talarico"—not only since the time when Fernandes took the course of the Escola de Polícia. "No one knows the present condition of that old friendship. It is licit, however, to conjecture." The bulletin also accused Fernandes of being a founder of the Centro de Criminologia Ademar de Barros and a leader of the pro-Vargas Movimento Universitário Nacional (MUN).

According to "Where Are Our Ideals?," the Libertadores in November 1940 had won an important victory over a group that was guided by dishonesty and "malign, concession-making connections (that tolerated the permanence of the tuition increase)." But the cost of the victory had been "the continuation of the presence in our ranks of people who were separated from our ideals, people who only recently joined our activity." The bulletin blamed the outcome of the 1941 *prévia* on the "evil interference" of the "adverse, archaic, and notorious" Conservadores. The outcome, it said, was a victory for the Libertador wing headed by the *candidato arrivista* (parvenu candidate). Pointing out that Fernandes had invited the head of the *casa civil* of the former *interventor* to be the *paraninfo* (spokesman) of his Escola de Polícia class, the bulletin said: "Imagine the situation of the P.A.L. [Partido Acadêmico Libertador] if this opportunist occupies the presidency of the Centro Acadêmico XI de Agosto."[1]

The anonymous bulletin was unfair to Fernando José Fernandes inasmuch as he had never been associated with the MUN or the so-called Centro de Criminologia Ademar de Barros (which never existed), and the selection of a *paraninfo* is made by all the graduating students, not just one. *O Libertador* and party speakers brushed aside the attacks and emphasized the "dynamism, intelligence, and loyalty" of the party's standard bearer. João Nery Guimarães praised his "firmness of character."[2]

In the meantime, in October, Cunha Bueno and other members of the Conservador fifteen-man *comissão diretora* (such as Domingos Luz de Faria, José Malanga, Nelson Coutinho, and Gilberto Quintanilha Ribeiro) issued a manifesto launching the candidacy of Oscar Augusto de Barros Bressane for Centro president.[3] Bressane, a close friend of Cunha Bueno, had been elected *procurador* on the ticket headed by Pupo Netto in 1938; in 1939 and 1940, as a *comissão diretora* member, he had campaigned zealously for Francisco de Paulo Quintanilha Ribeiro and Cunha Bueno.[4]

Surprisingly little interest was shown in the November 1941 election. *O Libertador* found two reasons for the apathy. One was what it called the reluctance of the students to group themselves into opposite camps after recent events, stemming from the honorary degree for Vargas, had "united the College in a single indestructible bloc." The other was what *O Libertador* called the certainty of the outcome of the election; it pointed out that since over half the student body had participated in the Libertador *prévia*, the *prévia* winners were sure to win in November.[5]

Articles in *O Conservador* (published by Rivaldo Assis Cintra and Fernando Melo Bueno) described the Partido Conservador as having a long experience, a serene position, and a broad view, which would prevent it from becoming "the apprentice of the witch doctor who liberated powerful hidden spirits and thus opened a box of tribulations." It recommended criticism that would be "constructive and optimistic" instead of criticism that was "destructive and skeptical."[6] After the second annual Baile das Américas, held on October 29, the Conservadores were able to point out that the event, under Libertador management, had provided less than 4 contos de reis (4:000$000) for the Casa do Estudante compared with over 28 contos when Quintanilha Ribeiro had run the Centro. Furthermore, Conservadores attracted the Juventude Universitária Católica (JUC) by arguing that Feijó, on the Libertador slate, was a Communist.[7]

The November election was an overwhelming success for the Conservadores. Out of seventeen Centro positions (including places on the editorial and *sindicância* commissions), the Conservadores won all but two. The only victorious Libertadores were Horácio Cherkaski ("o Menino de Ouro"), elected vice-president, and poet Péricles Eugênio da Silva Ramos, elected for the third time to serve on the editorial commission. In the presidential contest, where 963 votes were cast, Fernando José Fernandes lost to Oscar Bressane by 40 votes.[8]

Sometime later, when Arrobas Martins, Germinal Feijó, Renato Amaral Sampaio Coelho, and Ênio de Novais França analyzed their defeat of November 1941, they expressed some of the thoughts given in the anonymous bulletin of September 24, 1941. They concluded that the Partido Libertador, in marching to victory in November 1940, had collected much debris that it had been unable to digest. *Arrivistas* and *oportunistas* were mentioned.[9]

VI

Brazil Enters the War (1942)

1. The Liga Acadêmica de Defesa Nacional (May–June 1942)

Following the Japanese attack on Pearl Harbor in December 1941, the United States entered the war against the Axis powers (Germany, Italy, and Japan). Foreign ministers of the American republics met in Rio de Janeiro in January 1942 to consider whether all the republics should break diplomatic relations with the Axis. At the São Paulo Law School, Germinal Feijó became the coordinator of a plan whereby a group of students would go to Rio and gain admittance to the gallery during a session of the foreign ministers' conference in order to call attention to the Brazilian political situation by shouting, "We want democracy." But the plan was not carried out.[1]

Brazil's break in relations with the Axis, announced by Foreign Minister Osvaldo Aranha at the closing session of the conference, gave the activist São Paulo law students incentive to organize the Associação Democrática Acadêmica "to strive openly for liberty and democracy." But the Associação, formed in April, attracted only a small circle. It was, Arrobas Martins explained a little later, handicapped by its name and the lack of "the necessary climate."[2]

The theme of the *trote*, administered to the freshmen at the *arcadas* in April, was the ridiculing of Mussolini, Hitler, and Tojo. Paulistas watched while the freshmen, made up to resemble Axis leaders, marched and orated. After a bald "Mussolini" shouted at crowds at the Largo de São Francisco, a group of freshmen, including a bemedaled "Hitler" and a smiling "Tojo" (a freshman with a Japanese background), was conducted through the streets. The invitations to the *peruada*, issued in May, were decorated with caricatures of Mussolini, Hitler, and Tojo. The show, Arrobas Martins has written, "was an indirect way" of striking at the Brazilian dictator.[3]

In May the organizers of the unsuccessful Associação Democrática Acadêmica adopted a new name. They were, Arrobas Martins pointed out, "inspired by the nationalist movement which already existed in São Paulo" when they decided to call their association the Liga Acadêmica de Defesa Nacional. An appropriate manifesto, addressed "to Brazilian Youth," was signed by Rui de Azevedo Marques, Rodrigo Barjas Filho, Wilson Rahal, Edgard Barreira Matos, Petronio Fernal, Rubens Lessa Vergueiro, Roberto Costa Ferreira, Israel Dias Novaes, Péricles Eugênio da Silva Ramos, Rui do Amaral, João Nery Guimarães, and Ênio de Novais França.[4]

According to the manifesto, the war, once considered a struggle between large groups of incompatible ideological extremists, was now appreciated to be a war of repugnant conquest provoked by barbarians. The Axis powers were described as "storming, without pity and without glory, against the civilized world." Pointing out that prudence was cowardice and neutrality was unthinkable, the manifesto reminded its readers that the Brazilian people had "for a long time given constant and unmistakable demonstrations of their love of Democracy." It went on to say that "at the São Paulo Law School—the civic nucleus with the oldest presence in the pages of our history—there is now born the Liga Acadêmica de Defesa Nacional, as an affirmation of faith and willingness to struggle." The manifesto warned against "the treasonable Axis technique of infiltration" and defined the purposes of the Liga as the combat against anti-Brazilian activities and the defense of the democratic ideal.[5]

The Liga Acadêmica de Defesa Nacional learned with satisfaction that students in Salvador, Bahia, had recently put on a "monster parade" with signs calling for the dismissal of *professores verdes* (Integralistas). A message from the Liga congratulated the Bahians for having demonstrated their *brasilidade* and fondness for democracy.[6]

In Porto Alegre late in June, Arrobas Martins and second-year student Ênio de Novais França expressed the hope that students in Rio Grande do Sul would establish an association with ties to the Liga Acadêmica de Defesa Nacional. The two São Paulo law students warned the Gaúchos against fifth columnists, Integralistas, "the yellow peril," and members of foreign colonies who would "do their utmost because of their enthusiasm for fascism." They also told the Gaúchos that, in São Paulo, students hoped to make use of the radio and the Teatro Municipal for one week, building up publicity for a Noite Democrática (Democratic Night), when prominent people would give talks. Among the speakers they hoped to get was Lindolfo Collor, a Gaúcho who had supported the Constitutionalist Revolution of 1932 and the anti-Vargas putsch of May 1938.[7]

2. A New Libertador Manifesto (August 11, 1942)

It was not difficult to stir up demonstrations against the Axis starting in March 1942. The sinking that month by the Germans of a Brazilian vessel, the *Cairu,* cost fifty-three lives. Although the Vargas government, in retaliation, ordered the confiscation of some of the funds of Axis subjects in Brazil, the sinkings continued. The German torpedoing of eight more Brazilian ships in May, June, and July cost twenty-six more lives. Anti-Axis demonstrations throughout Brazil frequently led to the depredation of German-owned stores.

Under these circumstances, the Partido Acadêmico Libertador issued its manifesto of August 11 to the law students.[1] The manifesto noted that those same students who in the past had smiled in disbelief at the party's position, those same students whose cowardice had prevented them from taking a position, "are today the first to boast of democratic convictions, to enroll in the Pan American ranks." The Partido Libertador said that it did not propose to question the sincerity of the conversions. "If they increase our ranks," it said, "we want to view this simply as a reason for rejoicing."

The manifesto maintained that the law school had acquired a political conscience with the appearance of the Partido Acadêmico Libertador, and it pointed out that the party had adhered to its original position, announced in April 1940, despite skeptics who had believed that such consistency was impossible at a time of political about-faces and "last-minute adherences."

The manifesto stated that the Partido Libertador did not present merely a program of material accomplishments and did not propose, selfishly, simply to reform things at the law school: "It extended its vision, reaching all the borders of the Nation. It knew that, more than a century ago, the Academia de São Paulo brought to all of Brazil an appreciation of the worth of the Academia's enlightenment, the heat of its patriotic dedication, the din of its political struggles."

The manifesto noted that Brazilians had been hearing "the abominable hocus-pocus of the adepts of doctrines favoring the assassination of the human personality, presented as the only salvation of the world of our days." Youth, the manifesto said, had lost its fighting fiber. "The young people were living under the shadow of their tradition, with their arms crossed, in a criminal immobility. . . . Most of them shunned responsibility, fled from the perspective of struggle, and became cowardly in the face of danger. They were amorphous, pasty, undefined, accommodating." In this setting, the manifesto said, the Partido Libertador had unfurled its banner of "Liberty, Justice, and Democracy."

Two thousand copies of the four-page manifesto were printed. This opening gun for the annual electoral contest of November was signed by the libertador *comissão diretora*. Omitted from the printed version were the names of the members of the commission: Fernando Pereira da Rocha Filho, Ênio de Novais França, Fernando Jacob, Fernando José Fernandes, Germinal Feijó, Heitor Borelli de Alvarenga Freire ("Morango"), Horácio Cherkaski, João Nery Guimarães, Luís Arrobas Martins, Renato Macedo, Roberto de Abreu Sodré, Rui do Amaral, Rui de Azevedo Marques, Vítor Tieghi, and Zwinglio Ferreira.[2]

3. The Rally at the Praça da Sé (August 18, 1942)

Between August 15 and 17, five Brazilian ships were sunk by the Germans within twenty miles of the northeastern states of Bahia and Sergipe. In this savage attack about six hundred lives were lost. Brazil on August 18 was filled from north to south with anti-Axis demonstrations. In Rio de Janeiro a multitude, calling furiously for "war" and "revenge," surrounded Guanabara Palace. Leaders of the UNE, the CBDU, and university student associations in the federal capital assaulted the German Club of Rio de Janeiro on August 18.[1]

When the São Paulo law students reached the *arcadas* on the morning of August 18, they asked that classes be suspended to allow a meeting of professors and students. The request was granted and the João Mendes Júnior Room was filled that morning. After the national anthem was sung, Centro First Orator Luís de Azevedo Soares gave an opening speech that was interrupted by shouts against the totalitarian powers and in favor of Brazil and the democracies. The speeches that followed were given by faculty members.

Waldemar Ferreira declared that "Brazilian democracy is American democracy. Our support of the United States should be positive and unconditional." Professor Noé Azevedo became so emotional that he was reported to have wept as he called for a dike against the destructive wave of fascist imperialism and quoted Rui Barbosa about the impossibility of being neutral in a conflict between crime and what is right.[2]

Vicente Ráo said that for a long time the students had appeared to be cold and forgetful of the traditions of the *arcadas*, but he expressed the hope that, in the face of the recent affront to the nation, the spirit of the young people would be raised and they would demand loudly and clearly the "maintenance of our dignity and honor." Arrobas Martins, replying to Professor Ráo, said that "the soul of Brazilian youth never became frozen because it is like the symbol of the nation." He pointed out that the silence, noted by Ráo, had come about because "enemies of energetic statements and attitudes" had sought to postpone "manifestations of redress" until they could take a position without risking anything. Cardoso de Melo Neto closed the meeting by congratulating Arrobas Martins and announcing the suspension of classes that day as a sign of protest.[3]

Arrobas Martins seized the Brazilian flag and called on the students to go outside with him and hold a rally. But Arrobas was stopped by Major Olinto de França (known as "Major Bárbara"), the army officer who had been sent by the central government to head the Superintendência da Ordem Política e Social of São Paulo. The major, trying to maintain order, threatened to use machine guns to prevent the students from leaving the building. Professor Benedito de Siqueira Ferreira exclaimed, "I supposed that those machine guns were for fighting the enemy of Brazil; now I see that they are for killing students!"[4]

Despite the major, the students poured into the Largo de São Francisco. There and elsewhere in the city student orators exhorted the multitudes in the streets to attend a *grande comício* (large meeting) to be held that evening at 6:00 at the Praça da Sé.

The Centro Onze leaders named a commission to organize the evening meeting.[5] The commission, a sort of united front of different points of view,[6] consisted of Oscar Bressane (chairman), Arthur Octavio de Camargo Pacheco, Fernando José Fernandes, Fernando Pereira da Rocha Filho, Germinal Feijó, Gilberto Quintanilha Ribeiro (brother of the former Centro president), Horácio Cherkaski, Jarbas Teixeira de Carvalho, Jorge Mesquita Mendonça, Lenício Pacheco Ferreira, Luís de Azevedo Soares, Luís Arrobas Martins, Rivaldo Assis Cintra, Roberto de Abreu Sodré, Wilson Rahal, and Hélio Mota (who had transferred from the Faculdade de Direito de Niterói and joined the Partido Conservador).

The commission placed a large notice about the forthcoming *grande comício* in the afternoon *Folha da Noite*. The notice summoned people to "a vigorous demonstration of patriotism" and asked students to show up at the Largo de São Francisco one hour before the Praça da Sé *comício*. *Folha da Noite* also announced the reading, at the *comício*, of a telegram that was going to be sent to Vargas, in the name of the São Paulo students, asking for a declaration of war against the Axis. Furthermore, *Folha da Noite* revealed that the Centro Onze de Agosto had resolved to found a Legião Universitária Brasileira to bring students and others together to support democratic ideals and the United Nations.[7]

Members of the Centro commission to organize the meeting

started a movement to have all flags in São Paulo flown at half-mast. The members also visited the headquarters of the army's Second Region and the office of State Security Secretary Acácio Nogueira. Second Region Commander Maurício Cardoso, after meeting with the students, told reporters that he believed the students would display "perfect order, discipline, and respect for the authorities." Acácio Nogueira (a *bucheiro*) warned the student commission to avoid "undesirable turmoil." At the same time, he agreed to furnish a microphone and a police band for music. After the students left his office, he phoned the heads of the police units (Força Polícial, Segurança Política e Social, Guarda Civil, and Polícia Especial) in order that their men be on the alert to prevent "any disturbance of order." He also phoned Vargas' justice minister, Alexandre Marcondes Filho, to inform him of the scheduled evening rally.[8]

The rally, long remembered, attracted an enormous crowd ("a human wave" according to the press). Cherkaski held the law school banner aloft, an assignment traditionally fulfilled by the Centro vice-president. Large signs declared that "The Centro XI de Agosto Weeps with the Offended Nation" and "The Nation Was Outrageously Insulted!" Students were not alone in wearing black neckties and pieces of black crepe attached to their lapels. Professors and other special guests, invited by the Centro commission, took their places on the steps of the Cathedral da Sé. The band, furnished by the Guarda Civil, played the national anthem and the "Canção do Soldado" (Song of the Soldier).[9]

Centro Orator Luís de Azevedo Soares' opening speech ended with the words "the sword of Caxias, unsheathed at this moment, can only be sheathed with honor." He was followed by Germinal Feijó, Fernando José Fernandes, and Wilson Rahal (who warned against fifth columnists hidden everywhere and "disguised in the faded green shirt of *integralismo*"). Other speakers were Antônio Carlos de Abreu Sodré and Professor Cardoso de Melo Neto.

The telegram to Vargas was read. Bearing the signature of Centro President Bressane, it said that "the students and people of São Paulo, brought together at a rally on account of the mutual feeling of revolt at the barbarous aggression . . . , suggest to Your Excellency, as the proper reply . . . , the immediate declaration of war against the totalitarian vandals."[10]

Arrobas Martins told the crowd that for a long time people had been awaiting "this manifestation of the young people." "Today," he added, "youths have taken to the streets . . . to demonstrate that the young people, who brought about the Abolition and the Republic, who accompanied Rui in the civilian campaign, who acclaimed Bilac in the promotion of obligatory military service, are and will remain the same, always the first to cry when the nation cries, to vibrate with enthusiasm when the nation vibrates, to carry arms when the nation asks for their sacrifice."

The crowd, which included members of Paulista high society, heard a moving closing speech by Rivaldo Assis Cintra and then joined students in a march through the streets that ended at the Largo de São Francisco.[11]

4. The Campanha Nacionalista and Its *Caravana* (September–October 1942)

Following the Praça da Sé rally, the Centro Onze de Agosto was swamped with congratulatory messages, and it also received letters denouncing fifth columnists. To investigate the denouncements, the Centro officers set up a new department and named Camilo de Souza Coelho, a fifth-year student, to head it. The congratulatory messages were acknowledged with thanks in notices, published in the press, signed by Centro President Bressane. They expressed faith that the senders of the messages would not lose the enthusiasm that had brought them into "an indissoluble alliance with the aspirations of youth for the democratic destiny of the Nation."[1] The commission that had organized the Praça da Sé rally transformed itself into a permanent commission to coordinate a new campaign to be known as the Campanha Nacionalista do Centro Acadêmico XI de Agosto.

While the commission made plans for holding a large patriotic observance on August 25 (the Day of the Soldier), Vargas communicated with Roosevelt and then, on August 21, authorized Foreign Minister Aranha to send off notes advising the governments of Germany and Italy that the acts of war practiced against Brazil had created a state of belligerency. After a cabinet meeting on the twenty-second, a public announcement disclosed that Brazil was at war with Germany and Italy. Japan, it was "unofficially" reported, had committed no aggression against Brazil.

The declaration of war at the side of the democracies was seen by the anti-Vargas activists as a development that "would facilitate our fight against the dictatorship in Brazil and hasten its downfall."[2] It was hailed at a rally at the Largo de São Francisco on August 22 and gave special significance to the Day of the Soldier. Meeting on the twenty-fifth in the law school patio, the Centro decided to send a telegram to Vargas asking that the political exiles be allowed to return to Brazil. The telegram, signed by Bressane, contended that the moment was one "in which all Brazilians clamor for a sacred union, forgetting old partisanships and dissentions." Although copies of the telegram were sent to the press by the Centro's Departamento de Propaganda e Expansão, no newspaper published it. One newspaper blamed "a lack of paper."[3]

Despite the telegram and the anti-Vargas activists' use of the new situation to issue calls about "the democratic destiny" of Brazil, São Paulo Security Secretary Acácio Nogueira believed that Brazil's declaration of war, and his own psychological adroitness, had transformed the students into efficient collaborators of the government. "In São Paulo," he told the press, "the university students have brushed aside the last traces of their lack of understanding and have closed ranks around the interventorship."[4]

But to make sure that law student orators would not get out of hand during a *caravana* of the Campanha Nacionalista, Justice Secretary Abelardo Vergueiro César assigned two members of the Superintendência da Ordem Política e Social to accompany them.[5] The *caravana* of student orators, described to the justice secretary as a campaign to build up patriotic and anti–fifth columnist fervor in the north of the state, received financial assistance from the state government. It set out by train on September 25 and was made up of Horácio Cherkaski (leader), Arrobas Martins, Germinal Feijó, Roberto de Abreu Sodré, Wilson Rahal, Lenício Pacheco Ferreira, Luís Francisco da Silva Carvalho, Ruy Nazareth, Benjamin Augusto Pereira de Queiroz, Aluísio Álvares Cruz, and Martim Francisco Ribeiro de Andrada e Silva.

In São José do Rio Preto and many small towns, the students joined with local speakers in promoting "the struggle for the liberty of Brazil and for the United Nations." Notices posted ahead of time proclaimed the forthcoming messages to be brought by the "brilliant orators" of the *embaixada* from the law school, pioneer of "memorable civic campaigns." The receptions were encouraging. Before the completion of the campaign, which lasted well into the second half of October, the two government agents, supposed to control the *caravanistas*, became their friends.[6]

Martim Francisco Ribeiro de Andrada e Silva, who left the caravan in mid-October, told the *Diário de S. Paulo* of the particularly enthusiastic applause that greeted the speeches of Arrobas Martins and Benjamin Pereira de Queiroz.[7]

5. The Fifth Conselho Nacional de Estudantes (September 1942)

Arrobas Martins and Benjamin Pereira de Queiroz, praised by Martim Francisco Ribeiro de Andrada e Silva, had been chosen Libertador candidates for first and second orators at the party's *prévia* on September 16. Because of his stubbornness, Arrobas Martins had become known as "Potranca" (a young mare). Because of his appearance, Benjamin Pereira de Queiroz (son of a judge) had become known as "Basil Rathbone" (the movie actor).

At the *prévia*, Jarbas Teixeira de Carvalho defeated Astolfo Monteiro da Silva ("Biquinho") in the contest for nominee for president of the Centro. Jarbas, one of Roberto Victor Cordeiro's friends, was on the commission that organized the Praça da Sé rally and the Campanha Nacionalista. He had not been an early Libertador; as a third-party candidate for treasurer in 1940 he had been successful thanks to the deal with Cherkaski that helped place Libertador Luís Leite Ribeiro in the presidency. Among the others chosen at the 1942 Libertador *prévia* were vice-presidential nominee Paulo Henrique Meinberg (director of the *caravana artística* that visited Bahia in 1941) and *procurador* candidate Carlos Eduardo de Camargo Aranha (a relative of Foreign Minister Osvaldo Aranha and a participant in the anti-Vargas resistance).[1]

On the day before the Libertadores' *prévia*, Conservadores Bressane and Luís de Azevedo Soares (Centro first orator) played prominent roles in Rio as leaders of the delegation from the *arcadas* at the opening session of the fifth Conselho Nacional de Estudantes (the fourth had been held two years earlier). UNE President Luís Pinheiro Paes Leme and Luís de Azevedo Soares expressed the students' gratitude to United States Ambassador Jefferson Caffery for a letter and autographed photograph from President Roosevelt.[2] The event took place in the former German Club, which had become, thanks to Vargas, the headquarters of the UNE.[3]

The Conselho sessions, lasting for more than a week,[4] were marked by patriotic speeches and the suspense that preceded a close UNE officership election. Foreign Minister Aranha worked for the election of Rio engineering student Hélio de Almeida to the UNE presidency, while partisans of War Minister Eurico Gaspar Dutra favored Sebastião Pinheiro Chagas, law student in Minas.[5] José Gomes Talarico, a supporter of Hélio de Almeida, recalls that much money was spent on the campaign of Pinheiro Chagas and that the Mineiro's backers campaigned "every night at the Atlântico and Urca casinos"[6] to obtain votes (to be cast by over three hundred voting delegates).[7] Education Minister Capanema, a Mineiro with ties to Dutra, was felt to favor Pinheiro Chagas.[8]

Hélio de Almeida's supporters included outgoing UNE President Paes Leme, the Communist students, and the delegates from the Centro Onze de Agosto. Delegates from the other São Paulo colleges, considered pro-Vargas,[9] were expected to vote for Pinheiro Chagas. On the eve of the voting, Rio student Euclides Aranha took all the São Paulo delegates to the residence of his father, Osvaldo Aranha. The foreign minister told them that Hélio de Almeida was a better democrat than Dutra's choice, and he added that, if they would vote for Hélio de Almeida, "afterward I may be of help to you."[10] The São Paulo votes gave Hélio de Almeida the victory by a narrow margin.[11]

Capanema, informed that the UNE wanted to ask Vargas to remove Integralistas from the government, told the students to name a commission to go to Catete Palace after the close of the fifth Conselho de Estudantes. Paulistas on the commission of seven, Bressane, Naldo Caparica, and Luís de Azevedo Soares, had in mind Vargas' appointment, early in the year, of Miguel Reale to the Departamento Administrativo of São Paulo state.

Fifth-year student Luís de Azevedo Soares, who was chosen to do the speaking to Vargas, had met the president before as a member of a group of students that had been visiting the west coast of South America when the war broke out in Europe. With ships suddenly in short supply the students had managed to get aboard the last available ship for the return to Brazil, but because they had been unable to pay for the passages their baggage had been confiscated and placed in the customs in Rio. Vargas, informed of their difficulty, had called them to his office and arranged for the government to pay for the passages and get the baggage back to the students.

Now, in September 1942, Luís de Azevedo Soares explained to the president the purpose of the visit of the UNE commission. Reale's name was mentioned. The commission found Vargas patient and friendly. "Very well," the president said, "I'll take out the Integralistas and put students in their places!"[12]

6. Another Libertador Defeat (November 1942)

Rivaldo Assis Cintra, the outstanding Conservador orator, hoped to be his party's presidential nominee.[1] The decision was up to the party's fifteen-man *comissão diretora*, which included Luís de Azevedo Soares, Gilberto Quintanilha Ribeiro, Arthur Octavio de Camargo Pacheco, and Fernando Melo Bueno. Fernando Melo Bueno ("Mellinho"), a good orator who came from a poor family, held a government job and was frequently (and inaccurately) accused by Libertadores of being a Vargas supporter.[2]

The *comissão diretora* chose Hélio Mota to run for president and Assis Cintra to run for first orator. The decision was a tribute to

Mota's popularity and perhaps also to other qualities. Hélio Mota, although not known for his brilliance, has been described as open and brave. He had, Luís de Azevedo Soares recalls, an ability to act with firmness that was at least as important in a Centro president as the ability to orate eloquently.[3]

Hélio Mota, a nice person, good looking, and level headed, came from a wealthy Catanduva family and had an advantage enjoyed by very few students: he owned a car. He was one of those who might be seen occasionally in the socially prestigious Jequiti bar—so named by its founder, a grandson of Conselheiro Antônio Prado, because the *jequitibá* tree had been the symbol of the PRP.[4]

Mota had a united group of supporters in the circle to which Luís de Azevedo Soares belonged, and another one among the unusually large number of *vagabundos*, or transfers from the easy-going law school of Niterói. He was one of about fifty who came to the *arcadas* after one year at Niterói. As practically all of the participants in this most extraordinary mass transfer joined the Partido Acadêmico Conservador, it was assumed by Libertadores that their party affiliation was related to favors they undoubtedly owed to authorities who made the transfer possible.[5]

Like Rivaldo Assis Cintra, Mota belonged to the commission that organized the Praça da Sé rally and the Campanha Nacionalista. But Assis Cintra, who had delivered a strong speech attacking the honorary degree for Vargas, was regarded as a leading anti-Vargas orator, whereas Hélio Mota was regarded as nonpolitical and was certainly not an anti-Vargas activist. Mota's moderate stance was in sharp contrast to that of his roommate, Cory Porto Fernandes, who was attending both the law school and the nearby Escola Livre de Sociologia e Política. Cory Porto Fernandes, nephew of a well-known socialist medical doctor, belonged to the radical Left.

When an *A Noite* reporter asked Hélio Mota about his program, the presidential candidate replied that the most important thing for the nation was to react to the outrages practiced against it by the totalitarian nations. In that connection, he said, the Centro Onze de Agosto had an important role because college students influenced students attending less-advanced schools. "We young people," he told the reporter, "have much more to do than bear arms. We must arm ourselves spiritually with ideas, principles, and sentiments that serve the interests of Brazil."[6] Mota added that the Partido Conservador had two other objectives: (*a*) to secure funds to allow completion of the Casa do Estudante and (*b*) to obtain an authorization for law students who had reached the fourth year to use the title of *solicitador-acadêmico* and thus have access to official legal papers, helpful when training in law offices.[7] These two points were made in the party's manifesto, published in *O Conservador* (run by Fernando Melo Bueno and Pedro Brasil Bandecchi).[8]

O Libertador did not appear during this election campaign. But the party printed a one-page paper praising Arrobas Martins, which bore 172 signatures, and other pieces of propaganda. It lost no opportunity to reiterate that the Libertador Party "did not become the champion of Democracy at the last minute, after Brazil declared war on the totalitarians." It said that until war was declared the opponents of the Libertadores had sometimes accompanied the civic agitation of the Libertadores "without identifying themselves with it" and that at other times, fearful that the eloquence of the speeches might offend important personalities and harm their own "unconfessable subaltern purposes," they had retreated "into the easy and opportunistic convenience of silence."[9]

The Conservadores released sheets of propaganda attacking "the single and calamitous administration" of the Libertadores, when, with Jarbas Teixeira de Carvalho as treasurer, the Baile das Américas had furnished so little for the Casa do Estudante. The reduction in tuitions, for which the Libertadores took credit, was attributed by the Conservadores "exclusively to the dynamism of Antônio Sylvio Cunha Bueno."[10]

Furthermore, the Conservador directorship pointed out, an honest study of the manifestos presenting Conservador slates over the years showed that "every one of them expressed forcefully and clearly our democratic convictions. None, however, went beyond the bounds of academic dignity." In stark contrast, the Conservadores said, were the pamphlets issued by some oppositionists who were willing to go to any extreme, "even sacrificing national unity, trying to sow discord, and spreading distrust among the young people of this old law school." The Conservadores condemned "the disgraceful propaganda now aimed at Hélio Mota."[11]

The Libertadores were trying to make the most of the fact that Hélio Mota was a *vagabundo*. When it appeared that this tactic was backfiring because the law school had so many transfers, the Libertadores accused Hélio Mota, the "chief of the transferred students," of seeking to have all the *vagabundos* vote for him as though they lacked the intelligence to make a choice based on principles.[12]

Anacleto de Oliveira Faria mentions a samba that was being played in 1942 and that contained a line: "I am not from here, I am from Niterói." "On the day of the election," he writes, "a record player was set up in the law school patio" and was used to play the samba loudly. But he adds that the music did not last long. A "command group" of Hélio Mota "destroyed the record and the record player after a physical struggle that involved . . . dozens of students."[13]

When the votes were counted on the night of November 16, they revealed that the Conservadores had obtained the most votes ever given a party during the 39-year life of the Centro Onze de Agosto. Hélio Mota received 514 votes compared with 391 for Jarbas Teixeira de Carvalho. Mota's 123-vote majority was the largest in any recent election for president, and his total vote exceeded that of any of the Conservadores running on the slate with him.

No Libertador gained a place—not even on the Comissão de Redação and Comissão de Sindicância. Abel Newton de Oliveira Penteado's 490 votes won him the vice-presidency (against 382 votes for Meinberg). First orator candidate Rivaldo Assis Cintra received 470 votes compared with 315 for Arrobas Martins.[14]

Besides losing an election, the Libertadores were about to lose some of their leaders through graduation. The six graduating members of the *comissão diretora* were Roberto de Abreu Sodré, Fernando Pereira da Rocha Filho, Fernando José Fernandes, Horácio Cherkaski, Rui do Amaral, and Rui de Azevedo Marques. Among the other late 1942 graduates were Wilson Rahal and his friend Antônio Costa Corrêa (who had withdrawn from the school's *resistência* activities after marrying the sister of Germinal Feijó in March).

The São Paulo Law School in its early days and (*to the right*) the church and monastery of São Francisco de Assis. (*O Estado de S. Paulo*)

Law school liberal instructor Líbero Badaró on his deathbed after his assassination in 1830. Drawing by Hercules Florence, at the Instituto Histórico e Geográfico de São Paulo. (Courtesy of Brasil Bandecchi)

Law school liberal instructor Júlio Frank (1808–1841), founder of the Burschenschaft secret society. Reproduction, by Ana Rosa Coelho, of illustration in Spencer Vampré, *Memórias para a História da Academia de São Paulo*. (Courtesy of Brasil Bandecchi)

The first directorship of the Partido Democrático de São Paulo, 1926. *Left to right*: Professor Waldemar Ferreira, Paulo de Morais Barros (*front*), Paulo Nogueira Filho (*in rear*), Professor Francisco Morato, Prudente de Morais Barros (*in rear*), Antônio Prado (*center, front*), Antônio Cajado de Lemos (*in rear*), Professor Gama Cerqueira, Professor Cardoso de Melo Neto (*in rear*), José Adriano Marrey Júnior (*front*), and Luís Aranha. (Courtesy of Waldemar Ferreira)

Students in front of the law school volunteering to take up arms against the Vargas government, 1932. The drawing by Paulo do Vale Júnior, at the Instituto Histórico e Geográfico de São Paulo, shows the statue of José Bonifácio, o Moço, on its elegant pedestal. (Courtesy of Brasil Bandecchi)

Permanent Commission of the law school's Casa do Estudante, 1939. *Seated, left to right*: Noé Azevedo, José Carlos de Macedo Soares, Jorge Americano, Francisco Morato, and César Lacerda de Vergueiro. *Standing, left to right*: Cicero Augusto Vieira, School Secretary Flávio Mendes, Trajano Pupo Netto, and builder Alfredo Mathias. (Courtesy of Trajano Pupo Netto)

From left to right: students Domingos Luz de Faria, Fernando Pereira da Rocha Filho, Roberto de Abreu Sodré, and Germinal Feijó. (Courtesy of Paulo Meinberg)

Students Israel Dias Novaes and Antônio Costa Corrêa (*in CPOR uniform*). (Courtesy of Antônio Costa Corrêa)

Roberto Victor Cordeiro.
(Courtesy of João Nery Guimarães)

Miguel Reale, as an Integralista leader. (Courtesy of Flávio Galvão)

Partido Conservador campaigners, 1940. The smiling Centro presidential candidate, Antônio Sylvio Cunha Bueno, is at center (*with dotted necktie*). In the same row are Oscar Bressane (*second from left*) and Ulisses Guimarães (*third from left, with open mouth*). Nestor Bressane Filho is visible above Cunha Bueno's right shoulder, and Fernando Melo Bueno is among the kneelers (*at far left*). (*O Estado de S. Paulo*)

Partido Libertador campaigners, 1940. *Standing, from left to right*: Lenício Pacheco Ferreira (*far left, in full view*) and Rui Homem de Melo Lacerda (*third from left*). Wilson Rahal (*fifth from left, in light suit*) is next to Centro presidential candidate Luís Leite Ribeiro (*center, in dark suit*). Farther to the right is 1939 presidential candidate José Maria Ribeiro de Barros (*taller than Luís Leite Ribeiro*). Germinal Feijó is seated under Lacerda. (*O Estado de S. Paulo*)

Prévia polling by Partido Libertador to select its 1941 Centro election slate. *Seated, from left to right*: Luís Arrobas Martins, Alberto de Almeida Lima, and João Malheiros. *Standing, from left to right* (*after the ballot caster*): Arlindo Camargo Pacheco, Rodrigo Barjas Filho, Rubens Lessa Vergueiro, Fernando Pereira da Rocha Filho, Horácio Cherkaski (*tall, in white*), Wilson Rahal, Fernando José Fernandes (nominated for president), Roberto de Abreu Sodré (loser of presidential nomination), Germinal Feijó, and Gabriel Migliore. (Courtesy of *Revista da OAB São Paulo*)

The faculty, 1941. *Seated, from left to right*: Cardoso de Melo Neto, Sampaio Dória, Francisco Morato, Sebastião Soares de Faria, Ataliba Nogueira, Spencer Vampré, and Gabriel de Resende Filho. *Standing, from left to right*: Basileu Garcia, Ernesto Leme, Honório Monteiro, Jorge Americano, Joaquim Canuto Mendes de Almeida, Alvino Lima, Antônio de Almeida Júnior, Flávio Mendes (secretary), Cândido Mota Filho, Antônio Ferreira Cesarino Júnior, Teotônio Monteiro de Barros Filho (*half hidden*), Oscar Penteado Stevenson (*half hidden*), Noé Azevedo, and Benedito de Siqueira Ferreira. (Courtesy of João Nery Guimarães)

José Joaquim Cardoso de Melo Neto, faculty director, 1941–1943. (Courtesy of João Nery Guimarães)

Professor Mário Masagão. (Courtesy of Flávio Galvão)

Going through Direita Street on a march to protest an honorary degree for President Getúlio Vargas, September 1941. (Agência Estado photograph. Courtesy of *Revista da OAB São Paulo*)

João Nery Guimarães.

Renato Pintaudi Macedo.

Luís Gonzaga Bandeira de Melo Arrobas Martins. (Courtesy of Maria Alice Arrobas Martins)

Hélio Mota, president of Centro Onze de Agosto and the União Nacional dos Estudantes (UNE), 1943.

Part of a *peruada* parade. The carriage, with Oscar Bressane (*without hat*) in the front seat, is passing the *O Estado de S. Paulo* building on Boa Vista Street. The costumes are of sports clubs. (Courtesy of João Nery Guimarães)

São Paulo crowd listening to prowar speeches, August 18, 1942. (*O "XI de Agosto,"* 1942. Courtesy of João Nery Guimarães)

The law school standard, held by Centro Vice-President Cherkaski, at a prowar demonstration, August 18, 1942. At the far left is former Centro President Antônio Carlos de Abreu Sodré. Beside him (*next to standard*) is Centro President Oscar Bressane. (Courtesy of José Bonifácio Coutinho Nogueira)

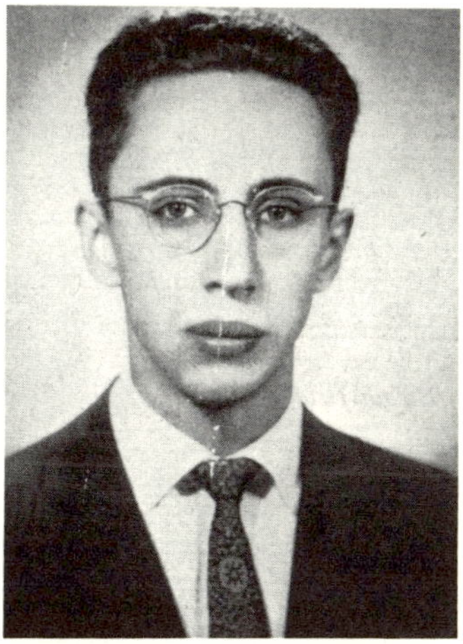

Poet Aloysio Ferraz Pereira, Centro presidential candidate of the Partido Conservador in 1944 and president of the Movimento Acadêmico Renovador in 1945. In 1943 he was wounded by the police.

Some law students in Italy during the war, 1944–1945. *Standing, left to right*: José Vasques Bernardes, Antônio Carlos Silveira Correia, Geraldo Vidigal, Celso Braga, and Rui Pereira de Queiroz. *Seated, left to right*: Antônio Leme da Fonseca Filho, Francisco de Assis Bezerra de Menezes, and Naldo Caparica. (Courtesy of Geraldo Vidigal)

Poet Geraldo Vidigal, president of the Frente Acadêmica pela Democracia until he left for the war in Italy.

Germinal Feijó protesting the government-forced closing of *Diretrizes* magazine, July 1944. *From left to right*: Francisco Morato de Oliveira, Paulo Henrique Meinberg, and Feijó. Wilson Rahal is second from the right. (Courtesy of Germinal Feijó)

Mass for the class graduating in December 1944. Pedro Brasil Bandecchi (*with mustache*) is in the front row at left, closest to Zamira de Sousa Toledo (*girl holding small book*). Farther along is Renato Pintaudi Macedo (*mouth partly open*), near Cardinal Carlos Vasconcelos Mota (*in the center*). Ester de Figueiredo Ferraz appears above the cardinal. Centro President Haroldo Bueno Magano (*with mustache, not in front row*) is the second clear face from the right. (Courtesy of Brasil Bandecchi)

Members of the Frente Acadêmica pela Democracia. José Bonifácio Coutinho Nogueira is at the far left. Second from the right is Luís Afonso Cardoso de Melo de Alvares Otero, who was wounded by the police in 1943. (Courtesy of Flávio Galvão)

"The students are with Eduardo Gomes, against Getúlio Vargas," according to the sign at the rally of February 24, 1945, in front of the law school. (Diários Associados photograph from the Arquivo *Nosso Século*, Abril Cultural. Courtesy of Elizabeth De Fiore di Cropani)

After the fall of Vargas in October 1945, his pictures were seized and destroyed by law students. Gabriel Cury (*smiling*) is at far left. Osmar de Almeida Prado is third from right. (Diários Associados photograph from the Arquivo *Nosso Século*, Abril Cultural. Courtesy of Elizabeth De Fiore di Cropani)

VII

Arrobas and the Front for Democracy (1943)

1. Arrobas Addresses the Sociedade Amigos da América (May 22, 1943)

The first months of the 1943 school year hardly gave the impression that 1943 would become the most memorable year of the anti-Vargas resistance at the São Paulo Law School. Freshman José Bonifácio Coutinho Nogueira, younger son of Paulo Nogueira Filho, wrote late in the year: "We entered the traditional Faculdade de Direito de São Paulo in an epoch in which the national political scene was dominated by the accommodative mentality of those who know how to breathe only in an atmosphere of apathy. . . . The first six months of the Academia confirmed our gloomy forecast. We lived a whole semester of inertia, silence, and cowardice until the National Congress of Students [July]."[1]

The months of "inertia" were notable for the development of the Departamento de Aeronáutica do Centro XI de Agosto, run by Lenício Pacheco Ferreira, Fernando Prado, and Tolstoi de Carvalho Melo. By mid-1943 three training planes had been donated to the *departamento*, thanks in part to the newspaper campaign of publisher Assis Chateaubriand to raise funds for the training of pilots. Law students took courses in aviation, received pilot's licenses, and were incorporated into the reserve of the Brazilian Air Force.[2]

On the anti-Vargas front, the principal development during the months of "inertia" was the interest shown by Centro President Hélio Mota in the ideas of Arrobas Martins. His interest coincided with a coolness in the relations between First Orator Rivaldo Assis Cintra and the controlling group in his party, which in October 1942 had picked Hélio Mota to be presidential candidate.[3] Arrobas has written that "when the president was Hélio Mota, in 1943, the Centro [as in 1941] was at the service of our cause, because Hélio, reaching a decision on his own, drew close to us, and he chose me to speak in the name of the Centro on almost every occasion although I had not been elected First Orator."[4]

By this time Arrobas had become a member of the Bucha, although no one would ever learn it from him. He attended the secret candle-lit sessions, held at night in residences that were blacked out from the street. On at least one of these occasions (this one at a mansion on Avenida Higienópolis), the head *porteiro* (janitor) of the law school, José Epaminondas de Oliveira, stood guard in the garden outside. At the school, Epaminondas, a black, supervised the work of the *porteiros* who were assigned to the professors.

Hélio Mota turned to Arrobas to speak on behalf of the São Paulo students at the meeting held at the Municipal Theater in May 1943 for the installation of local officers of the Sociedade Amigos da América. The Sociedade Amigos da América had been founded late in December 1942 at the Rio residence of General Manoel Rabelo. Rabelo, a member of the Supreme Military Tribunal who criticized what he called the government's failure to implement its decision to enter the war, had been acclaimed by UNE officers and other student leaders, such as Germinal Feijó.[5] Early in January 1943, after becoming president of the Sociedade Amigos da América, Rabelo spoke in São Paulo. "São Paulo," the general exclaimed, "never was, never will be, at the service of tyranny, oppression, deceit. Let us march together, struggling for liberty." War Minister Dutra complained to Vargas that Rabelo's conduct was demoralizing for the government and could be an "alarming cause of subversion," and he stressed that Rabelo, while in São Paulo, had been "always surrounded by elements believed to be Communist." Rabelo, giving his version to Vargas, criticized the war minister's "obstinate and morbid preoccupation with perceiving the Communist danger everywhere" and he argued that "no one any longer feels the imminence of this peril, above all since Russia joined the United Nations in the struggle against the totalitarian countries, and principally since the Comintern's extinction and Russia's adherence to the Atlantic Charter." "Brazil," Rabelo added, "also belongs to that alliance."[6]

When Rabelo returned to São Paulo on May 22, 1943, it was to install the Sociedade's local directorship, headed by 69-year-old medical Doctor Sinésio Rangel Pestana. The evening ceremony, at the crowded Municipal Theater, featured speeches by Sinésio Rangel Pestana, Arrobas Martins, General Rabelo, and Professor Ernesto Leme.[7] The speech of Arrobas electrified the audience. He was constantly interrupted by applause and, after he finished, the audience rose to cheer him. Arrobas, who disliked writing out speeches ahead of time, used the briefest of notes. Nevertheless, his sentences were so well constructed that listeners could hardly believe that they had not been prepared.[8]

Arrobas opened by saying that his only credential for giving an address was his having always belonged to a group of young people that had kept alive and blazing the democratic ideals of justice, liberty, respect of persons, active Pan Americanism, and human solidarity. He declared that students had accepted the constitution and principles of the Sociedade Amigos da América "with the unshakable desire to crush the Nazi viper which, in our land, dresses in green; with the firm desire to take theoretical Pan Americanism out into the streets; with the undeterrable resolution to consolidate, among our people, truly democratic principles." To give what he called the testimony of the young people about the situation, he quoted Disraeli: "We live in an epoch in which it is no longer possible that youth and indifference be synonymous."

Arrobas accused the "Integralista gang" of sabotaging Brazil's future and traitorously trying to assassinate the Brazilian vocation of liberty. In conclusion, he quoted Rui Barbosa's words about the first world war: "God unleashed the conflagration not to destroy mankind but to save it. From the catastrophe will emerge great renovations. Governments of despotism will fall, to be replaced by governments of law."[9]

General Rabelo, reviewing for his São Paulo audience the progress made in the past year, praised the allied victories in Stalingrad and Tunis. He praised Brazil's plan, announced by Vargas on December 31, 1942, to send a large infantry force to fight overseas.[10] Upon leaving São Paulo, Rabelo traveled around Brazil, setting up more local chapters of the Sociedade Amigos da América, and, while he did so, Feijó joined students at the various São Paulo colleges in helping to found the Departamento Universitário da Sociedade Amigos da América.[11]

2. The Partido Libertador Schism (June 1943)

A schism in the Partido Acadêmico Libertador had been brewing for over a year. The aggressively anti-Vargas wing accused the more moderate faction of using only nominal and ineffective methods to oppose the Brazilian dictatorship.[1] The more moderate faction accused the aggressive wing of making unfair charges against it and of considering itself the only possessor of the truth. The moderate Libertadores felt that the aggressive, *apaixonado* (ardent) wing of their party had connections with political exiles who had cooperated with Vargas in the mid-1930s and only broken with him because of their ambition.[2] The leaders of the moderate Libertadores, such as João Nery Guimarães, were strongly and actively opposed to the Brazilian dictatorship and did not wish to be confused with Conservadores, who, they said, took the attitude that students should not get involved with national political matters. But the leaders of the moderates refused to identify themselves with what they considered to be extreme methods, sometimes rude, of the *apaixonado* group. From the practical viewpoint, the Libertador moderate wing felt that the best way to have the *arcadas* oppose the dictatorship was to have the Libertador Party defeat the Conservadores and that this would be difficult as long as the attitude assumed by Germinal Feijó, Hiram Mayr Cerqueira, and other *apaixonados* alienated, or scared, not a few student voters. The Libertador moderate wing was much less inclined than the *apaixonados* to associate with supporters of the far Left. It planned to attract many of the quieter students (unconnected with the "Paulistas of four hundred years"), who had hesitated to get involved in political matters (such as studious Camilo Ashcar Filho). Some of them would be given places on the party's *comissão diretora*.[3]

The quieter students, journalist Flávio Galvão reminds us, made up the large majority, which was democratic in spirit and whose time away from studies was almost entirely devoted to earning a living. He describes the *apaixonados*, or *democratas exaltados*, who complained that the Libertadores had become ineffective, as a minority within a minority. These *democratas exaltados*, he points out, had the means and the connections with ousted politicians that were uncommon and should not be regarded as typical of the law students.[4]

The *apaixonados*, who felt that the failures of the Libertadores were due to the inclusion of "opportunists" in the party, held a minority position on the Libertador *comissão diretora*. When the party members met in May 1943 to fill the six *comissão* vacancies caused by graduation, the aggressive wing (*apaixonados*) won two of the six new posts. One of the two went to second-year student Renato Amaral Sampaio Coelho, a courageous anti-Vargas activist known as "Trombone" due to his deep voice. The other went to fourth-year student and poet Geraldo de Camargo Vidigal. The movement to put the much respected Geraldo Vidigal on the *comissão diretora* had been initiated by a group of his friends who wanted the party to intensify its opposition to the Brazilian dictatorship. The group was made up of fourth-year student Rui Pereira de Queiroz (often referred to as "our De Gaulle" because of his height and appearance), freshman José Bonifácio Coutinho Nogueira and his brother Paulo Nogueira Neto (a third-year student), and Geraldo Vidigal's younger brother, Marcello de Camargo Vidigal (a second-year student).[5]

The June installation meeting of the Libertador's fifteen-man *comissão diretora* was brief and stormy, despite Geraldo Vidigal's efforts to prevent a schism. So-called moderates, such as João Nery Guimarães, were determined to eliminate Germinal Feijó from the *comissão diretora*.[6] Renato Amaral Sampaio Coelho recalls that his own tenure on the *comissão* lasted for about thirty minutes.[7] He walked out together with Feijó, Arrobas Martins, and Ênio de Novais França. Geraldo Vidigal (who had been chosen, along with Naldo Caparica, to publish *O Libertador*) broke with the Partido Libertador about a month later. That left the party with ten *comissão diretora* members: Zwinglio Ferreira (president), João Nery Guimarães, Fernando Jacob, Heitor Borelli de Alvarenga Freire, Renato Macedo, Vítor Tieghi, and four who had been chosen in May: Astolfo Pio Monteiro da Silva, Joaquim Franco Garcia, Renato de Sales Abreu, and Sílvio de Campos Melo Filho.[8]

Arrobas, Feijó, Renato Amaral Sampaio Coelho, and Ênio de Novais França issued a manifesto, which appeared in printed form in June together with the signatures of fifty-three who joined them in leaving the Partido Libertador. Among the fifty-three were Hiram Mayr Cerqueira, Israel Dias Novaes, Paulo Henrique Meinberg, Péricles Eugênio da Silva Ramos, Júlio de Mesquita Neto, Antônio Cândido de Melo e Souza, Lenício Pacheco Ferreira, Carlos Eduardo de Camargo Aranha, Rômulo Fonseca, Luís Francisco da Silva Carvalho, Severo Gomes, and Benjamin Augusto Pereira de Queiros ("Basil Rathbone"—a distant cousin of "our De Gaulle").

The manifesto reviewed the original purpose of the Partido Libertador: "to struggle for democratic ideals, spreading them in the life of the *academia*, and beyond the law school walls." It reviewed also the manner in which "opportunists of every sort" had joined the "triumphal Libertador train, at first as . . . clandestine and irksome baggage, then, thanks to our tolerance, as conspicuous personalities, and, finally, today, . . . with the control in their hands." Most of the students, according to this review, had lost the faith they had originally placed in the party and refused to support it any longer because it limited itself to routine electoral maneuvers for gaining Centro officerships. The manifesto attacked those who, motivated by personal ambition, now repeated "thoughts drawn from earlier manifestos" of the party although they had remained in hiding during the early days of arduous combats. According to the manifesto, it was inadmissible that "sizeable groups of students" at the *arcadas* should support these insincere and "inexpressive little leaders" at a time when "the youth of the whole civilized world, with students and intellectuals in the vanguard, is joined in gigantic struggles for the survival of humanity's conquests."

The signers of the manifesto promised to continue upholding their position of "intransigent defenders of the democratic ideals" by militating in other organizations and "opposing law school politics if they continue in their present framework of pettiness and depravity."[9]

The ten remaining members of the Partido Libertador lost no time in publishing a manifesto declaring that the party remained after four years "the same in the coherent exercise of democratic virtues, which it never neglected, never having served . . . as an instrument for hidden individual interests or inadmissible ambitions of office." The party was described as having the support of the group that had fought during the bitter early reverses, that had not been numbed by the first victories, and that had always known how to uphold "the same inalterable line of behavior, superimposing the objectivism of the collective interests above personalism." The *comissão diretora* spoke of the party's "exuberant vitality and irrevokable will to continue fighting for the same ideals that inspired its foundation."[10]

When *O Libertador*, directed by Fernando Jacob, appeared in September, it carried an article by João Nery Guimarães (member of the school's Academia de Letras), which took a more direct aim at those who had left the party. One of the worst defects of the "democrats of the São Paulo Law School," he wrote, "is that of jealousy, that attitude of ownership which they assume about Democracy, as though they had the patent on the idea or the invoice for its purchase. They speak of Democracy at rallies but do not pratice it." He likened "'democratic' meetings" at the law school, where the so-called democrats tried to resolve everything by hurling insults, to meetings of "adepts of the Third International." He wrote that "they apply the terms reactionary, fascist, peddler of the law school conscience to anyone who does not dance to their music. They involve the majestic figures of Rui Barbosa, Joaquim Nabuco, Castro Alves, Álvares de Azevedo in their chimerical projects."

"The 'defenders of Democracy,'" João Nery Guimarães wrote, "close their eyes to many forms of totalitarianism. And they betray Democracy because they do not know the rudimentary principles of Democracy. . . . Without any knowledge of the fundamentals of politics, they erroneously invoke the principle that the majority should not prevail over the minority."[11]

3. Hélio Mota, UNE President (July 1943)

Education Minister Capanema's plan to create a youth organization, Juventude Brasileira, was resisted early in 1943 by the UNE, which considered the plan fascist and an attempt to have the Education and

War ministries control Brazilian youth. Despite this resistance, Capanema named the national officers of the new organization, including army Major Jair Dantas Ribeiro, who became general secretary of Juventude Brasileira.[1]

On April 1, Capanema issued Regulation 225 appointing Juventude Brasileira administrator of the building used by the UNE (the former German Club of Rio de Janeiro) and alloting space in the building, such as that used by the CBDU, to Juventude Brasileira. Consequently, Hélio de Almeida resigned from the UNE presidency. In his letter of April 3 to Capanema, Hélio de Almeida pointed out that the education minister had broken his promise to take no step without consulting the UNE and, in any event, not to place Juventude Brasileira in the building used by the UNE.[2]

After students throughout Brazil threatened to call strikes in support of Hélio de Almeida, Capanema told UNE leaders Tarnier Teixeira and Paulo Silveira that he would modify Regulation 225 as the UNE wished, on the condition that Hélio de Almeida not return to the UNE presidency. Hélio de Almeida accepted the condition.[3] Major Jair Dantas Ribeiro then resigned as Juventude Brasileira general secretary.

On the night of July 19, shortly before Vargas accepted the major's resignation, the sixth Congresso Nacional de Estudantes held its opening session at Rio's Escola Nacional de Música.[4] There Capanema, Federal District Police Chief Alcides Etchegoyen, and the much acclaimed General Manoel Rabelo joined over three hundred students in hearing a speech by Arrobas Martins, named official orator of the Paulista delegation by Hélio Mota.

Arrobas was at his best, defending democratic regimes and condemning dictatorships. Speaking of the "green struggle," he declared that the students at the São Paulo Law School were unwilling to attend the lectures of Professor Miguel Reale because Reale, as an Integralista, represented the fascism with which Brasil was at war. In response to Arrobas' words, his friends in their fifth year at the *arcadas* organized a strike to protest the planned return of Reale, on July 21, to teach philosophy of law, a fifth-year course.[5] In Rio the sixth Congresso Nacional de Estudantes adopted a resolution repudiating professors who had been Integralistas.[6] The Congresso also named a commission to take up the Reale case with the authorities; one of its members was Germinal Feijó, president of the Sociedade Amigos de Rui Barbosa.[7]

At the Congresso, Arrobas assumed the leading role to secure a "Paulista victory"—the election of Hélio Mota to the UNE presidency. On July 25, after working with the delegations from other states, he offered a slate, in the name of the delegates from São Paulo, that was headed by Hélio Mota.[8]

The outgoing UNE administration had been strongly Communist because both acting President Tarnier Teixeira and Paulo Silveira, who were running the UNE, were associated with the Communists' Comissão Nacional de Organização Provisória (CNOP). To oppose the slate offered by Arrobas, this group put up a slate headed by Fernando Santana, of the Escola Politécnica da Bahia. Santana had been serving as a UNE officer with Tarnier Teixeira and Paulo Silveira.

Communist leaders of the CNOP were starting a campaign of "National Union" at the side of Vargas. The CNOP's strongly pro-Vargas propaganda, appearing almost to be government inspired, alienated Communist intellectuals and many students. Paulo Silveira, who did not favor this policy of the CNOP (and later left the CNOP), feels that the policy contributed to the defeat of the slate headed by Santana.[9] All the candidates in the slate worked out by Arrobas were elected.

On July 26, at the "fraternization lunch" at the UNE headquarters (attended by Capanema), Hélio Mota defended democracy. "By democracy," he said, "we understand the real intervention of all the citizens in the investiture and exercise of the power—the participation of all in the public life of the Nation. Only in that way will the peace of tomorrow be a peace of harmony and general satisfaction."[10]

Arrobas received a "Vote of Praise" signed by Hélio Mota and twenty-two other members of the São Paulo delegation. It mentioned his "inestimable service" and "lofty points of view" and said that "without doubt the eloquence of his words and the brilliance of his intelligence were decisive for the Paulista victory."[11] A reporter of *O Jornal* interviewed Arrobas, "outstanding member of the São Paulo student movement and strong *cabo eleitoral* of the candidacy of Hélio Mota." "São Paulo," Arrobas told the reporter, "came to the sixth National Congress of Students to place itself, as it did, in an intransigently democratic position."[12]

Reflecting thirty years later on the São Paulo student resistance movement of 1943, Arrobas wrote: "We always repudiated the alliance that the Communists insisted on making with us. This, I believe, was one of the finest aspects of our struggle. We were democratic students fighting for the restoration of democracy in Brazil, inspired by the noblest idealism, without any spurious contamination. When we won, for São Paulo, the presidency of the União Nacional dos Estudantes in 1943, we were opposed by the candidate of the Communists."[13]

On the other hand, students who were not too fond of the hard-hitting group of *democratas exaltados*, to which Arrobas belonged, criticized it because of its inclusion of leftists. They would have more to complain about in 1944 when some of the *exaltados* launched a publication, *Resistência*, appealing for a broad support, including that of extreme leftists, socialists, Communists, and partisans of the Aliança Nacional Libertadora (of which imprisoned Communist Luís Carlos Prestes continued to consider himself a leader).

4. Reale Faces the Students (July 21, 1943)

In São Paulo on July 20, the strike against Miguel Reale was organized by fifth-year students Hiram Mayr Cerqueira, Israel Dias Novaes, Celso Galvão, Rômulo Fonseca, Astolfo Pio Monteiro da Silva, Paulo Henrique Meinberg, Lenício Pacheco Ferreira, and others. One of the organizers was arrested and taken to the Superintendência da Ordem Política e Social. During the ensuing negotiations, the students agreed that Reale would not be prevented from giving his lecture on July 21 and Reale agreed that a few questions from students would be permitted during the lecture. The students chose Israel Dias Novaes to take the lead in asking questions. Some help in the questioning would be furnished by Hiram Mayr Cerqueira and Astolfo Pio Monteiro da Silva ("Biquinho," who had remained with the Partido Libertador).[1]

When Reale reached the law school to give his lecture, students, in front of the building, were burning a pile of Integralista papers and insignia that they had collected.[2] Reale, after entering the crowded classroom and being greeted by shouts in favor of democracy, opened by expressing his pleasure at the large attendance. The interest, he said, was justified because his subject, generally considered a dry one, took on importance during periods of great social transformations. He promised not to make his course a political one.[3]

Voices: Very good! We agree!

Reale: Gentlemen! I am giving a lecture! I am not presiding over a rally!

Israel Dias Novaes: But this is turning into a rally regardless of your opinion!

Reale: You gentlemen belong to a Law School, where there are professors and students and where harm can be done, above all, to the institution to which you belong.

Voices: We agree! Psiu! . . . [Mutterings.]

Reale: I don't want to hear "we agree" or "we don't agree"! I simply want the right to develop my subject. You called for Democracy when I entered. One of the democratic principles is freedom of opinion!

Israel Dias Novaes: There was, however, in Brazil, a certain political party that wanted to deny that liberty!

Reale said that he had not come to speak about political parties. Pointing out that Brazil was in the midst of war, he suggested that two types of people were pernicious: those who adhered to liberal parties in order to disturb much-needed national unity, and those who believed that they alone were patriots and worthy of loving the nation. Following the vocal support given to these thoughts, he went on, undisturbed for a while, to contemplate the social "order of tomorrow." It would not, he said, be found in Nazism or fascism, nor in liberalism. "We are marching," he declared, "to a more human, more social order, in which Democracy will be a reality." As Reale said that he had already expressed these opinions in his books, Israel Dias Novaes brought up Reale's *O ABC do Integralismo*.

Reale handled this interruption by saying that he did not pretend to think as he had thought in 1936 and 1937. He explained that at the law school he had once been active in the Marxist ranks. "Today," he added, "I view problems more objectively." When he repeated that Brazil's tomorrow would be democratic, with a greater participation of the people, Israel Dias Novaes interrupted again to say that "all of Brazil knows you as one who has been, up to now, a supporter of Integralismo." "Of fascism," shouted another student. Israel Dias Novaes proceeded to read a message, received that day from the sixth Congresso Nacional de Estudantes. It expressed the support of "all Brazilian students" to the São Paulo law students "for opposing the ignominious intrusion of the fascist Miguel Reale" into the faculty of their school. "The students of all Brazil," it said, "cannot remain indifferent to this fifth-column maneuver."

Although Reale repeated that he would not permit his lecture to turn into a political meeting, Israel Dias Novaes continued to read the message from Rio: "At this moment when Brazil dedicates every effort to a tremendous war against the Nazi-fascist ideology, represented in this country by Integralismo, of which Sr. Miguel Reale was the supreme formulator of doctrine, it is Brazil itself that rises to its feet to protest, through the voice of its true representatives, demanding that public execration and police action be used to isolate one who was an agent for the destruction of national unity. Carry on, Paulista students, in your struggle, for national unification. . . . You must tenaciously oppose the entry of Miguel Reale into your traditional College, bulwark of democratic ideals in Brazil." The message, Israel Dias Novaes added, bore the signatures of the presidents of all the *centros acadêmicos* of Brazil.

Reale: You feel you have the right to read that message which involves an attack . . . on one who has a clear conscience. Young people, listen to me! If any one of you feels more patriotic than me, if any one of you has done more than I have done for the good of Brazil, raise your arm!

A student: That type of salutation is not accepted here! [Laughter and prolonged applause.]

Reale: With jests and wisecracks one does not escape from an imperative of moral order.

Voices: We agree! We don't agree!

Reale: I do not want either handclapping or contradictions. This is a lecture in which, as a demonstration of my spirit and my moral conduct, I give you the right to express yourselves, so that you can see how different is the Miguel Reale who is described from the Miguel Reale who came into this building! I am not afraid of your words, nor of your accusations, because I have a fortress within me . . . [laughter] . . . which is the conscience of a duty fulfilled. . . . Brazil at this moment needs moral and mental unity. If you want a collaborator for this unity, without bias . . . , you will find in me a friend, a sincere collaborator who acts now, as always, with sincerity, with courage. . . . I believe that those who address remarks to me do not know me.

Israel Dias Novaes: I, for example, know you only through your books.

Reale: I hope, then, that through personal contact there will develop a better understanding among us.

The request of a student to leave the room was followed by a conversation among the students. When the students quieted down, Reale went on, explaining that he had not come into the room "to suffer any diminution" in his authority of professor. "It is because you got in touch with me, as students, that I agreed to this exceptional meeting. I want to tell you that I shall give my lectures and I am counting on your collaboration. May the Law School never fail its traditions. I shall never do anything against those traditions!"

As Professor Reale left the room there was some clapping but it was quickly drowned out by cries of "Viva Democracia."[4]

5. Reale's Declarations End a Strike (July 31–August 2, 1943)

Neither Reale's lecture nor his statements made at about the same time to the press satisfied the student strike leaders. They went ahead with their strike while mimeographed sheets, written in verse and prose, ridiculed Reale's "hymn to Democracy," given in the classroom, and put his recent statements alongside older statements.[1]

Reale suspected that the movement against him was led by Arrobas Martins ("of the Partido Democrático group") and inspired by the wish to demonstrate against Vargas.[2] Arrobas confirmed this when he wrote later that the movement resulted from "an opportunity to strike a new blow against fascism and give trouble to the dictator who had named Professor Reale to the Administrative Department of the state."[3]

The strike in São Paulo was so warmly supported by the UNE that strikes appeared likely to break out at many universities.[4] One of the letters to the São Paulo strike leaders, this from "the university students of Rio de Janeiro," implored them to clear up rumors that put in doubt "the purity of our academic movements from north to south." The letter was prompted by a newspaper report that "the São Paulo university students are troubling Professor Reale on the orders of politicians Altino Arantes and J. J. Cardoso de Melo Neto in order to sabotage the war effort and in return for promises of jobs in the DEIP and other departments controlled by those two politicians." The São Paulo strike leaders were advised by their Rio colleagues to persuade *Diário da Noite* to ask Cardoso de Melo Neto why he held on to the title of "Comendador da Itália," "given him by Mussolini," and why Altino Arantes retained the title of "Baron of the Rising Sun," "for which, when he was governor of São Paulo, he sold the state to the accursed Japanese. . . . These are false democrats, bad Brazilians."[5]

In São Paulo the Miguel Reale matter was of particular concern to army Major Hildeberto Vieira de Melo, who had been sent by Vargas in December 1942 to become Superintendente da Ordem Política e Social in the place of tough army Major Olinto de França ("Major Bárbara"). Vieira de Melo, close to Getúlio and Benjamin Vargas, was determined to use tact—and his large "secret expense account"—to "neutralize" the anti-Vargas elite of São Paulo. He did favors for Aureliano Leite and the wife of Armando de Sales Oliveira. And he tried to be helpful to Júlio de Mesquita Filho when the newspaper publisher, unable to cope with the expenses of living abroad, returned to Brazil in 1943 and was interned on a family fazenda not far from the state capital.[6]

After the strike broke out at the law school, Vieira de Melo spoke with Miguel Reale and learned that the professor had disassociated himself from Integralismo around 1937. The students, however, wanted some clear public statements about a number of questions. Luís Arrobas Martins, after returning from his UNE work in Rio, drew up a questionnaire for Reale: "1. What is the position of Professor Miguel Reale about Integralismo? 2. What are his thoughts about the participation of Brazil in the War? 3. What does he think of the struggle in which Brazil is engaged against all forms of fascism? 4. How does he understand the movement of the youth of the *academia* with respect to his return to the College? 5. What attitude should the intellectuals assume about the democratic reconstruction of the postwar world? 6. How does he view the attitude of former Integralistas who separated themselves from the war policy of Brazil? 7. Does he consider the Integralista ideology simply inopportune or definitely condemned?"[7]

The questions for Reale were submitted to Major Vieira de Melo, and on July 30 Reale answered them in the office of the Superintendente da Ordem Política e Social. On July 31 a *Diário da Noite* reporter, having obtained the questions from a group of students, went to the residence of Reale, who said that he could answer them easily because he had already gone over them with Major Vieira de Melo. The professor pointed out that the authorities and his friends knew that he was no longer an Integralista. "The simple duty of social discipline," he said, "requires that all good Brazilians renounce any point of view that might even remotely conflict with the cause embraced by the nation." Furthermore, he said, "from 1937 to the present, social conditions in Brazil and the world have changed in a way that requires a careful revision of convictions, which were mere hypotheses awaiting experimental verification. . . . In the special case of Brazil, there is no doubt that Integralismo, which had its historic moment and reason for existing, was pushed aside by events." Reale also said that his "preoccupation at this time" was to collaborate with thinkers in order to bring about the "common ideal of a truly democratic order."

From the professor's residence, the *Diário da Noite* reporter went to see Vieira de Melo to get the major's approval to publish the statements. The major expressed his satisfaction with them and congratulated the Diários Associados newspaper chain and the law students. Reale's words appeared in *Diário da Noite* on July 31 and in *Diário de S. Paulo* on the next morning.[8] The published version, Reale felt, contained some distortions in large type that were particularly pleasing to the student strikers and that he attributed to Major Vieira de Melo.[9]

Leaders of the strike told reporters that their movement had achieved its purpose and that they wished to "receive Professor Miguel Reale as a legitimate son of our Academia." "Now," Astolfo Monteiro da Silva said, "the students and people of Brazil know that Professor Reale has condemned fascism and is participating in our democratic army. We fulfilled our obligation." According to Hiram Mayr Cerqueira, "the democratic youth of the Arcadas has once again demonstrated its valor and courage; it was victorious in the name of democracy." Germinal Feijó said that he considered the outcome "a settlement of accounts with our generation and the future." The outcome was also hailed in statements to the press by Arrobas Martins, Libertador Party President Zwinglio Ferreira, and Francisco Camargo de Almeida Prado, a member of the *comissão diretora* of the Partido Conservador.[10] At a Centro Onze de Agosto meeting held on Monday morning, August 2, the strike was declared at an end.[11]

6. The Frente Acadêmica pela Democracia's Incisive Manifesto (September 1, 1943)

During August 1943, while the Partido Acadêmico Libertador prepared for its annual *prévia*, some of those who had left the Libertadores, such as the poet Geraldo Vidigal, organized a new party, the Frente Acadêmica pela Democracia. Geraldo's younger brother, Marcello, suggested the name.

The new party satisfied a good many anti-Vargas activists, such as the Vidigals, who wanted a vehicle for launching the candidacy of fourth-year student Rui Pereira de Queiroz for the Centro presidency.[1] And it provided the sort of organization that satisfied those who had argued in June that the Partido Libertador had disappointed students by taking on "irksome baggage" and concerning itself too much with routine electoral maneuvers. José Bonifácio Coutinho Nogueira observed, shortly after the party was formed: "We founded the glorious Frente Acadêmica pela Democracia in order that we might struggle, in the loftiest association, with the noblest bravery, with the highest idealism, for the cause that grips our whole heart today, as yesterday and tomorrow: liberty of the people, emancipation of the needy classes, and the right of representation by all people, to whom God has given the good fortune of life."[2]

Fifth-year student Arrobas Martins drafted a manifesto for the new party. Although the revision by fourth-year student Geraldo Vidigal adhered to Arrobas' ideas, Arrobas objected to the changes, and they turned to fourth-year student José Carlos Moraes Abreu, who wrote the final version, with some help from Vidigal for the opening paragraphs.[3] It appeared in printed form, with 112 signatures, on September 1.

The manifesto reviewed student politics since the founding, in 1936, of the Partido Conservador, "in the first effort . . . to defend sacred individual liberties." Many Conservadores, the manifesto said, had feared that a clear affirmation of the principles of liberty would deprive them of the goodwill of the regime and alienate the colorless electorate. The manifesto described the world events of 1940, the crushing of France by the Nazi hordes and the talk in so-called neutral countries about "a new order," as making the task of the Libertador Party a difficult one—but one in which it became clear who were opportunists and adversaries. The Libertador Party was pictured as losing much of its idealism and taking in false converts after its "ruinous" success in 1940 and persisting, even after the 1941 defeat, in the "counterproductive policy" of "rounding up votes of every sort."

With the world events of 1942, the manifesto said, the Brazilian situation changed and *democracy* ceased being a prohibited word. Under those circumstances, the Libertador Party "should have reformed itself and intensified the struggle." According to the Frente Acadêmica pela Democracia, it did not do so and thus lost its reason for existing.

The new Frente called for freedom of thought, of expression, and of holding meetings. "We want," its manifesto said, "to choose freely those who govern us. We want a Constitution that is discussed and voted by the representatives of the people." To reach these objectives, the Frente added that "it is indispensable that we do not limit our activity to the milieu of the *academia*. We are a group of young people who want to take hold of all the other young people for the democratic reconquest of Brazil. Let us engage in every struggle that might help our ideal. . . . And within the Law School let us act to prevent the directorship of the Centro XI de Agosto from being taken over by students of dubious or undefined orientation."[4]

As Arrobas Martins wrote thirty years later, students at the *arcadas* published prodemocracy manifestos that appeared before the famous "manifesto of the Mineiros" (of October 24, 1943) and that were much more incisive.[5] The manifesto launching the Frente Acadêmica pela Democracia was one of these. But, as Arrobas added, "our manifestos were of mere students, whereas that 'of the Mineiros' was signed by people who were well known and respected throughout the nation."

7. Prelude to the Centro Elections (September–October 1943)

Centro President Hélio Mota chose Arrobas Martins and *O Libertador* First Secretary Roberto Fleury Meirelles to join him as delegates from the *arcadas* to attend the Pan American Congress of Students in Santiago, Chile, in September 1943. Before leaving the country, the Brazilian delegation of twelve or thirteen students from various universities called on Vargas, who suggested that they not speak poorly of Brazil while abroad because dirty laundry should be handled at home.[1]

Arrobas, addressing the inaugural session in Santiago, ignored the suggestion. He said: "I bring you the word of my democratic country, excuse me, I mean I bring you especially the word of the democratic youth of my country despite the grave circumstances that exist in my country. . . . In Brazil the young people want democracy and they fight for it." Calling for "freedom of speech, freedom of opinion, political freedoms," he was heartily applauded.[2]

Arrobas had already left for Chile when Germinal Feijó received a letter in which Monteiro Lobato grieved over the lack of freedom in Brazil. The author reluctantly declined to speak at a meeting of the Sociedade Acadêmica Amigos de Rui Barbosa because he felt that what he would have to say would make his reimprisonment certain. In a pessimistic mood, Monteiro Lobato wrote Feijó that "nothing that might be done or said—or that you people might do or say—will hold back the process of moral decomposition, which, as I see it, is turning the world into waste matter." He described Vargas ("the short-legged one") as a fascist trying to "worm his way" into the company of world democratic leaders, who were sending forces to exterminate fascism, and he wrote that "the main task is to unmask the big hoax." In conclusion, he wrote: "Adieu, my dear Germinal Feijó. You all filled me with enthusiasm and my wishes are that you continue to bring enthusiasm to the mountain of skepticism and disbelief that makes up this old and useless Monteiro Lobato."[3]

At the *arcadas* in September, the student political parties chose their slates of nominees for the November Centro election. The new Frente Acadêmica pela Democracia surprised no one when it nominated Rui Pereira de Queiroz for president of the Centro. Rui Pereira de Queiroz ("our De Gaulle") belonged to a prominent São Paulo family, as did quite a few of the Frente leaders. Rui's aunt, Carlota Pereira de Queiroz, had been a federal congresswoman until Vargas closed Congress in 1937, and had connections with Armando de Sales Oliveira and the anti-Vargas underground. Rui's father (who had named his son for Rui Barbosa) sent money to help exiles in Buenos Aires.[4] In the course of the Centro election campaign, Rui Pereira de Queiroz and two of the other Frente candidates issued invitations to a "cultural" program featuring a speech by José Eduardo do Prado Kelly. Prado Kelly, anti-Vargas jurist and federal congressman (until November 10, 1937), came from Rio and spoke about democracy in the Barão de Ramalho Room on October 30.[5]

The Partido Conservador picked a strong ticket headed by presidential candidate Waldir Ribeiro de Lima and vice-presidential candidate Pedro Brasil Bandecchi. Waldir Ribeiro de Lima, considered "a second Cunha Bueno" because of his intelligence and well-earned popularity,[6] was a son of PRP supporter Diogenes Ribeiro de Lima, a lawyer willing to defend students, without charge, who were to be tried for subversion by the Tribunal de Segurança Nacional of the Estado Novo. Bandecchi, also a lawyer's son, had recently published (in *O XI de Agosto*) his "Ode to Young People," which declared death was preferable to living without liberty.[7]

The Conservadores took credit for having been at the helm when São Paulo students demanded a declaration of war in August 1942, for having instituted the annual Baile das Américas, for having obtained *carteiras de solicitador* for law students, and for progress in constructing the Casa do Estudante.[8] The Conservadores, assisted by the Libertador schism, were expected to win in November. Pre-election polls showed them ahead.[9]

Evidently the Conservadores felt that Haroldo Bueno Magano would be a weak Libertador presidential candidate. When they infiltrated the Libertador *prévia*[10] they helped him win the nomination from Cicero de Toledo Piza and Eduardo Gomes Freitas Martins (who had written that his former party, the Conservador, was made up of accommodating Iscariots).[11] Magano was a poor speaker and was unconcerned about his appearance. He dressed poorly and often seemed not to have shaved. But his association with the Libertadores had been of long duration: he had helped launch the José Maria Ribeiro de Barros candidacy in 1939.

Magano was assisted by able Libertador campaigners, such as his chief *cabo eleitoral*, fifth-year student Astolfo Pio Monteiro da Silva ("Biquinho"). Astolfo Monteiro da Silva had been *chefe do gabinete* (office chief) of the state's important Departamento de Municipalidades, directed by his brother, Dr. Gabriel Monteiro da Silva, but he had resigned lest a place in the government of Fernando Costa conflict with his work with the anti–Estado Novo Partido Libertador.[12]

Other effective, hard-working members of the Libertador *comissão diretora* were fourth-year student Renato Macedo and third-year student João Nery Guimarães. Both were able vote getters, having come to know all the law students by name, a remarkable feat. And both were friends of Roberto Victor Cordeiro, whose partiality for the Libertador Party, which he had helped found,[13] was not disrupted by the schism of 1943. Cordeiro, as interested as ever in law school electoral matters, had not been involved in the creation of the Frente Acadêmica pela Democracia.[14]

Renato Macedo ("Renatinho"), who won the Libertador nomination for Centro vice-president by defeating Flávio Prestes in the *prévia*, had been arrested some time back in Belo Horizonte, Minas Gerais, together with Wilson Rahal and Germinal Feijó, when they had honored opposition politician Pedro Aleixo. (Rahal's stirring oration had brought on the arrests.)[15] At the *arcadas* Renatinho was the *mola mestra* (master source of action) of the electioneering politics of the Partido Libertador. He went out of his way to befriend new students and sought to protect them from the *trote* that they feared.[16]

The Libertador *comissão diretora*, having lost five members due to the schism of 1943, was back to its normal size of fifteen due to the addition of Naldo Caparica, Aloísio Marcondes Barbosa Ferreira, Ênio Antônio Monte Alegre, José Correia de Almeida Morais, and José Gonçalves Santana.[17] Santana, known by everyone as "Juca Santana, the composer of verses," had written the "Hino [Hymn] do Partido Acadêmico Libertador," whose opening stanza went as follows:[18]

Somos contra a inação submissa,
Nossa gente é de grande valor,
Liberdade, Direito e Justiça
São princípios do Libertador.[19]

VIII

Repression by the Special Police (1943)

1. The Baile das Américas (October 30–31, 1943)

It has been said that "everybody in São Paulo" was at the 1943 Baile das Américas, held at the Esplanada Hotel on the night of October 30–31 (Saturday–Sunday). This was a few days after the appearance of the "manifesto of the Mineiros," which declared that "a people reduced to silence and deprived of the faculty of thinking or expressing itself is a corroded organism" and that, "if we fight against fascism at the side of the United Nations so that liberty and democracy may be restored to all people, certainly we are not asking too much in demanding for ourselves such rights and guarantees."[1]

The ball, according to a government report issued some days later, proceeded normally (with considerable consumption of alcoholic beverages by students) until around 3:00 A.M., when rumors began to circulate that leading Mineiro politicians, such as Pedro Aleixo and Artur Bernardes, had been jailed and some of their supporters wounded.[2] Except for this report, which blamed the ensuing disturbances on these unfounded rumors, no evidence exists that would tie the disturbances to anything but the exuberance of partying students, eager to express their democratic yearnings dramatically.

Among the group of students who resolved to do so were Paulo Henrique Meinberg, Hiram Mayr Cerqueira, Lenício Pacheco Ferreira, and Luís Arrobas Martins. By lot Lenício Pacheco Ferreira was chosen to start the manifestation. At about 3:15 A.M. he went to the orchestra, which was playing a Glen Miller dance tune, and persuaded the leader to have a loud drum flourish.[3] With everybody's attention thus gained, Lenício announced: "At this Baile das Américas, the most traditional social gathering of the Centro Onze de Agosto, we are going to take the opportunity to recite:

Oh! valente legionário
Do Corpo Expedicionário:

Por que vais lutar a esmo
Se a luta cruente e fria
É pela Democracia.
Vamos travá-la aqui mesmo!"[4]

The verse, suggesting that the prodemocracy struggle of the Brazilian Expeditionary Force should be carried out in Brazil, is said to have been written by José Gonçalves Santana (Juca).[5] It was already popular. Typed on small pieces of paper, it had made the rounds in anti-Vargas circles. The recital of the verse at the Baile was followed by shouts of "Down with the dictatorship" and "Death to Vargas." The shouts were led by Paulo Henrique Meinberg, who was in a balcony overlooking the dance floor, and who called attention to himself by whistling loudly. Simultaneously, from the bandstand, Lenício Pacheco Ferreira led the shouting.[6]

Germinal Feijó made a pronouncement: "We proclaim the following enacted: (1) the Third Republic is installed; (2) Cândido Mota Filho [director of state censorship and propaganda] is not acceptable as a professor; and (3) these resolutions are immutable." Meinberg shouted his agreement and led more antidictatorship and anti-Vargas cries.[7]

Lenício Pacheco Ferreira spotted Centro President Hélio Mota, who was with his girlfriend and who, Lenício could see, felt uneasy about the scene being made by some of his most radical schoolmates. But Lenício persuaded Hélio Mota to raise his voice against Vargas and the dictatorship, and the brief, clear shouts of the Centro president were acclaimed. Then Hélio Mota went to the orchestra. Seizing the microphone, he called for "music, much music," and added, "Viva a democracia!" After that, Lenício recalls, the ball went on until 5:30 A.M. amidst a "feeling of great euphoria, as though we had overthrown the dictatorship and Vargas."[8]

Police Delegado Antônio Pinto do Rego Freitas, who attended the Baile to see that it was orderly, was reluctant to make arrests during a gathering of the elite. He tried to calm the students, gathered testimonies that Hélio Mota had been subversive, and invited Hélio Mota to appear on October 31 at the Superintendência da Ordem Política e Social. For his feeble performance, Rego Freitas was later suspended by Coriolano de Góis, who had become the state secretary of Segurança (Security).[9]

When Lenício Pacheco Ferreira left the Baile at 5:30 A.M. with Meinberg and other friends, he was asked by two police agents to accompany them because, he was told, Elpídio Reali, *delegado* of the

Superintendência da Ordem Política e Social, wanted to speak with him. Remarking that it would be "an honor to be jailed by the cops of the dictatorship," Lenício was about to be taken away, when a group of fifteen or twenty students, including Meinberg, Arrobas, and Hiram Mayr Cerqueira, pulled him away from the police. He was thus able to change from his formal clothes at his apartment and participate a few hours later as a pilot in the program of the Centro's Departamento de Aeronáutica, of which he was a director.

Meinberg, who lived in the same building as Lenício, came to the Aeroclube later in the morning to report that DOPS agents had searched Lenício's apartment and made away with books and papers. Meinberg also reported that the police had arrested Hélio Mota, Arrobas Martins, and Germinal Feijó.[10]

2. Arrobas' Manifesto Condemning the Estado Novo (November 1, 1943)

Arrobas Martins and Germinal Feijó were not held long after being questioned by the police, and they went to the Feijó country place in Guararema. But Hélio Mota was kept in prison and was declared a "confessed criminal." An official report (which went to Vargas) said that "the Police, who could not countenance disrespect to the highest authority of the Nation and who sought also to avoid more serious developments, imprisoned Hélio Mota, the president of the Centro Acadêmico XI de Agosto and the most fanatic of the demonstrators."[1]

After Hélio Mota was transferred from the Superintendência da Ordem Política e Social to the Casa de Detenção (prison) and held there *incomunicável*, steps were taken to secure his release. In the presence of Superintendência Director Vieira de Melo, law school Director Cardoso de Melo Neto and banker Gastão Vidigal spoke by phone to Vargas, who said that the police should drop their charges against the students and release Hélio Mota. An order for Mota's release was expected to arrive from Rio the next day.[2]

State Security Secretary Coriolano de Góis, who had served as Rio police chief in the government of President Washington Luís, took his time about releasing Hélio Mota. On Monday afternoon, November 1, Coriolano was asked about the release when he was visited by a commission consisting of law school Secretary Flávio Mendes, three students, and recent graduate Luís de Azevedo Soares, lawyer of the Centro Onze de Agosto.[3] Luís de Azevedo Soares was familiar with the temperament of Coriolano, for he had called on him before with Wilson Rahal; when Rahal had suggested that a map of Brazil would be a more fitting wall decoration than the picture of Vargas, Coriolano had flown into a rage and shouted, "Vargas is Brazil."[4] Coriolano was in no better mood on November 1, 1943, and was apparently suffering from a neuralgic pain in the neck.[5] After stating that he needed time to resolve the Hélio Mota matter, he added: "Thank God I do not have to go to the school, for if that happens I shall not weigh the consequences, and, if necessary, I'll order shooting of the students, causing blood to flow."[6]

Students, holding an emergency session of the Centro, had felt that the situation was becoming serious. Therefore, Renato Amaral Sampaio Coelho and first-year student Álvaro Roberto Mendes Gonçalves (nicknamed "Febre") had set out for the Feijó country place in a car (equipped with a *gasogênio* for producing fuel from charcoal) belonging to Gonçalves' father. They returned from Guararema with Arrobas Martins and Germinal Feijó.

Before going to the law school, the group stopped at the home of Joca (João Batista Silva Azevedo) in the Liberdade district of the city of São Paulo. Arrobas sat down and wrote out, without deliberating, a manifesto to the nation for the Centro to consider at its prolonged emergency session.[7]

The manifesto recalled that a little over a year had passed since "we law students, together with the other São Paulo university students, placed ourselves at the front of our people, in the streets, to demand a decision of the nation in the face of the fascist aggression." This demand that Brazil struggle at the side of free nations had been made by the students, the manifesto said, in the hope that "the rulers of our land would be honest enough first to make Brazil democratic, because only that step would bring about the national union so necessary at that moment and so much desired by all Brazilians."

According to the manifesto, the failure of Brazil to implant an effective legal and democratic regime had filled the people with despondency and was preventing Brazil from availing itself of the opportunity to become included among the great nations of the postwar world. The manifesto described Brazil as having made no effective contribution to the war, and the Brazilian people as becoming apathetic, and it blamed this "deplorable situation" on the general distrust of "the present political regime of Brazil."

Arrobas went on to write in the manifesto that "we law students of São Paulo have remained silent" hoping for an honorable and patriotic attitude by the government. "However," he continued, "it is no longer possible to temporize. A distinctly fascist act of the government has wounded completely the heart and spirit of youth. For the first time in the history of our glorious Centro Acadêmico XI de Agosto, its president was arbitrarily jailed. Why? Because he expressed 'ideas opposed to the regime,' according to those responsible for his jailing. Would this be a crime in a democratic country? No!"

For this reason, the manifesto said, "we fulfill today the duty we have long postponed. We denounce, at last, publicly and solemnly, the so-called 'Estado Novo' as a regime absolutely incompatible with Democracy."

The manifesto explained that by democracy the students meant a state in which the citizens elected the government and fiscalized its performance efficiently by means of representatives in congress and the unrestricted right to criticize, through freedom of thought and expression. "By democracy," the manifesto added, "we mean the state in which all citizens enjoy the fundamental right of being able to organize public opinion in political parties." The manifesto expressed the students' belief that "a Republic exists only when the rulers are chosen for predetermined and short mandates."

The manifesto also said that all of its signers were familiar with the character and viewpoint of Hélio Mota and were certain that he would not disagree with the thoughts being expressed. The signers declared formally before the Brazilian nation that they fully supported the position he had assumed and were adopting as their own any of his words that might have caused him to become incriminated. Therefore, the manifesto argued, legal proceedings should be undertaken against all the signers similar to those undertaken against Hélio Mota.

"Let the reprisals come," the manifesto concluded. "The Brazilian Nation will know how to judge us."[8]

3. The Special Police Invade the Centro (November 2, 1943)

Late on the afternoon of November 1, Arrobas Martins, Germinal Feijó, Renato Amaral Sampaio Coelho, and Álvaro Roberto Mendes Gonçalves went from Joca's home to the assembly of the Centro Onze de Agosto. Arrobas' manifesto was acclaimed and the crowded Centro became a busy place for typing it. Different sheets were typed simultaneously on several typewriters.[1] Signature sheets were passed around to add to the last typed page, on which Arrobas was the first to sign. The 180 authentic signatures included that of Evaristo Pan Gomes, who was not a law student but headed the student Centro Acadêmico Horácio Berlink of the Faculdade de Ciencias Econômicas de São Paulo. Another signer, Antônio Melo Bueno ("Toti"), was a cousin and admirer of Antônio Sylvio Cunha Bueno but was not a student. At least a few of the signers had been considered lukewarm in opposing Vargas. Even the openly pro-Vargas José Barbosa signed. Some of the strongly anti-Vargas students were not present at the Centro and therefore friends signed on their behalf, bringing the grand total of names on the original document to 205.[2]

One copy of the manifesto was delivered to the Rossolilo printing firm on Rua Asdrubal do Nascimento (near the law school).[3] Another (the first carbon) was turned over to students, who went to confer with Major Vieira de Melo.[4] Among these students were Geraldo Vidigal, Rui Pereira de Queiroz,[5] Antônio Cláudio Fernandes Rocha (who had designed the emblem of the Frente Acadêmica pela Democracia),[6] Roberto Fleury Meirelles, and Cory Porto Fernandes, roommate of Hélio Mota and president of the Grêmio da Escola de Sociologia e Política.[7]

The students were not admitted to the major's office until about 1:00 A.M. on November 2. He read the manifesto and proposed a solution: since Vargas had already called for the release of Hélio Mota, the release would be carried out immediately provided the manifesto was not printed and circulated. The students returned to the Centro Onze de Agosto with the proposal, but as only about fifty students remained at the *arcadas*, it was decided that a few students should advise the major that no decision could be reached until a majority of the signers of the manifesto could be heard.[8] Geraldo Vidigal, Antônio Cláudio Fernandes Rocha, and some others set out for the Superintendência da Ordem Política e Social with this message.

The Centro Onze de Agosto assembly had already turned into a noisy forum for antidictatorship speeches. Renato Macedo, in a bar in the neighborhood, was told by a policeman that the students should not be holding their assembly, but, despite the denouncement, he returned to the *arcadas*.[9] There, Lenício Pacheco Ferreira shouted: "We are surrounded but the dictatorship does not have the courage to confront us; a breach has been opened for the victory of democracy." That as many as fifty students remained at the law school at about 2:30 A.M. was due to the decision not to leave the Centro weakly guarded. Some students had brought mattresses.[10]

The students' fears of an invasion were justified. During the night, state Viação (Transport) Secretary Luís de Anhaia Melo, whose office was near the law school, phoned Interventor Fernando Costa to advise that a "big movement" was going on at the law school. Soon Segurança Secretary Coriolano de Góis received a call from the *interventor*. What was happening, Coriolano de Góis learned, was "worse than the Baile das Américas."[11] According to other reports that reached him, the Centro had assumed "a seditious position, absolutely revolutionary, during which the walls were decorated with pornographic drawings and inscriptions ridiculing the President of the Republic." Coriolano ordered the tough Special Police, under Major Anísio Cardoso de Miranda, to send shock troops to arrest the students and close the Centro.[12]

The invasion was led by Anísio Miranda, who had once been a corporal shoeing horses for the Força Pública (state troops) and had risen in the ranks without formal course work.[13] At about 2:30 A.M. he brought trucks and armored cars, with over 150 members of the Special Police, to the law school. Armed with portable machine guns, rifles with bayonets, and apparatuses for releasing gas, the policemen unleashed a vigorous attack. Rifle butts, wielded with authority, sent students sprawling and wounded about thirty. Machine gun fire and revolver shots damaged the walls. Furniture, manuscripts, and relics were destroyed, and a bayonet was used to slit holes in a valuable old painting of Pedro II. Chico Elefante, hoping to save himself from the wrath of the Special Police, put on the apron and cap that he never used. But the policemen decided that he must be a student trying to fool them, and he was given a thrashing.

As the students were put in police cars, they were struck with rifle butts and billies. The cars made stops at restaurants and bars, where other students were picked up. Most of the students were jailed at the Superintendência da Ordem Política e Social on the Largo General Osório (near the Sorocabana and Luz railroad stations), and it was there that Geraldo Vidigal, Antônio Cláudio Fernandes Rocha, and others who had returned to see Major Vieira de Melo again were already being held. A few students were sent to the Casa de Detenção. Law Professors José Soares de Melo, Waldemar Ferreira, and Ernesto Leme were put under house arrest.

Among those who had set out before midnight to help negotiate with Major Vieira de Melo were Conservador Arthur Octavio de Camargo Pacheco and Antônio Melo Bueno, the cousin of Antônio Sylvio Cunha Bueno. The two young men had trouble finding a taxi so late at night and never reached the major's office. They changed their plans when it became clear that policemen in the streets, firing pistol shots, were eager to arrest them.

Eventually they reached the home of Law School Director Cardoso de Melo Neto, where asylum had already been found by Israel Dias Novaes and Rômulo Fonseca—a thin, cultured, fifth-year student nicknamed "Professor Picard" by Israel Dias Novaes because he looked like the Swiss balloon man. Around 4:00 A.M., when the young men were telling Cardoso de Melo Neto about the attacks by the Special Police, approximately thirty members of the Special Police, with revolvers in hand, arrived at the home of the law school director and demanded that the students there be turned over to them. Cardoso de Melo Neto phoned Gastão Vidigal and asked him to come to the house.

After the banker and the law school director discussed the situation, Gastão Vidigal phoned Coriolano de Góis. It was agreed that the young men would be turned over to the police, but only briefly, in order to give testimonies. The agreement, however, was not kept. The young men were locked up.[14]

4. Days of Imprisonment (November 2–5, 1943)

Cardoso de Melo Neto was furious. On November 3, he advised a specially called law school faculty meeting that the government had broken its promise to him to release the students and therefore he was submitting his resignation as the school's director. His resignation letter, made known to the faculty, informed Interventor Fernando Costa of the behavior of the Special Police.

The faculty named two commissions of professors, one to assist the jailed students and the other to assist the three law professors who were under house arrest. Antônio de Sampaio Dória acted as interim law school director for two days and was succeeded by Alvino Ferreira Lima (professor of civil law).[1]

Prominent Paulistas sent messages to the *interventor* protesting the aggressiveness of the police. One was written by Alcides da Costa Vidigal, president of the Institute of Lawyers of São Paulo and father of Geraldo and Marcello.[2] Teotônio Monteiro de Barros Filho, state secretary of education and law school professor of finance, rushed to Rio and obtained Vargas' order for the release of the students.[3] But about half of the arrested students remained locked up until November 5 because Coriolano wished to have thorough interrogations.

During the Estado Novo, the imprisoned students in São Paulo were almost always treated well, with the jailers assuming a paternal attitude. But the interrogators were sometimes less considerate. Lenício Pacheco Ferreira recalls interrogations of early November 1943 that were accompanied by blows to the head and ears. In response to questions, Hélio Mota assumed responsibility for having shouted against the dictatorship at the Baile das Américas, and Arrobas said that he had written the manifesto of November 1.[4] Many of the students were asked about the printing of the manifesto. The police already suspected the Rossolilo firm and, when they invaded it and found the manifesto, they prevented its distribution by destroying the type set up to print it and by threatening the shop manager with imprisonment and closure of the shop.[5]

The interrogators, inquiring of the arrested students about the "extent of the movement" and the students' "relations with political figures,"[6] sought to show that the law school subversion, begun at the Baile, was connected with a large, organized movement. Investigators wrote that "components of various groups of the old Partido Democrático, among them Srs. Júlio de Mesquita Filho, Cardoso de Melo Neto, Horácio Lafer, Waldemar Ferreira, etc.," had developed a plan for an outbreak that would not be confined to São Paulo and would seek to provide elections and a new constitution. The plan was felt to call for demonstrations by university students, principally those of the São Paulo Law School. While the students remained in jail, these investigators reported, "manifestos by politicians of São Paulo and other states were distributed together with the manifestos of support for the law students issued by the directorships of the other academic associations."[7]

During the imprisonment of the students, an avalanche of messages protested the rough invasion of the once inviolable "free territory of the Largo de São Francisco." Copies were circulated widely in São Paulo. One of the first was addressed to the education minister by the directors of the Centro Acadêmico Cândido de Oliveira, student body of the Faculdade Nacional de Direito of the federal capital. It said that "rarely in the entire history of Brazil have students been so outrageously insulted" and "professors so much disparaged." Besides mentioning the patriotic traditions of the São Paulo Law School, the message extolled democracy and quoted Rui Barbosa as saying that the nation was made up of all the people, "each with the same right of opinion, words, and association."[8]

On November 4 the presidents of the São Paulo student associations, in a joint message to the people of the state, advised that they had informed Interventor Fernando Costa that all school work would be suspended until "the university student class has been indemnified morally for the damages inflicted." In separate manifestos each association made somewhat similar statements. The medical students, for example, resolved to return to their studies only after the law students had received "moral and material indemnization" and the authorities responsible for the invasion had been dismissed.

The Grêmio da Faculdade de Filosofia said that a return to the classroom depended on the opening of an inquiry to determine who were responsible for the vandalism and beating of "completely unarmed and defenseless young people." The students of schools unconnected with the university (such as the two-hundred student Escola de Engenharia Mackenzie) also went on strike and issued statements.[9]

Although most of the jailed students were together in large cells, some, like Germinal Feijó, Hélio Mota, Arrobas, and Lenício Pacheco Ferreira, were held in solitary confinement. Lenício Pacheco Ferreira received a visit from Major Vieira de Melo, who advised him to stop fighting the government and sign a statement asking Vargas for clemency. By suggesting to the major that he would try to persuade Hélio Mota and Arrobas Martins to follow that advice, Lenício was able to talk with those two. He proposed that Mota gain his freedom by telling the major that he planned to speak with Vargas but wanted first to hear the opinion of the leadership of the São Paulo student strike. "Outside prison," Lenício told Mota, "you can explain that we are all firm in our convictions and you can give new life to the movement." With the release of the last of the students on November 5, it became unnecessary to consider Lenício's suggestion.[10]

While Arthur Octavio de Camargo Pacheco was still in jail, he received a proposal from Vieira de Melo that he go to Rio to speak with Vargas and Capanema. He was allowed to shave and bathe, and the police made arrangements to take him to the station from which the Cruzeiro do Sul train would leave for Rio. However, Pacheco first sought the advice of Gastão Vidigal and the banker argued that it would be unwise for students to follow the suggestions of the police that they leave for Rio.[11] There was no telling what might happen to them in Rio even if they arrived there safely. Their "base of protection" was in São Paulo. Pacheco told Major Vieira de Melo that he had decided not to go to Rio. He was rearrested but it was only a matter of hours before he was set free. However, Vargas' order that released the students did not cover the three professors. They remained under house arrest, their homes under police vigilance.

Lenício Pacheco Ferreira, before being released, was ordered to sign a statement that the police claimed was based on information furnished during several interrogatory sessions. Lenício, who had not cooperated with information, argued that the statement was incorrect, and he refused to sign despite threats of being tortured and then sent to an island prison. The police finally agreed that Lenício's signature be accompanied by a written protest that the statement had been obtained after beatings and threats.[12]

5. Reactions to the Assaults and Jailings (November 5–8, 1943)

The last of the jailed law students, about thirty in number, were released on November 5. As it was the anniversary of the birth of Rui Barbosa, they gathered at once around the statue of the statesman in Anhangabaú Park. Then they paraded through the streets in the direction of the law school, yelling vivas for democracy and death to the dictatorship and Vargas.[1]

Cory Porto Fernandes, invited to the home of Justice Secretary Abelardo Vergueiro César, found "Abelardinho" in the company of Education Minister Teotônio Monteiro de Barros Filho. While explaining details of the students' recent troubles, Cory Porto Fernandes learned that the two state secretaries were so upset with Coriolano de Góis that they planned to inform Vargas of their discontent.[2]

Hélio Mota addressed a letter to Fernando Costa to advise that the Centro Onze de Agosto, informed of Cardoso de Melo Neto's resignation letter, would not accept a new law school director unless the school and Cardoso de Melo Neto received "complete and public redress for the arbitrary acts" and unless Cardoso de Melo Neto still insisted on resigning after the redress had been made.[3] Law school student leaders worked with Centro lawyer Luís de Azevedo Soares and three other graduates of December 1942, Wilson Rahal, Roberto de Abreu Sodré, and Antônio Francisco Leonel Costa, in the preparation of a legal case demanding indemnization. In the apartment shared by Hélio Mota and Cory Porto Fernandes, Luís de Azevedo Soares picked up information for the case.[4]

Francisco Morato de Oliveira received a visit in his law office from Roberto de Abreu Sodré and students Renato Amaral Sampaio Coelho, Marcello Vidigal, Luís Arrobas Martins, and José Bonifácio Coutinho Nogueira. The first president of the Sociedade Acadêmica Amigos de Rui Barbosa suggested to his visitors that the university students sponsor a prodemocracy rally on November 9, the eve of the Estado Novo's sixth anniversary. This step, he said, would force the São Paulo police to choose between two alternatives: they could prohibit the rally, "unmasking themselves in the eyes of the public," or could permit the demonstration and thus open the way for a series of rallies that would bring an end to the dictatorship. The proposal appealed to the lawyer's visitors. José Bonifácio Coutinho Nogueira composed a brief notice to be distributed on the eighth: "The students of our University invite the people of São Paulo to attend the prodemocracy rally that they will hold tomorrow, November 9, at 6:00 P.M. in the Praça do Patriarca."[5]

The notices were prepared clandestinely. Seventeen-year-old Rui Mesquita (a son of Júlio de Mesquita Filho and not yet a law student), Celso Medeiros, Adolfo Nardy (a cousin of Celso Medeiros), and second-year law student Severo Gomes used a stolen key to enter the Sociedade Harmonia de Tênis, and they went off with its mimeograph.[6] At the home of Celso Medeiros they used the mimeograph to produce copies of the invitation to the rally. To gather support for the rally from oppositionist circles in Rio, Antônio Carlos de Abreu Sodré and Antônio Pereira Lima (who received his *resistência* student friends at the Automóvel Clube) provided Lenício Pacheco Ferreira with a round trip railroad passage to the federal capital.[7]

While preparations for the rally were being made, São Paulo was informed about the November 2 invasion of the law school, not by the press but by mimeographed verse and prose. The nearest the press came to saying anything was a little item that coupled the names of Coriolano de Góis and Special Police Major Anísio Miranda: "In a city of the interior Coriolano Miranda, angry at a neighbor for offending the captain of his favorite soccer club, invaded the house, breaking the furniture and beating the residents." The item was reproduced at the top of a mimeographed sheet of verse written by José Gonçalves Santana.[8] According to the last stanza:

Está dito e está provado
Que um governo faz um povo.
Se somos um povo atrasado
Ora viva o estado novo.[9]

Another sheet of verse, "As 'Carícias' do Coriolano" (The "Caresses" of Coriolano) mocked the "stool pigeon" who had been "dismissed" as finance secretary and made *segurança* secretary by Gegê (Getúlio Vargas); it described the assault of November 2 against the "Onze of Rui Barbosa" by "the irascible Gestapo" and mentioned the subsequent interrogations made under threat. In conclusion it said:

E os ratos da embarcação,
Sentindo o barco afundar,
"Resolveram" a situação
Dando ordem pra saltar.[10]

Some verses had made the rounds among the imprisoned students. In these, and in a two-page parody of a samba, references were made to Jorge Americano ("George, o Americano"), who had sought to give Vargas an honorary degree, and Miguel Reale ("Mick, el Reale"). DEIP Director Cândido Mota Filho was also mentioned.[11]

More serious was the motion adopted on November 8 by twenty law professors (including Jorge Americano and Professor Emeritus Francisco Morato) and given publicity in mimeographed copies.[12] Addressed to Vargas, his education and justice ministers, Interventor Fernando Costa, and the state education secretary, it was not signed by Miguel Reale. Nor was it signed by the three arrested professors or by Education Secretary Teotônio Monteiro de Barros Filho (one of the addressees). Like most of the *livres-docentes*, DEIP Director Cândido Mota Filho did not sign.

A commission of professors, the motion said, had confirmed the reports about the barbarous acts of the "two hundred" members of the Polícia Especial who had broken into the *arcadas*, wounding "over thirty" students and violating "the old tradition of respect for the Law School." Although the motion admitted that the authorities might have had the right to arrest students who were meeting at their *centro* in a semipublic session and promoting disturbances to the public order, it condemned the physical aggression. It requested a thorough investigation and the punishment of the authorities who were responsible for such an act, carried out just when the young people were reaching an agreement with the Superintendente da Ordem Política e Social.

In a reference to this motion, an emotional anonymous mimeographed "manifesto to the São Paulo law students" pointed out that the faculty had fearlessly taken a position—"with the exception, of course, of Cândido Mota Filho and Miguel Reale. The first is the apologist of the incredible 'Democracia Autoritária' and director of the Department that stifled the freedom of the press. The second is the stand-in for Plínio Salgado and today also the defender of the *caudilho* of São Borja [Vargas]. Outside of those two, who lecture against the will of all of you, the teachers support the revolt against the Getulista power." According to this anonymous manifesto, the cry of revolt had begun in Minas and spread rapidly to other states. "In São Paulo, this glorious São Paulo," the manifesto declared, "once again it is the law students who deliver the first blow against the destroyers of liberty." Pointing out to the law students that everyone backed their attitude, the manifesto told them of their moral obligation to hold more and more rallies.[13]

The presidents of the associations of twelve São Paulo colleges joined with the student representative on the university's governing Conselho in signing, also on November 8, a report about recent events, which was mimeographed and circulated. It accused Coriolano de Góis of demonstrating, from the moment he took office, "hostility and prejudice" against the São Paulo university young people, especially those in the law school. The report spoke also of the "insolent and sadistic attitude of Major Anísio Miranda," commander of the Special Police.[14]

6. The March of Silence (November 9, 1943)

When the mimeographed notices appeared on November 8, announcing the "democratic rally" to be held the next day by university students, Coriolano de Góis ordered the police to prevent the rally, and he explained to the new Second Military Region commander, General Horta Barbosa, that the rally was "clearly designed to disturb order on the eve of the November 10 commemorations." Coriolano de Góis also prepared a notice to be published in all the São Paulo newspapers on the ninth to advise that the Secretaria da Segurança Pública, considering the rally a plan to disturb the peace, would not permit it and would "act with maximum force against anyone attempting to carry out the disturbances."[1]

Hélio Mota was unpleasantly surprised on the afternoon of November 8 by the appearance of the mimeographed invitations to the rally. He told General Horta Barbosa that the Centro Onze de Agosto had not planned the rally. Aided by friends, he spent the rest of the day and part of the night convincing students not to participate in it. After reading at lunch on the ninth the notice that Coriolano de Góis had put in the newspapers, he continued to persuade law students not to become involved in a rally. He arranged with Arnaldo Sena, president of the Centro Acadêmico Horácio Lane of the Mackenzie Engineering School, and Cory Porto Fernandes, president of the Grêmio da Escola de Sociologia e Política, to hold a meeting at which the heads of various student associations were expected to sign a joint statement in favor of canceling the rally. Although the meeting did not take place as planned in the apartment of Hélio Mota and Cory Porto Fernandes, General Horta Barbosa was nevertheless able to report to Coriolano de Góis that representatives of the students of some of the colleges, including the law school, would see to it that the "democratic rally" would not take place. Coriolano, taking no chances, sent a large police contingent to the busy, store-filled Praça do Patriarca during the warm, sunny afternoon.[2]

Following a polite request by Major Vieira de Melo, the law school building was closed at 5:00 P.M. Around 5:30 several hundred law students were at the Largo de São Francisco and the nearby Largo do

Ouvidor. With the rally banned, Ênio de Novais França suggested a *passeata de silêncio* (march of silence) to the Praça do Patriarca, in which the students would walk with their mouths covered by handkerchiefs. The walk was organized at once by students Abel Newton de Oliveira Penteado, Celso and Cássio Queiroz Ferreira, Carlos Pinto Alves, Carlos Adolfo Schmidt Sarmento, Plínio Simões, Eduardo Whately, the Nogueira brothers, and others.[3]

Hélio Mota and three of his friends had been at the Praça do Patriarca, in the center of the city, noting the police contingent and were walking up São Bento Street on their way to the Largo de São Francisco when they met about three hundred silent students, handkerchiefs across their mouths, marching in the opposite direction. He warned them to remain silent during their pacific march; then, reflecting that by leading them he could probably get them back quickly from the Praça do Patriarca, he took his place at their head. When the silent students appeared in the Praça they found it crowded. After being acclaimed by many people there, they returned, quiet and orderly, to the Largo de São Francisco, where Hélio Mota urged them to go to their homes.[4]

7. Coriolano de Góis Dispatches the Special Police (November 9, 1943)

Most of the students did not go home. About 150 decided to advance again into the Largo do Ouvidor and down São Bento Street in order to close their manifestation with cries for democracy at the Praça do Patriarca. Again, Hélio Mota decided to accompany them. As they were about to enter the Praça they were stopped at Direita Street by Police Delegado Gustavo Cordeiro Galvão, who reached for his revolver and ordered the students to go no farther. While Hélio Mota argued with the *delegado*, the students made their shouts for democracy and were applauded.

The police authorities contended that they had been tolerant in allowing the *passeata silenciosa* but that the new outbreaks were turning the affair into precisely what had been prohibited and was a breach of an agreement made by student leaders.[1]

Coriolano de Góis sent fifty *guardas civis* to help bring order to the Praça do Patriarca. Then, at the suggestion of Major Vieira de Melo, a water truck of the Corpo de Bombeiros (fire department) was also dispatched. The large truck, making its way down São Bento Street, was surrounded by a mob, including students, and its occupants were booed. But the students, having given their shouts for democracy, decided to return to the Largo de São Francisco. Hélio Mota, agreeing to abide by the order of Delegado Gustavo Cordeiro Galvão, told the students that the manifestation was over and that on the next day, November 10, they were to wear black neckties in public.

Coriolano, believing that "the rally was turning into a veritable riot," had the colonel commanding the Força Policial send a part of a cavalry regiment to help quell the riot. Furthermore, Coriolano took the extreme step of ordering the commander of the Special Police, Anísio Miranda, to go to the scene with shock troops in cars and break up the rally "at any cost." The cars, some of them armored, brought bombs of gas, rubber billies, and firearms (rifles, pistols, and Schmeisser portable machine guns). At the Praça do Patriarca and nearby Direita Street the shock troops fired into the air. Most of the people, frightened, ran away.

Following "the evacuation of the Praça do Patriarca," Major Anísio Miranda pursued students by going up São Bento Street with his "tico-tico reis" (a nickname given to the special policemen because their red caps brought the tico-tico rei bird to mind). As the policemen, some in an armored car, approached the Largo do Ouvidor, the students, under the direction of Hélio Mota, formed a line (or a wall of students) as though to prevent the police from advancing from the Largo do Ouvidor to the Largo de São Francisco.[2]

Hélio Mota left the line to negotiate with the "tico-tico reis" at the point where São Bento Street joins the Largo do Ouvidor. He was approaching the armored car, when a police *delegado*, law school graduate Nicolau Ulrico Mário Cêntola, got out of a nearby automobile. Mota, who had met the *delegado* before, said: "Cêntola, for God's sake, get the Special Police out of here." Such a step, Mota argued, would bring everything to a peaceful conclusion in fifteen minutes. Cêntola said that it would be difficult to obtain a "counterorder" to reverse the role of the Special Police and he asked Mota to get the students to leave, but Mota refused to do this as long as the Special Police remained. When Cêntola drove down São Bento Street a few minutes later (violating the one-way street sign), Mota believed that he had gone to see if he could obtain the "counterorder."[3]

8. Shootings by the Special Police (November 9, 1943)

After Delegado Cêntola left, Hélio Mota spoke with the special policemen in the armored car. He found them holding machine guns and so aggressively excited that he tried to calm them by explaining that they had nothing to do because the students were unarmed and had concluded their manifestation. During the conversation, Special Police Commander Anísio Miranda arrived from the Praça do Patriarca. Hélio Mota had had an altercation with the major a few days earlier in the office of Delegado Elpídio Reali, when the major had spoken arrogantly about the arrest of students on November 2 and had added that the time had come to go after the professors. Seeing him now, Mota became silent and retreated a few steps.

Anísio Miranda, recognizing Hélio Mota, told the men in the armored car: "This is the one!" He ordered Mota to send the students away but Mota asserted forcefully that the Special Police should leave first. During the argument, the furious major hit Mota in the face. Before Mota could retaliate, "tico-tico reis" sprang into action, hitting Mota with their billies.[1]

Swarms of unarmed students and observers cried out and moved against the Special Police. The policemen reacted quickly. Some fired toward the ground but others used their machine guns and pistols to shoot directly at the advancing crowd.[2] The shooting killed Jaime Carlos da Silva Telles, a 20-year-old worker in commerce who was coming out of a store, and Domingas Covelli, a 65-year-old Italian woman. The wounding of a boy, José Emigdio de Barros, required the amputation of his left leg. Of the two dozen others wounded, more than half were students. Seven were taking courses at the *arcadas*: João Brasil Vita, Haroldo Bueno Magano, Idel Aronis, Sílvio de Campos Melo Filho, Aloysio Ferraz Pereira, Luís Afonso Cardoso de Melo de Alvares Otero, and Ciro Amaral Alcântara.[3]

People fled in panic. Hélio Mota, getting away from the policemen who had been beating him, ran down José Bonifácio Street and reached the União Cultural Brasil–Estados Unidos (on Santo Antônio Street), where many others also found refuge.[4] Lenício Pacheco Ferreira, who had been making his way with Meinberg from the Praça do Patriarca when the tragic shootings occurred, found asylum in the home of a lawyer friendly to his family.[5] Renato Macedo and others, already soaked with water from the Corpo de Bombeiros, ran to the law school and hid behind the large columns at the front of the building. But that was a poor place to hide because special policemen, tearing down Centro electioneering posters,[6] were looking there for students to arrest, and so Macedo and a friend made their way to the garage of the nearby Secretaria de Viação.[7] Aloysio Ferraz Pereira, wounded by a bullet that pierced his neck and emerged at the lower part of his back, was able to hide with a group in a building around the corner from the Largo de São Francisco before being conveyed in a vehicle to the Casa de Saude Santa Rita.[8]

Second-year student João Brasil Vita, the Conservador candidate for second secretary of the Centro, fled to a nearby garage after noticing blood all over his chest. He was fortunate to be alive because the bullet, which went through his chest and lodged in his back, barely missed his heart. First-year student João de Toledo Lara (whose sister later married Rui Mesquita) put him in a taxi and took him to the Santa Casa de Misericórdia, a hospital for poor people, long directed by Sinésio Rangel Pestana.[9]

Track star Sílvio de Campos Melo Filho, a law student covered with blood from his bullet wound, was also taken by taxi to the Santa Casa de Misericórdia. João Nery Guimarães and the others who took him there judged the lung wound of the silent and bloody Sílvio more serious than that of the talkative and less bloody João Brasil Vita, whom they found lying on the table next to that on which Sílvio was put. But Alípio Corrêa Neto and other doctors said that Vita's condition was the more serious because blood was getting into his lungs.[10] Vita called for a priest to administer the last rites, and his mother reached the hospital room while the rites were being administered. That he survived may have been due to the decision of doctors to let the organism react by itself without the appliance of the operating knife. He left the hospital, the bullet unremoved, after a little more than a week.[11]

Shortly after 8:00 P.M. on November 9, Antônio de Almeida Júnior, professor of medical law, was visited at his home by Astolfo Pio Monteiro da Silva and José Bonifácio Coutinho Nogueira. The professor, shocked at what he heard, went with the two students to the hospitals, including the Sanatório Esperança, where Jaime da Silva Telles died. "It was," Almeida Júnior has written, "one of the greatest emotions of my life to see those young people on their sick beds, some in serious condition, and only because, in a moment of civic exaltation, they had hailed Democracy in a public square."[12]

Haroldo Bueno Magano, the Libertador candidate for the Centro presidency, had received a wound in the left leg, which kept him hospitalized for over two weeks.[13] Luís Afonso Cardoso de Melo de Alvares Otero, a relative of the recently resigned law school director, had received a wound (also in the left leg) when shots were directed at a group that was completing the *pré-jurídico* course.[14] Otero recovered in the Sanatório Esperança and, after November 9, was occasionally called O Tiro na Perna (The Shot in the Leg).

Among the hundreds who called on the convalescents was Jorge Americano. At the Casa de Saude Santa Rita the *reitor* received a brief lecture from Aloysio Ferraz Pereira, a Conservador who had once hoped for good things from the Estado Novo. In his hospital bed Aloysio Ferraz Pereira argued that the sacrifice of November 9 was necessary to get the authorities, and the *reitor* himself, "to see, finally, that we live under a dictatorship."[15]

Thirty years later Luís Arrobas Martins wrote: "Starting on November 9, 1943, the battle was won. The blood of the young people, shed in a public square, would stir up the entire nation. That date, therefore, stands as a landmark in the history of the democratic struggles of Brazil."[16]

IX

Aftermath of the Shootings (1943–1944)

1. Resignations and Dismissals (November 9–13, 1943)

On the night of November 9, Interventor Fernando Costa received a visit from industrialist Horácio Lafer and three state cabinet secretaries: Abelardo Vergueiro César (Justice), Teotônio Monteiro de Barros Filho (Education), and Luís de Anhaia Melo (Transport). Luís de Anhaia Melo had witnessed the shootings from a window of the office of the Transport Secretaryship, close to the law school. Appalled, he had phoned the *interventor* from his office.[1]

Now the *interventor*'s visitors insisted on the immediate dismissal of Segurança Secretary Coriolano de Góis; as the *interventor* did not acquiesce, the three state cabinet members submitted their own resignations. Later that night Abelardo Vergueiro César wrote the law school director to say that "the people, perplexed and hurt, want to know if the men who make up the government support or condemn the outrages. . . . That is what Luís de Anhaia Melo, Teotônio de Barros Filho, and I told Dr. Fernando Costa tonight."[2]

On the tenth, the press reported that Coriolano de Góis had ordered an investigation. The report, released by the Secretaria da Segurança, explained that on the ninth "people interested in disturbing order disobeyed the police and tried to carry out an ostensively seditious rally." It added that the police had sought to act mildly but had been aggressively received, with the result that some people, including policemen, had been wounded.[3] The press also advised that the *interventor* was closing the law school temporarily pending the receipt of more information about the tragedy.

In the afternoon, while the Estado Novo's anniversary was observed in the Municipal Theater,[4] thousands braved the rain and went to the Consolação Cemetery to attend the burial of Jaime Carlos da Silva Telles, a cousin of *livre-docente* Gofredo da Silva Telles Júnior (whose father, "Gofredão," was president of the State Administrative Council). Among those at the burial were Júlio de Mesquita

Filho, Francisco Mesquita, Euclides Figueiredo, Roberto Simonsen, Gastão Vidigal, César Lacerda de Vergueiro, Herbert Levy, Horácio Lafer, and members of the Macedo Soares and Abreu Sodré families. While the throng sang the national anthem, the casket was lowered into the grave, and then representatives of the student bodies of the São Paulo colleges gave speeches, some of them inflammatory.[5]

On the eleventh, Fernando Costa left by car to confer with Vargas in Rio, and, while he was away, mimeographed leaflets containing manifestos, bulletins, and verses were distributed in São Paulo. The *interventor* was referred to as an "inconsequent puppet," "plump, goofy, and made of nothing," whereas Coriolano de Góis and Anísio Miranda drew more fearful descriptions. A bulletin released by student associations in the state of Paraná condemned the "sadistic" Special Police of São Paulo. The "dauntless" Jaime da Silva Telles was extolled in a leaflet of verse entitled "M.M.D.C.J." (adding Jaime's initial to MMDC) and distributed at night, largely by students at the Escola de Politécnica.[6]

Many of the leaflets were produced at the home of first-year law student Fernando Barjas Millan on the mimeograph "borrowed" from the Sociedade Harmonia de Tênis. As Millan's parents, Spaniards, were worried about their home becoming a *resistência* center,[7] the leaflets were stored elsewhere, some of them at the residence where Severo Gomes lived with his parents. Severo Gomes had been in the front line during the demonstration of November 5, but, as his father had been worried about how things would develop in the city, Severo had been at the Gomes fazenda at São José de Campos on November 9.[8]

Many students were infuriated by a bulletin that advised that the students of the Faculdade de Medicina, the Escola Paulista de Medicina, the Escola de Politécnica, and the Escola de Engenharia Mackenzie "affirm categorically that they do not support the movement of some colleagues of the Faculdade de Direito and BLAME STUDENTS HÉLIO MOTA, GERMINAL FEIJÓ, and ARROBAS MARTINS for the grave events that occurred." These bulletins, law students decided, were written by the DEIP and distributed (principally in front of the Faculdade de Medicina) by police investigators.[9] A quickly circulated reply, refuting the bulletin "distributed by persons unconnected with university students," was signed by the presidents of the Centro Acadêmico Osvaldo Cruz (Faculdade de Medicina), Centro Acadêmico Pereira Barreto (Escola Paulista de Medicina), Grêmio Politécnico (Escola Politécnica), and Centro Acadêmico Horácio Lane (Escola de Engenharia Mackenzie).[10]

In the meantime, Fernando Costa spent two hours with Vargas at Catete Palace on November 12 and then set out for São Paulo. When he reached the Palácio dos Campos Eliseos after midnight, he found state cabinet secretaries Abelardo Vergueiro César, Teotônio Monteiro de Barros Filho, and Luís de Anhaia Melo waiting for him. He advised them of the decisions reached in Rio, one of which was to release São Paulo political prisoners against whom no formal charges had been drawn up. (This brought an end to the eleven-day house arrest of Professors Waldemar Ferreira, Ernesto Leme, and José Soares de Melo.) Another decision was to revamp the state cabinet, finding replacements for the *interventor*'s three visitors (who had already submitted their resignations) and Segurança Secretary Coriolano de Góis. Major Anísio Miranda would not remain as commander of the Special Police, at least during the period of investigation. The resignation of law school Director Cardoso de Melo Neto was to be accepted.[11]

Speaking to the press after his three visitors left, Fernando Costa announced that he had acceded to their requests to resign. Then he closeted himself with Coriolano de Góis and Major Vieira de Melo, recent arrivals at Campos Eliseos. Their visit had been prompted by a telephone call in which Benjamim Vargas had told Vieira de Melo: "Go tell Coriolano to submit his resignation because, if he doesn't, his dismissal will be ordered from here [Rio]." The *interventor*, already familiar with the news transmitted by Benjamim Vargas, accepted Coriolano's resignation and suggested that Vieira de Melo take his place. But the major, a member of the Army General Staff on temporary assignment to work tactfully on Vargas' behalf, preferred to remain in the post he held and recommended that Coriolano be succeeded by Alfredo Issa Assaly, the young general director of the Secretaria da Segurança.[12] For the time being Fernando Costa announced no new appointments. He ordered the reopening of the law school.

2. Law Student Reactions (November 13–16, 1943)

Vieira de Melo returned to Campos Eliseos at 9:00 A.M. on November 13, this time with the presidents of the student bodies of the colleges, who expressed their pleasure at the removal of Coriolano and Anísio Miranda, the release of students recently arrested, and the cancellation of an order for the patrolling of streets by the cavalry. The young visitors showed the *interventor* a note they had drawn up asking students to return to their classrooms.[1]

Diário da Noite that afternoon described the latest developments as filling the law school with "happiness and delirious satisfaction," whereupon the law students released another mimeographed bulletin, this one to reprimand the newspaper and blame the "malicious distortion" on *métodos motafilhares* (methods of Mota Filho, recent DEIP director). The bulletin pointed out that not a week had passed since the death of Jaime Carlos da Silva Telles, "martyr of a noble cause, symbol of an ideal," and that many other young people, "victims of the irrational fury of the Brazilian Gestapo, still wail on their beds of pain." The bulletin admitted that the "great sufferings" had produced some consolation, but it pictured the dismissals of "the outlaw Anísio Miranda and the hoodlum Coriolano" as "only a dose of morphine for public opinion" furnished by a government that had not really changed its ideas.[2]

The supporters of Coriolano sent Vargas an incredible story that blamed the deaths and injuries on a single special policeman, who, "seeing his commander threatened . . . , shot a few bullets from his pistol into the ground, resulting in the wounding of 21 persons . . . and the death of commerce worker Jaime da Silva Telles." In the opinion of the report, Coriolano and the Special Police had, by their "energetic and wise actions," prevented "more deplorable events," and it was therefore unfortunate that Coriolano had been dismissed, due to the *interventor*'s "weakness" and the collaboration of some state cabinet secretaries with the subversive work of old Democratic Party members. The report said that the effects of the *interventor*'s "unhappy solution" could be seen in the repeated "manifestations against the Regime and the President" in movie theaters, cafés, and eating places. It pointed out that, "in the São Paulo movie theaters, students and everyday citizens are arrested daily because they boo the President whenever he appears in films."[3]

José Bonifácio Coutinho Nogueira wrote a letter for his father, Paulo Nogueira Filho, but the letter, instead of reaching Buenos Aires, fell into the hands of censors and was transcribed in one of the official reports that went to Vargas and other authorities concerned with the "national security."[4] The letter said, in part:

> As you must already know, I am alive, simply as a matter of luck. The events of the 9th almost cost me my life. . . . I had to be one of those who was at the front of my colleagues, and, in fact, the bullets of the "especial" came when I was in my proper post. I do not have the pretension to be a "leader." . . . But in a movement such as we are going through, without doubt the most serious of all we have experienced, it would be impossible to flee from my duties, from my family tradition. . . . Our traditional

law school distinguished itself, gave a tremendous lesson of courage and patriotism. . . . We overthrew a state cabinet, we threw a Coriolano out of São Paulo, but all of this is little—we know that—compared with the blood shed. . . . From now on our steps must be taken with great care. . . . The nation is at war, and public opinion will be entirely with us if we know how to keep it mindful of two things: the combat abroad against Nazism, and, at home, in favor of a moral uplifting. We must know how to be idealists!

As for the matter at hand, I must praise, in first place, Cardoso; and, after him, Anhaia Melo; and in third place, Teotônio and Abelardinho, these two far from the others. Major Vieira de Melo also did not act badly within his area of authority; on the contrary, he knew how to be a first-rate diplomat. . . . [He has been] praised as the example of a smart and intelligent man. However, he crossed his arms in the face of the slaughter that the Anísios and Coriolanos were delighted to carry out, and he was clearly seen by everyone.

The law school has no director up to now, for none of the *catedráticos* wants to run it. Mota Filho has been prohibited from entering the school.

On November 16 the acting director of the law school, Alvino Lima, presided at a faculty meeting, which named a commission of professors to keep in touch with the investigation announced by the *interventor*. During the meeting, Professor José Soares de Melo, having just spent eleven days *incomunicável* under house arrest, used some appropriate expressions when he mentioned the police, who, he said, had given him the opprobrious label of "conspirator."[5]

Following the faculty meeting, professors joined students in the Barão de Ramalho Room to witness the closing of the Centro's "permanent session" (begun on October 31). With Hélio Mota presiding, Germinal Feijó greeted visiting representatives of student bodies of São Paulo and Rio de Janeiro, and he expressed the Centro's thanks for the support received from them and the professors during the crisis. Unanimous approval greeted his motion of appreciation of the attitude that Cardoso de Melo Neto had assumed and his motion making Jaime Carlos da Silva Telles an honorary member of the Centro Onze de Agosto. Professor Waldemar Ferreira, speaking on behalf of the other law professors, especially José Soares de Melo and Ernesto Leme (who had suffered house arrest with him), recalled the "preponderant role always exercised by the São Paulo law school, together with that of Recife, in the nation's destinies." At the students' insistence, José Soares de Melo and Ernesto Leme also spoke.[6]

The students, along with thousands of others, had spent a part of the morning at the Consolação Church and Cemetery, for the sixteenth was the seventh day following the death of Jaime da Silva Telles.[7] Many students returned to the cemetery on the seventeenth to help observe the one-hundredth anniversary of the birth of Martinico Prado, brother of Antônio Prado and an early supporter of the republican cause. The speech on behalf of the São Paulo law students was delivered by Afrânio de Oliveira, a fourth-year student from Minas who had been jailed two years earlier for a Rui Barbosa anniversary day speech and who had lost his job teaching history at the Liceu de Artes e Ofícios because police agents found his views strongly opposed to the Estado Novo. He told the crowd at the Consolação Cemetery that "only a week has passed since we were here at the side of the grave of a 20-year-old youth who fell in the public square, victim of the murderous bullets of a despotic and anti-Brazilian regime."[8]

3. Magano, Centro President-elect (late November 1943)

The events of the first half of November 1943 cost the Partido Acadêmico Conservador the commanding position it had held earlier. Its candidate for the Centro presidency, popular Waldir Ribeiro de Lima, was not the only student to have been withdrawn from the city by worried parents who had foreseen the danger of police violence. But his absence during the shooting left him at a disadvantage.[1] His chief opponent, Libertador presidential candidate Haroldo Bueno Magano, lay wounded in the hospital, a fact that Magano's principal *cabo eleitoral*, Astolfo Pio Monteiro da Silva, did not let the student electorate forget. Magano, a rather quiet individual, had not been enthusiastic about Lenício Pacheco Ferreira's aggressive pronouncements at the Baile das Américas, but he had given good support to the post-Baile antigovernment movement.[2] Following his imprisonment from November 2 to 5, Magano had participated in the demonstration of the fifth and the March of Silence on the ninth.

The Conservadores had a wounded contestant in João Brasil Vita, candidate for second secretary. But even this circumstance was used to strengthen Magano's position.[3] The Partido Libertador and Vita's Libertador opponent, Otávio Reis, issued announcements saying that Otávio Reis was stepping aside out of respect for the hospitalized Vita and that everyone should vote for Vita, "unity candidate."[4]

Just before the election, Libertador leaders Fernando Jacob and Astolfo Pio Monteiro da Silva persuaded Magano's doctor to allow him to be present at the election.[5] While the students voted, he lay nearby on a stretcher. Under these circumstances Magano and the Libertadores won a sweeping victory (and João Brasil Vita became second secretary).[6]

For president:	Haroldo Bueno Magano (Libertador)	396
	Waldir Ribeiro de Lima (Conservador)	302
	Rui Pereira de Queiroz (Frente pela Democracia)	199
For vice-president:	Renato Macedo (Libertador)	390
	Pedro Brasil Bandecchi (Conservador)	245
	Olavo de Almeida Pinto (Frente pela Democracia)	239

Following the election, Magano got in touch with Colonel Tasso Tinoco, the new head of the staff (*estado maior*) of the army's Second Region, and Major Nelson de Aquino, also of the Second Region. He assured them that as Centro Onze de Agosto president he would lead a strong campaign in favor of Brazil's Expeditionary Force (the FEB) abroad, preferring this to movements that might disturb the war effort. Later he gave a similar assurance to new Secretary of Segurança Alfredo Issa Assaly. This was not the type of Centro administration that the Vargas-hating activists wanted. But Magano believed that it would be the most useful to Brazil and he believed that the authorities to whom he had spoken were working to bring about the democratization of Brazil.[7]

Major Vieira de Melo, who had defied Coriolano de Góis by attending the funeral of Jaime da Silva Telles and visiting the wounded, disliked Vargas' nomination of Tasso Tinoco to head the staff of the army's Second Region. Tasso Tinoco, he soon noted, was inclined to "punish" students he considered troublemakers by drafting them to serve in the FEB[8]—provided they had not become lieutenants in the reserve by completing the two-year CPOR course.[9] The first four, named at the beginning of January 1944 to become FEB privates, were Naldo Caparica, member of the *comissão diretora* of the Partido Libertador, and three active members of the Frente Acadêmica pela Democracia: Geraldo Vidigal (Frente president), Rui Pereira de Queiroz, and José Vasques Bernardes. Some of them received the first news of their selection from poet Péricles Eugênio da Silva Ramos, who continued with his newspaper work after graduating late in 1943 and learned about the FEB calls because some of his work was with the official news agency, Agência Nacional.[10]

Relations worsened between Tasso Tinoco and Vieira de Melo, who had no wish "to alienate the young people who would later be important." Vieira de Melo, critical also of what he called the "weakness" of Fernando Costa, left São Paulo in February 1944 to take a position in the Casa Militar of Vargas.[11]

4. Closing Out the School Year (December 1943–March 1944)

Among the São Paulo law school students, the Vargas supporters, a small minority, remained very discreet; the only exception was José Barbosa, a self-declared supporter. Barbosa, having completed his fourth year and having been elected president of the Academia de Letras da Faculdade de Direito, accepted an invitation to speak on December 21, 1943, in the presence of Vargas, at the inauguration of the Serviço de Assistência aos Trabalhadores Intelectuais. After he spoke, he was ordered by the Centro Onze de Agosto to appear before an assembly for judging him. Although he failed to appear at the assembly, he published his defense in a leaflet that explained that his speech had been given simply in his own name as a student and journalist. "During my speech," he wrote, "I invoked the name of the proletarian students, the poor students, but the poor students of all Brazil—those who struggle at writing and editing newspaper stories, those who receive small pay and work long hours into the night to support themselves and carry on their studies."[1]

Barbosa stressed the need of the union of all Brazilians in wartime. He accused his detractors of violating freedom of thought and thus practicing "democratic fascism, . . . much more dangerous than all the other forms of fascism." He pointed out that he had, in his speech, asked the government for wage increases for journalists, and to allow him to become an FEB volunteer, and that Vargas, in his improvised speech, had made a special reference to the first request.

In conclusion, Barbosa said that, in order to avoid discord in a law school class to which he had always been proud to belong, he was submitting his resignation from the traditional and glorious Centro Onze de Agosto. He added, "It is sorrowful for me to do this shortly after Christmas and with the doors of the new year about to open." On December 29 a notice in the press advised that the Centro, at an extraordinary assembly on the twenty-seventh, had resolved unanimously to expel José Barbosa.[2] The report was not quite accurate because two students, Geraldo Vidigal and Teófilo de Siqueira Cavalcanti, voted against expulsion.[3]

Centro First Orator Rivaldo Assis Cintra also ran into trouble because some of the anti-Vargas activists maintained that he had changed and had become a fence-sitter.[4] A venomous leaflet, signed "Os Contra-DIP," argued that the former enemy of the Estado Novo had become "the Assis Cintra of Integralista times . . . , without character, without opinion, without scruples, worshipping the rich and the distributors of . . . the national treasury. . . . Undoubtedly the big shot Macedo Soares and the ass Osvaldo Aranha will be able to give him one of the many posts they have available." The leaflet asked Assis Cintra not to forget that "wretches of your sort—and many exist—will be the objects of public loathing."[5]

But Assis Cintra, the Conservador, was chosen to be the class orator at the commencement exercises because his speechmaking was considered better than that of Libertador Israel Dias Novaes and the Frente's Arrobas Martins in a *concurso* judged by a panel of eight (professors and students). Thus, at the Teatro Municipal on the evening of January 14, 1944, he shared the limelight with Mário Masagão, whom the graduating class picked to be its *paraninfo* (honored spokesman). Masagão, a 44-year-old professor of administrative law, had served in 1933 as secretary of justice and secretary of *segurança* in the state cabinet of Armando de Sales Oliveira, and in December 1937 he had given up his judgeship on the state court of appeals in compliance with a regulation of the Estado Novo. Masagão made his students work hard and earned their respect.[6]

At the Municipal Theater, Assis Cintra spoke with erudition and eloquence about the opportunities to uphold the traditions of law, Christian civilization, democracy, and liberty despite the discouraging moment in which tribunals of emergency were improvised and administrative functions were replacing "true judicial power."[7] The orator, reviewing the contributions of the São Paulo Law School to Brazilian civilization and leadership, declared that recently "the young people of this Academia, compelled to preserve their self-respect of free citizens," had spilled their blood in their protest against totalitarian violence.

Participants in the *resistência* were more enthusiastic about the speech of Mário Masagão that followed.[8] "In truth," the professor said, "I tell you that, although I have never experienced self-esteem from investitures that might have given me satisfaction in the days of my youth, I now find myself, in my maturity, filled with pride at being *paraninfo* of the class of this year of 1943, in which the ruby red of our [college] colors stained the asphalt of the streets." He added that "the Faculdade is pleased with you and you cannot have higher praise."[9]

Masagão asserted that

> the armies of democracy are immersed in fire and blood so that, in the future, no government anywhere should feel that it fulfills its mission by devoting its attention to what is material and transitory, with disregard of what belongs to the dignity and civic life of the nation; so that no one be obliged to do or not to do anything except by virtue of law; . . . so that the home constitutes an inviolable haven of the citizen, with no one able to invade it except in accordance with the law; so that no one can be arrested without a formal charge of crime, except in flagrant cases or by judicial decision; so that everyone might be able to meet peacefully . . . and discuss public affairs; so that expression of thought in the press and tribune might be unhindered, with each person responding for abuses he might commit; so that, in one word, there be restored and reguilded that which civilization has created at great cost and which ennobles human life. Because, without these rights and fundamental guarantees, people become herds afflicted by the audacity of adventurers.

(Flávio Galvão, writing in *O Estado de S. Paulo* years later, called Masagão's speech "a defiance of the organs of repression and the DIP censorship.")[10]

Sinésio Rangel Pestana, of the Sociedade Amigos da América, presided at a banquet given at the Esporte Clube Pinheiros to honor twenty of the new graduates who were deemed to have distinguished themselves, during the five-year course, "in civic movements of the São Paulo Law School." According to one description of the event, "the presence of representatives of the various democratic currents of Brazil made the meeting a sort of political reconciliation brought about to define positions in the face of the problems created by the imperative need to democratize the nation." The main speakers were Lenício Pacheco Ferreira (who spoke on behalf of the new graduates) and Germinal Feijó.

Lenício Pacheco Ferreira declared that the law school class had been imprisoned and machine-gunned and, while manacled, had witnessed the most fearful of spectacles, the destruction of its most sacred convictions, of all it held dear. Feijó contended that Vargas, by making use of "the danger of Communism" in the 1930s, had adopted "that old instrument of fascist propaganda." Turning to the current situation, Feijó maintained that the university students had achieved unity of action and thought, on behalf of democracy in Brazil, and were appealing for a similar demonstration by those who had been associated with the PRP, the Partido Constitucionalista, the Aliança Nacional Libertadora, the *tenentista* movement, and the Partido Socialista. "We know," he said, "that among you there still remain resentments that should be forgotten and divergences that should be overcome."[11]

X

The Resistance in High Gear (1944)

1. Calls for Army Service (1944)

Luís Arrobas Martins, who joined the law firm of Professor José Soares de Melo late in 1943, applied to the British Council in Rio for a scholarship that would allow him to study at a university in England or Scotland. He wrote that he wanted the chance to study "in a country where democratic principles are practiced," and that his ambition was to become a professor at the University of São Paulo.[1]

On January 26, 1944, soon after the application was mailed, Arrobas received orders to serve in the coastal artillery in Santos. Already in June 1942, his political views had caused him to be excluded from the CPOR although he had trained in it, and now he felt that his wish to serve overseas was denied for the same reason.[2] He therefore appealed to anti-Vargas minerology Professor Reynaldo Saldanha da Gama, who had become a major in the FEB.[3] But the appeal was of no avail and on March 9 Arrobas became a soldier in the 6° Grupo Motorizado de Artilharia de Costa in Santos. As he wrote to José Bonifácio Coutinho Nogueira on July 12, he found himself "vegetating in the unproductive torpidity of the barracks." Although his scholarship application to the British Council was approved, the Brazilian military authorities would not allow him to take advantage of it.[4]

In the meantime, many of his former schoolmates were inducted into the FEB. Geraldo Vidigal, Rui Pereira de Queiroz, Naldo Caparica, and José Vasques Bernardes, already called up early in January 1944, became soldiers in the 6° Regimento de Infantaria (Regimento Ipiranga) and took their leave of the *arcadas* on March 28, 1944. Caparica, in his farewell speech, said: "Liberty! Justice! Democracy! It was for you that we went to die in the Largo do Ouvidor!" And he expressed confidence that the young people remaining at the "old and beloved Faculdade" would keep it a barrack of liberty, "alert for the struggle in Brazil."[5] Vidigal crossed the seas to Italy as a member of the first contingent that departed from Rio on the *General Mann* on July 2, 1944. The other three left on the second contingent on September 22.

By January 1945, when Professor Ernesto Leme spoke as *paraninfo* of the Expedicionaríos Acadêmicos, the number had grown to fifteen,[6] and still later it became twenty-five: Antônio Carlos S. Correia, Antônio Leme da Fonseca Filho, Antônio Moreno Gonzalez (officer), Antônio Teodoro de Freitas (officer), Armando Veiga Castelo (officer), Cândido Teobaldo de Souza Andrade (sergeant), Carlos Mendes Coelho (officer), Celso Braga, Clovis Garcia (officer), Eduardo Ramos de Oliveira, Euripedes Simões de Paula (officer), Fernando Correa da Rocha (airforce officer), Francisco da Silva Prado (officer), Francisco de Assis Bezerra de Menezes, Geraldo de Camargo Vidigal, Hélio Barreto Mateus (officer), José Vasques Bernardes, Kioschi Sakai, Naldo Caparica, Paulo Gomes, Roger Jules de Carvalho Mange (officer), Rui Caldeira Ferraz (officer), Rui Pereira de Queiroz, Túlio C. Campelo de Souza (officer), and Ubirajara Dolacio Mendes (officer).[7]

Those with officer's rank had completed the CPOR course. Túlio Campelo, who entered the FEB as a second lieutenant and lost a leg to a German mine in Italy, ended up with the highest rank of the twenty-five, lieutenant-colonel in the reserve. Sergeant Cândido Teobaldo de Souza Andrade, at the fighting front the whole time, became a second lieutenant in the reserve. Pilot Fernando Correa da Rocha, who flew seventy-five air missions, was decorated several times for his heroism.[8]

Quite a few of those who had not completed the CPOR course were assigned to the Special Services section, which was not at the fighting front and which was directed by democracy-minded Major Reynaldo Saldanha da Gama, veteran of the 1932 anti-Vargas revolution. Among those who published the FEB newspaper *O Cruzeiro do Sul*, a Special Services activity, were Naldo Caparica, Rui Pereira de Queiroz, José Vasques Bernardes, and Antônio Leme da Fonseca Filho.[9]

From Italy on August 11, 1944, Geraldo Vidigal sent a declaration to the Centro Onze de Agosto expressing confidence in "the great bastion of the Brazilian democratic rear guard,"[10] and it was published in several newspapers in Brazil and reproduced in the invitation to the Baile das Américas that year. Vidigal was editor of the first numbers of *E a cobra fumou!*, published for the First Battalion of the Regimento Ipiranga in Tarquinia in August 1944. (Some numbers bore the notation "Not registered with the DIP.") By the end of 1944, when his book of poetry *Predestinação* was receiving good reviews in Brazil, Vidigal was publishing *Vanguardeiro* in northern Italy, where the winter had reduced combat action.[11] Naldo Caparica, busy editing *O Cruzeiro do Sul,* wrote law student Ruy Nazareth that Vidigal "was cited in a bulletin for an act of bravery; he assumed the command in a dangerous situation."[12]

2. *Resistência* and the Proletariat (April–August 1944)

The anti–Estado Novo law students, unable to get subversive material printed, relied solely on mimeographs until around April 1944, when, in the words of Paulo Duarte, they obtained "a small printing press and enough type for rapid composition."[1] José Bonifácio Coutinho Nogueira took the lead in using the small press for launching a subversive publication, *Resistência.* It was directed by him and Germinal Feijó and three alumni: Antônio Costa Corrêa, Roberto de Abreu Sodré, and Francisco Morato de Oliveira.[2] Its first number, consisting of four pages and dated April 1944, explained that its purpose was

> to bring together and organize to some extent this enormous discontent of the nation and to polarize some of those irrepressible aspirations of liberty that stir in the spirit of all Brazilians. RESISTÊNCIA is an organ of the democratic opposition in Brazil. . . . It brings together people of all national, democratic currents from the liberals to the extreme leftists, people from the liberal party organizations existing before November 1937, from the old socialist organizations, communists, and from the Aliança Nacional Libertadora, [and] from the new democratic organizations that are operating in the national territory. . . .
>
> RESISTÊNCIA will be an illegal journal . . . because the right to criticize and organize political activities, existing in any democratic nation, is not allowed Brazilians under the laws of the present regime.[3]

Resistência wrote that the Estado Novo, "a regime of social stagnation and widespread corruption," spent most of the federal budget on propaganda, police organization, and the concession of special privileges to the military, whose support was bought in a manner worthy of the most backward South American *caudilhos.* To get the approval of the United States, the Estado Novo was said to have made concessions that went far beyond cooperation between allies.

Resistência recommended the use of sabotage, propaganda, public manifestations, strikes, noncooperation, and the isolation of supporters of the regime in order to bring about the *Resistência* program. The program called for (*a*) immediate elections for a constitutional assembly; (*b*) the immediate suppression of the DIP and censorship (except in the case of military secrets); (*c*) the dismissal of fascists from government posts; (*d*) amnesty for exiles and political prisoners (except fifth columnists); (*e*) liberty of speech, the press, meetings, strikes, and political party organization; (*f*) anti-inflationary measures; (*g*) better wages, especially for farm workers; (*h*) support for agriculture; and (*i*) effective participation in the war.[4]

Resistência praised Monteiro Lobato, Mário Pinto Serva, Anísio Teixeira, Oswald de Andrade, and Heráclito Sobral Pinto ("five outstanding intellectuals recently prohibited from writing for the press"), and added that the government's most serious recent act of censorship was the prohibition of the sale of the novel *Fronteira Agreste*, written by Ivan Pedro de Martins, a leftist long in exile.[5] Other articles in the April number described the "massacre of November 9, 1943," and the events leading up to it.[6]

Resistência asserted that Vargas, coming to São Paulo to address the workers at Pacaembu Stadium on May 1, would explain the November 9 shootings as just "another 'unfortunate mistake,'" and would attempt "to 'prove' how much he is loved by the people." "The workers of the Antartica and Brahma Companies," *Resistência* said, would be "forcibly put in large trucks in order to witness the arrival of the new God."[7]

Resistência was not alone in disparaging Vargas' plan to speak in São Paulo. The law school's Frente Acadêmica pela Democracia distributed a mimeographed circular that said the purpose of the great "labor demonstration" would be to mock the good faith of the workers. They would, it predicted, present a petition for better conditions, which Vargas would promise to adopt, only to advise later that his war minister's veto made it impossible for him to grant their meritorious aspirations—just as Vargas was in the habit of saying that Dutra and the army opposed the return to democracy. It was time, the circular declared, for Vargas to assume the responsibility for his acts and not blame the war minister, who was patriotically organizing the Expeditionary Force to fight in Europe for the permanent removal of dictatorial governments in the world. "Either the head of the nation really wants a democratic regime," the circular said, "or he desires to perpetuate the regime of November 10, as his brother Viriato Vargas insinuates daily in the newspaper *Brasil-Portugal*. And, if he does not want to give satisfaction to the people, let him assume the responsibility for his acts and not put the blame on others."[8]

A multitude estimated at well over fifty thousand packed Pacaembu Stadium to acclaim Vargas' May Day pledge that a bright postwar future awaited labor, especially if enemies at home, such as "the intransigence of private interests" and "class egoism," were defeated. He argued that the people could not satisfy their hunger with the right to vote or educate their children with the right of assembly. Promising an expanded system of retirement benefits and government social assistance for the workers and their families, Vargas urged all workers to join their unions. On May 2, before he flew back to Rio, he joined workers at a ceremony in which the cornerstone was laid at the Casa do Trabalhador (House of the Worker) in the Brás district.[9]

When *Resistência*, in its fourth and last number, commented on the May Day speech, it agreed with observers who believed that Vargas' announcement of "a vast social program" was the political speech of a candidate for the presidency. *Resistência* also pointed out that, during the two weeks preceding the speech, all the newspapers had undertaken a propaganda campaign to remind readers "of everything the Estado Novo and Getúlio Vargas have done for the workers." *Resistência* called the newspaper reports "a complete falsification of recent historical facts," which left public opinion divided.[10]

Following Vargas' May Day speech (and the first number of *Resistência*), leftist Antônio Cândido de Mello e Souza suggested that *Resistência* was directed to the middle class and contained nothing for labor. Like the other leftists, he was also concerned with the need of the movement for which *Resistência* spoke to give attention to the proletariat. The movement, an illegal one, had become known as the Frente de Resistência. Among its principal leftists, some of whom had formed the Grupo Radical de Ação Popular (GRAP), were 27-year-old Paulo Emílio Sales Gomes (a recent graduate of the College of Philosophy, Sciences, and Letters), Antônio Costa Corrêa, Germinal Feijó, journalist Paulo Zingg, and Antônio Cândido de Mello e Souza. The majority of the Frente de Resistência was liberal but the leftists willingly went along with them because of mutual opposition to the Vargas dictatorship.[11]

Resistência's fourth number, published in August 1944, contained a front-page article, "Proletariado brasileiro," that said "the Brazilian urban and rural workers constitute one of the greatest hopes for social and political regeneration because they are a vital force. The proletariat tends to have good faith, when stripped of class consciousness, but has never had the naïvete attributed to it by the despots of the Estado Novo."[12] According to the article, the urban worker, aware of many things, knew that he had no friend in anyone who "reduced him to misery by the comedy of the minimum wage," a sleight of hand that fostered inflation and therefore wiped out wage increases. He also knew, the article said, that the unions were nests of exploiters who transformed institutions, theoretically free to defend the working class, into the worst instruments of oppression. On the other hand, *Resistência* said, the rural worker knew nothing and lived in misery.

Resistência pictured the government as simply making speeches while the peasants and urban workers tightened their belts and the unions crushed class liberty. Concluding that workers had become aware they could no longer put their faith in the "incredible buffoonery" of the government, *Resistência* summoned the proletariat to the "*resistência* against the fascist Estado Novo!"

3. The Pursuit of Democracy by Libertadores and the Frente (April–August 1944)

The banquet for honoring students, given after the close of the 1943 school year, had been inspired by the minority group of *democratas exaltados*. On April 20, 1944, the more popular Partido Libertador gave a dinner at the Casa Anglo-Brasileira to honor three December 1943 graduates who had contributed mightily to the party but had not been honored at the Esporte Clube Pinheiros: Astolfo Pio Monteiro da Silva, Jarbas Teixeira de Carvalho, and Zwinglio Ferreira. The speeches contrasted with those given by Feijó at the earlier banquet. Centro President Magano, opposed to agitation that might hurt the war effort, pledged that the Libertador Party would carry out "a democratic policy that is not quixotic or deceitfully ostentatious."[1]

Libertador President João Nery Guimarães, who had been giving much thought to democracy, pointed out in his speech that rights ought to be accompanied by attention to responsibilities. He declared that "if, nowadays, one notes everywhere, and on the part of everyone, a disrespect for the authority of the law, creating an irrespirable atmosphere of unrest, we are not going to find the reason for this trouble in the law, but in the individuals themselves, who for the most part, reveal alarming symptoms of a lack of religious faith, a disparagement of paternal authority, and indiscipline at school, clear indications of social disaggregation." He went on to quote German legal theoretician Hans Kelsen as saying that "the multitude accepts, without wavering, the prerogatives of democracy, but few understand the depths and extent of its principles. It is easy to shout: Liberty, Equality, Fraternity!"[2]

João Nery Guimarães told his fellow Libertadores that "if we might use the word *totalitarian* in the sense of political intolerance, it fits well in the nomenclature of our democrats—totalitarian democrats.

Recent democrats, very recent democrats, democrats of the Right, democrats of the Left (who are now the fashion), democrats with the exclusive use of the term, democrats of words and tyrants in action, democrats to give a pleasing personal effect, all this exists in abundance at the College of Law of São Paulo. One thing, however, is as scarce at the Arcadas as water in the desert: democratic democrats. Democrats who think, practice, and defend Democracy, serving it and not using it to serve themselves for personal or party purposes."

While the Libertadores pursued their policy of practicing a democracy that was not "deceitfully ostentatious," members of the Frente Acadêmica pela Democracia distributed anti–Estado Novo manifestos. The police, raiding a boardinghouse, seized thousands of copies of a manifesto that Gabriel Cesário Cury had helped prepare. Cury, who was locked in a cell, received several blows to the head while interrogators sought to learn where the manifesto had been mimeographed.[3] The police also invaded the home of Severo Gomes and his parents at about the time of the Vargas May Day visit and they found more than anti–Estado Novo bulletins transferred there from the residence of Fernando Millan. Severo's wealthy father had an arsenal of machine guns dating from the mid-1930s, when Armando de Sales Oliveira had created the Special Police of São Paulo and suggested that the elder Gomes and other people store some of its arms at their homes. Severo Gomes and his father were held for ten days in cold cells, and even Severo's mother had to put up with about twelve hours of detainment while she was interrogated.[4]

Early in July 1944 the Estado Novo instituted a wave of repression. Oppositionist magazines, such as Samuel Wainer's *Diretrizes* in Rio and Paulo Zingg's *Ilustração* in São Paulo, were closed down, and Coriolano de Góis was named Federal District police chief.

Fernando Millan decided that a "message from the Paulistas to the people of Rio de Janeiro" about Coriolano should be distributed in Rio. He worked so hard on the idea that the "message" became known as his. In its production in August, on one mimeographed sheet, he was assisted by his older brother Roberto (a medical student), José Bonifácio Coutinho Nogueira, Paulo Nogueira Neto, and Luís Francisco da Silva Carvalho.[5] When he arrived by train in the federal capital (his first visit there), one of his two suitcases full of copies of the "message" fell open in Rio's Central do Brasil railroad station and copies spilled over the floor; but policemen, unaware of the nature of the papers, helped him put them back in the suitcase. In distributing the "messages," Millan was assisted by São Paulo law students vacationing in Rio, such as Benjamin Pereira de Queiroz (especially effective), Olavo de Almeida Pinto, and Ênio de Novais

França, and by Naldo Caparica, awaiting embarkation to Italy.[6] It was a courageous act because the Rio police, under Coriolano de Góis, were rounding up suspected enemies of the Estado Novo with greater energy than had been evident in Rio for at least several years.

Fernando Millan's message advised the Cariocas that the dictator Vargas had called Coriolano de Góis to Rio in order to maintain himself in power in a fascist regime and in order to carry out "the cruelest of undertakings that our people have suffered in all their history." The message pointed out that Coriolano, confidant of Catete Palace, had thrashed democratic law students, meeting peacefully, and then had been responsible for the assassination of "men, women, and children" by ordering the deployment of the tanks and machine guns of the Special Police, commanded by Major Anísio Miranda—"presently a person of prominence in the Carioca police." The message concluded with a call for the Cariocas to defend themselves by sabotaging the acts of Coriolano and by reminding him they knew that "his courage consists only of assassinating unarmed and defenseless people."[7]

Members of the Frente Acadêmica pela Democracia participated in the rally celebrating the liberation of Paris in August 1944. This demonstration, not an exclusive affair of the Frente, took place in the Largo de São Francisco. Students held up flags of countries fighting the Axis. As no flag of the Soviet Union could be found, an appropriate one was made out of red material, against which the likenesses of a hammer and sickle were affixed, and it was given to Rui Mesquita to hold. Speakers, such as Germinal Feijó, used the occasion to attack the Vargas dictatorship. Following the ceremony, many of the participants were arrested at the Jequiti Bar and held for two days at the Superintendência da Ordem Política e Social. A few of those arrested were Feijó, Afrânio de Oliveira, Rui Mesquita, Celso Medeiros, Jorge Mesquita Mendonça, and Alfredo Mesquita (a brother of Júlio de Mesquita Filho and the founder of the Escola de Arte Dramática).[8]

4. The Mota Filho Case (June–August 1944)

On March 18, 1944, the press carried the news that "the government of São Paulo named Cândido Mota Filho to the chair of constitutional law at the Faculdade de Direito" and that "this act of Interventor Fernando Costa has been received with the highest praise in the nation's university and juridical circles."[1]

Forty-six–year–old Cândido Mota Filho, a longtime *livre-docente,* had been an aide to São Paulo Governor Pedro de Toledo during the Constitutionalist Revolution and had been elected to the state assembly in 1934 as a member of the Partido Constitucionalista. His interest in helping abandoned children had led Vargas to call on him to draft a statute to create the National Department for Children, and in June 1941 Vargas had named him head of the Departamento Estadual de Imprensa e Propaganda (DEIP) of São Paulo. He resigned from the DEIP in September 1943.[2]

Early in June 1944, the São Paulo law students declared themselves on strike to get the cancellation of the professorial appointment of the former DEIP director (made without the usual competition). The strike lasted through the July vacation and into August.[3]

In June, soon after the strike began, Centro President Magano, regretting the agitation, sought a settlement. During his negotiations with Cândido Mota Filho and the *interventor,* it was agreed that, if the students would return to their classes at once, arrangements would be made for Cândido Mota Filho to step aside and not give his lectures.[4]

Opponents of Magano and his negotiation released a mimeographed leaflet that berated "those who, gratuitously, for the simple pleasure of humiliating us, pour forth insults, accusing us of being disorderly hooligans, *bons vivants.* . . . Many more defend us than accuse us." The leaflet went on to say

> our objective was, and is, to depose Sr. Mota Filho from the post of professor. This was the decision of all. . . . Let us not accept dilatory measures. . . . We therefore do not agree with the compromise, inopportunely devised without our approval. Would it be right, perchance, for us to return to the classrooms and tranquilly wait until September for the dismissal of Sr. Mota Filho . . . ? . . . To postpone . . . the dismissal of Sr. Mota Filho is to whitewash him, proclaim him the victim of slanders. . . . To have him step aside is not enough. He stepped aside before the strike, and to accept only that, on the terms proposed, is to be badly defeated. . . . Colleagues: let us not accept promises which usually turn out to be vague.[5]

When Magano presented his negotiated settlement to a Centro assembly, he found feelings running high. A majority wanted a clearcut resignation by Mota Filho from the chair and were unwilling to end the strike while anything remained to be worked out. Besides, they criticized Magano for negotiating without the Centro's authorization and for doing it alone. Magano's proposal was defeated by a margin of roughly two to one.[6]

Magano therefore took a leave of absence from the Centro presidency and Renato P. Macedo became interim president. The strike ended on August 14 when the Centro heard the reading of a letter from Mota Filho that made it clear the former DEIP director would not accept the *interventor*'s appointment to a full professorship or give lectures on constitutional law.[7]

This victory of the Centro succeeded another one announced to the membership by interim President Renato Macedo on July 27. Judge Clovis de Morais Barros (a cousin of the father of Hermann de Morais Barros) had awarded damages for the material destruction inflicted when the Special Police invaded the law school on November 2, 1943.[8] The judge (whose decision was upheld unanimously in the appeals court) ordered the state to pay over four thousand cruzeiros (formerly called milreis) to the Centro and additional amounts to the concessionaires of the bar and barber chair. He ruled that the authorities should not have beaten students and carried out acts of vandalism even if reasons had existed for making arrests. He reported that no evidence supported the prosecution's claim about insulting inscriptions on law school walls and added that even such evidence would not have justified the behavior of the police.[9]

5. Advice from Arrobas (July 1944)

On July 12, during the strike against Mota Filho's appointment, Arrobas Martins wrote from Santos to José Bonifácio Coutinho Nogueira to advise that further public demonstrations against the "ex-director of the DEIP" would be counterproductive because the problem concerned only the law school. He recommended that the law students, having firmly established a position, should leave the initiative for negotiating to "the other side," and, while awaiting a reply, should issue propaganda and exert pressure for a general university strike.[1]

But, Arrobas wrote, taking the case to the "public square" would give undeserved importance to the "adulator of the dictator" and confirm the more or less generalized reputation of the students as being hooligans, or street rioters. He added: "If we appeal to the people all the time, and in cases of inferior importance, such as this one, we shall build up our own discredit. . . . Let us reserve the precious collaboration of the people for key occasions, when we have something substantial to tell them or ask of them, when we can present ourselves as young people concerned with the broad social and national frontiers and not as children who amuse themselves with firecrackers. We should take to the people only problems that they feel and understand."

In his letter, Arrobas expressed interest in the forthcoming campaign of Luís Francisco da Silva Carvalho, of the Frente Acadêmica pela Democracia, for the Centro presidency. A year earlier, when Luís Francisco was a third-year student, Arrobas had arranged for him to join the Bucha, which was still trying to recapture some of its former glory. Luís Francisco had been one of no more than 10 members of a class of 182 who became *bucheiros*.[2]

"How," Arrobas asked José Bonifácio Coutinho Nogueira, "are the understandings with the Ruy Nazareth group? An alliance with them, based on well-defined political principles, in both internal and external areas, will bring valuable help to the candidacy of Luís."[3] Ruy Nazareth, to whom Arrobas referred, was showing leftist tendencies not appreciated by some of his fellow Libertadores. He was popular and deeply interested in politics at the *arcadas*. A resident of São José do Rio Preto and the son of a medical doctor in Bahia, Ruy Nazareth was wealthy, married, and older than most of the students.[4]

Arrobas, in his letter, warned against repeating collusions based on mere electoral objectives. "The suspect chemistry of combinations worked out for reasons of vanity or empty self-conceit," he wrote, would lead to new schisms. And he urged the exclusion from "our group" of all who were not perfectly identified with it, thus avoiding "the mixture of wheat and tares, of which the Scriptures speak."[5]

Agreeing with José Bonifácio on the need of student support for "our movements," Arrobas wrote that "we never forgot that need, but were never able to obtain the support. At the end of 1941, Bé [Roberto de Abreu Sodré], Germinal, and Costinha [Costa Corrêa], and others decided to leave school politics and devote themselves simply to external politics. They even drew up a manifesto to that effect. When they sought my opinion, I resolutely opposed their idea. . . . I explained that our campaigns would have repercussion only if they had the conscious or forced adherence of our student body. And that we would obtain that adherence only if we had prestige there. The prestige, you know, comes from internal political activity. They agreed with me. Therefore they reluctantly remained in militant academic politics." But, Arrobas added, "we never had the knack of winning voters. We were always a closed circle. We always revealed ourselves better at criticizing than pleasing. We formed a group of splendid friends and very bad *cabos eleitorais*."

6. Authorities React to Centro Electioneering (October–November 1944)

Campaigning for the annual Centro election, significantly set for November 10, [1] aroused the interest of more students than ever before and received more publicity in the daily press than in the past. But some of the student leaders ran into trouble because the growing clamor for an end of the Estado Novo, evident in the electioneering, coincided with the period of increased repression begun in July.

When 396 law students met on September 15 to choose the Libertador slate, the popular Ruy Nazareth had no trouble winning the nomination for Centro president.[2] If some Libertadores were displeased by his leftist tendencies, they took comfort in the point of view represented by most of the other candidates on the slate.[3]

Earlier in the year the Libertadores had suffered another of their schisms, this time because six *comissão diretora* members, citing Magano's "undercover pro-government ways" and handling of the Mota Filho case, had left the party.[4] The six were verse writer "Juca" Santana, Vítor Tieghi, Cicero de Toledo Piza, Aloísio Barbosa Ferreira, Rui Junqueira de Freitas Camargo, and Fernando Jacob (who was considered to be attracted to leftist ideas). After the nomination of Ruy Nazareth, the six issued a circular explaining that, although they were unconnected with any party, they felt obligated to participate in the election and recommended voting for him. Their circular called attention to the economic hardship of poor students, "explicable only in a typically bourgeois society," and called for free education at all levels.[5]

The circular was inspired in part by a determination to prevent a victory of the Libertadores' strongest rival, the Conservadores.[6] Conservador presidential candidate Aloysio Ferraz Pereira, the poet who had the virtue of having been wounded on November 9, 1943, was telling the press that, while his party stood for "the immortal democratic principles," it was not made up of "extremists" and was not attracted to "poorly studied ideologies." He called for "renovation tempered by good sense."[7] The manifesto of the Partido Conservador advocated the "union of everyone" in favor of the democratization of Brazil and regretted to find that its adversaries, rejecting the union, insulted Conservadores. Replying to the insults, the Conservadores insisted that the fruits they had provided over a period of almost ten years could have come only from a "thoroughly democratic" party and pointed out that Conservadores had been in charge of the Centro during the great prowar rally of August 1942 and the struggle against "the bullets of the tyranny" in November 1943.[8]

In an attack on the Libertadores, the Conservador manifesto said that never had a Conservador, in the Centro presidency, "reached a decision without the knowledge of, and against the declared wish of, the democratic *assembléia*," nor had his agreement been rejected by the student body. Nor had "members of our *comissão diretora* ever found it necessary to abandon the party due to the incoherence of positions." In closing, the manifesto said that "those who today sneakily try to attack" Aloysio Ferraz Pereira "were forced a year ago to hail his heroism. . . . The blood he shed for Democracy . . . reveals the resolute attitude he will maintain as President of the Centro Acadêmico XI de Agosto."

Members of the Frente Acadêmica pela Democracia met on September 26 at the Clube Escandinávia and accepted by acclamation a slate headed by Luís Francisco da Silva Carvalho. At the same time they chose a new party directorship consisting of José Carlos Moraes Abreu (president), Afrânio de Oliveira, Wilson Minervino, Antônio Cláudio Fernandes Rocha, Benjamin Pereira de Queiroz, Olavo de Almeida Pinto, Carlos Eduardo de Camargo Aranha, Jair Carvalho Monteiro, Renato Amaral Sampaio Coelho, José Bonifácio Coutinho Nogueira, Roberto Brotero de Barros, Carlos Eduardo Barreto, and José Bueno de Aguiar.[9]

The daily press gave especially good coverage to the Frente, which was not expected to win the election but seized every possible opportunity to promote public manifestations in favor of democracy.[10] On Saturday, October 23 (anniversary of the fascist march on Rome), the Frente took the lead in bringing crowds of students (among them first-year student Paulo de Tarso Santos and fourth-year student Francisco Chagas Rodrigues) from the *arcadas* to a *churrasco* (barbecue party), where a band played and speeches extolled "the democratic citizens of the world" and the collapse of Italian fascism.[11] Luís Francisco Carvalho's distribution of copies of Rui Barbosa's 1920 "Oração aos Moços" prompted *Diário da Noite* to praise the law school for its devotion to democracy.[12] The press also gave publicity to the votes for Luís Francisco that were mailed from Italy in correspondence addressed to José Carlos Moraes Abreu by Gerald Vidigal and Cândido Teobaldo de Souza Andrade.[13]

The Frente issued an "authentic copy" of Arrobas Martins' "manifesto of November 2, 1943, cornerstone of the events that resulted in the slaughter of November 9." Besides being misdated, it was not authentic in the wording or in the signatures. Among the signatures omitted was that of José Barbosa, who had been expelled from the Centro in December 1943.

The mimeographed election manifesto of the Frente was written by José Carlos Moraes Abreu with some help from Luís Francisco Carvalho and (in the section about "the Democracy of Tomorrow") from Arrobas Martins.[14] After reviewing the history of the "handful of passionate adversaries of the dictatorship" who had, from the start, shown the courage to react against the Vargas regime, it called for the democratization of Brazil. This change, it said, should not be by means of the "carta" of November 10, 1937, or a plebiscite about the "carta," for that path would make a pact with the regime that "gave us the Gestapo, imprisonments, and political exiles, censorship and the DIP, the Tribunal de Segurança condemning Brazilians simply for being oppositionists, monetary inflation, and the increasing misery of the workers." In contemplating "the Democracy of Tomorrow," the Frente's manifesto criticized the liberal regime in effect in democratic societies of the past century, made up of the privileged classes. Democratic ideas of equality and liberty, it said, should be reinterpreted to the extent necessary to prevent economic inequalities from creating political inequalities.[15]

Unlike the Frente, the Libertador Party issued a manifesto that was printed. It described "the political regime established by the 1937 coup" as "writhing in agony under the clamor that can no longer be stifled." "The youth of the *academia*," it said, "must be on guard against attempts that neo-fascism will use to remain in power, under the affectation of being democratic, using the whitewash of a plebiscite that we are obliged to denounce to the Nation as a sneer to the sacrifice of our brothers who fight in Europe against oppression, and as a mockery to the Brazilian people who demand, prior to elections, liberty of the press, liberty of meetings, liberty to organize parties, and amnesty for the exiles and political prisoners."[16]

The Superintendência da Ordem Política e Social decided that the manifestos of the Frente and Partido Libertador were subversive. Therefore, the authorities drew up legal cases against the signers of each and forwarded the cases to the Tribunal de Segurança Nacional in Rio. Twenty-six students were indicted in the case against "Luís Francisco da Silva Carvalho and others" because the Frente manifesto had been signed by its candidates as well as its *comissão diretora*. The indicted Libertadores were the fourteen members of its *comissão diretora*, including party President João Nery Guimarães and Centro Vice President Renato P. Macedo.[17]

Furthermore, as the Libertador manifesto had been printed, agents of the Superintendência da Ordem Política e Social wrecked the press that had been used and arrested the printer (at his home at 2:00 A.M.). He was locked up for three weeks.[18]

7. The Centro Elects Nazareth and Expels Celio Costa (November 1944)

The campaign of Ruy Nazareth went so well, and the vote-getting organization headed by party President João Nery Guimarães (candidate for a *comissão de redação* post) was so efficient, that the pre-election betting heavily favored the Libertadores. Despite the odds, the interest in the outcome continued intense. The columns of the daily press were filled with the statements of contestants and described the attention given by the *população paulista* to the democratic battle at the urns of the *arcadas*.

With the Centro's membership estimated at 1,200, a record of 1,063 votes were cast. They included the votes of former Presidents César Lacerda de Vergueiro, Eduardo Vergueiro de Lorena, Antônio Pereira Lima, Roberto Victor Cordeiro, Antônio Carlos de Abreu Sodré, Trajano Pupo Netto, Francisco de Paula Quintanilha Ribeiro, and Hélio Mota. First- and second-year students voted in the Barão de Ramalho Room and those in the other classes used the João Mendes Júnior Room. At 8:00 P.M. Magano and his assistants presided over the count in the presence of a multitude, while thirty party representatives checked the count.[1]

The final results, reported after midnight, gave an overwhelming victory to the Libertadores, who won all the places on the two *comissões* and all the officerships except for first secretary (won by Conservador Antônio de Castro Assunção). The outcome of the presidential race was 543 votes for Nazareth, 356 for Aloysio Ferraz Pereira (Conservador), and 164 for Luís Francisco Carvalho (Frente).[2]

Naldo Caparica in Italy was delighted at the victory of his close friend Nazareth and sent his congratulations in a letter dated December 11. "You know," he wrote, "how much our 'little school' means to me. My friends there and the struggles in which we participated are probably the most important part of my life." Describing the effect of the election news on six former law students, who were about to have supper when the mail arrived, Caparica wrote Nazareth that much good wine was consumed and "De Gaulle [Rui Pereira de Queiroz] was forced to join us in toasting you with a *quin-quin-querum* [law school battle cry in 'macaroni Latin']. Besides, as good democrats, we offered good luck to the Frente and our friend Luizinho [Luís Francisco]. The only party not getting in on that was the Conservador, whose illustrious representative, Dr. Bezerrote [Francisco de Assis Bezerra de Menezes of the class of 1943] has just left us for other parts, where Bernardes [José Vasques Bernardes] awaits him." Nazareth also received congratulatory notes from Bezerra and Bernardes.[3]

Shortly before the election, fifth-year student Célio de Oliveira Costa dropped his Superintendência da Ordem Política e Social employment identification card near one of the two billiard tables in the Centro Onze de Agosto and it was picked up by Renato Amaral Sampaio Coelho.[4] It bore the words "Agente Reservado" and, consequently, on November 8, Célio Costa, a quiet person, was summoned before Centro leaders, who put him in a state of shock by accusing him of being a secret agent, or spy, of the police. His accusers issued an unsigned bulletin that bore a facsimile of the identification card and proclaimed that "Getúlio Vargas transformed this young student into a spy, into a traitor of his law school colleagues." The bulletin warned of other spies and asked the students to seize them all and turn them over "to the justice of the people."[5]

Célio Costa was ordered to defend himself at a Centro assembly in the Brasílio Machado Room (on the law school's third floor) on November 9. His request for more time was denied and he faced a hostile assembly, with Germinal Feijó acting as chief accuser.[6]

Célio Costa's work as a clerk at the Superintendência had nothing to do with spying, but his explanations were to no avail, and only one student, Quintino Ferreira Millás, raised his voice to defend him.[7] When Célio Costa pointed out that he had been beaten up by the police and arrested on November 2, 1943, his accusers declared that this treatment had been carried out to mislead the students.[8] The defendant was found guilty.

After Célio Costa's appeal to the Centro for a more careful study and a reexamination at another assembly were denied, he issued a declaration likening his condemnation to the findings made by fascist tribunals. He ridiculed the charge that he telephoned reports to the police and added that his lack of association with the student political leadership placed him in the position of having no knowledge that would interest the police. His declaration reported in detail on the clerical functions he had carried out at the Superintendência since 1942 to earn a monthly stipend of 400 cruzeiros to help pay for his law studies. These functions, which included filling out pages about Italians seeking "safe conduct" papers, had become necessary after Brazil broke relations with the Axis and were financed from a fund known as the *verba reservada*, which led to the classification of some employees as *agentes reservados*.[9]

8. Anti-Vargas Activities (December 1944–January 1945)

After Vargas accepted an invitation of the Associação Comercial de São Paulo to attend its fiftieth anniversary celebration on December

7, 1944, a group of students belonging to the Frente Acadêmica pela Democracia spoke about the need to protest the dictator's visit. A smaller group decided to act. It liked the idea of Benjamin Pereira de Queiroz of filling the city with leaflets attacking the visit and chose José Bonifácio Coutinho Nogueira to devise a plan for distributing them. The plan eventually adopted was to have the leaflets thrown simultaneously from tall buildings.[1]

Benjamin Pereira de Queiroz ("Basil Rathbone") drafted the leaflet, and José Bonifácio took the draft to the residence of Fernando Millan, where copies were mimeographed. The leaflet read, in part:

> Insensible to the suffering of the working population and the disdain of the Paulistas, the dictator Getúlio Vargas again degrades São Paulo with his presence. Brazilians! Paulistas! While you starve and your children die from a lack of milk, this same man, creator of the fascist Estado Novo, constructed Quintandinhas with your money and banqueted with the bankers and capitalists who exploit your work: they are always the same Roberto Simonsen, Brasilio Machado, Horácio Lafer, Gastão Vidigal, and others, who, together with the cabinet ministers and creatures of the Estado Novo, have made money while you hungered. . . .
>
> All who applaud or are seen at the side of the dictator Getúlio will be noted, and, as happened in Paris and Rome, judged on the day of victory.
>
> All of São Paulo in mourning when the dictator Getúlio is here! . . .
>
> Brazil and São Paulo demand immediate elections for the national constitutional assembly![2]

The mimeographers were Luís Francisco Carvalho, José Bonifácio Coutinho Nogueira, Benjamin Pereira de Queiroz, Ênio de Novais França, and Fernando Millan. By a 3-to-2 vote they decided to leave the name of banker Gastão Vidigal although he was uncle of Geraldo and Marcello Vidigal. But, after fifteen thousand leaflets had been printed, Ênio de Novais França changed his mind and agreed with Luís Francisco and José Bonifácio that Vidigal's name be deleted.[3] Therefore, the stencil was changed, and it may have been changed more than once because some of the circulars deleted the name of Horácio Lafer while retaining that of Vidigal.[4] By 4:00 A.M. on December 6 the dangerous work of turning out thirty thousand copies had been completed with some assistance from Frente enthusiasts José Carlos Moraes Abreu and Antônio Cláudio Fernandes Rocha.

José Carlos Moraes Abreu recalls hiding a little later in the home of Antônio Cláudio because police would hardly suspect the residence of Antônio Cláudio's father, Sinésio Rocha, *procurador geral* of the state. Sinésio had no idea that his residence was used for anti-Vargas work.[5]

At 5:00 P.M. on the sixth, after the leaflets had been put in packages, a meeting was held in the office of Roberto de Abreu Sodré. There Germinal Feijó opposed the plan for distributing the leaflets, but it received strong support from Roberto Sodré and Cory Porto Fernandes (a law school graduate of December 1943 but still a student leader at the Escola Livre de Sociologia e Política). College of Philosophy graduate Paulo Emílio Sales Gomes, an anti-Stalinist far leftist, meditated about the matter.[6]

That night at 2:00 A.M. Paulo Nogueira Neto, Benjamin Pereira de Queiroz, and Fernando Millan reviewed the plan in the apartment of Hélio Mota and resolved to execute it at noon, but the hour was postponed at a 10:00 A.M. meeting held in the law office of Wilson Rahal. A 5:30 P.M. distribution was agreed upon by Rahal, José Bonifácio, Millan, Sérgio Brotero Junqueira, Renato Amaral Sampaio Coelho, and Afrânio de Oliveira.

Rahal, José Bonifácio, and Ivo Cariani (a dentist) moved the thirty thousand leaflets from the home of Carlos Eduardo de Camargo Aranha to the office of José Bonifácio at the Nogueira family firm, the Sociedade Predial Ester, where they were guarded by Paulo Nogueira Neto. In the afternoon the plotters picked up their quotas.

Paulo Nogueira Neto, making the rounds, was pleased. Fernando Millan was at Barão de Itapetininga Street; Luís Francisco Carvalho, helped by his sister Lygia (expert at throwing subversive circulars), was at the Mappin Building; Afrânio de Oliveira was at Xavier de Toledo Street; Armando de Morais Barros (grandson of Paulo) was at Marconi Street; Sérgio Brotero Junqueira was at Boa Vista Street; Renato Amaral Sampaio Coelho was at the Central Building; Maurício Freitas Guimarães Hess and Flávio Pinho de Almeida were at the Praça do Patriarca; Carlos Eduardo de Camargo Aranha was at Líbero Badaró Street; Ênio de Novais França was at the Paulista de Seguros building; Benjamin Pereira de Queiroz was at the Largo de São Francisco; Álvaro Roberto Mendes Gonçalves was at the Sulacap building; and José Bonifácio was at the Banco de São Paulo building on São Bento Street near the Praça Antônio Prado.

José Bonifácio, writing on the night of December 7 about the episode, recorded the trepidation he felt as he mounted stairways, tossed out hundreds of leaflets, and made his descent, alone, fearful that each person he passed might be a "truculent soldier of the Special

Police." When it was all over, and the subversive leaflets had caused "a great repercussion throughout the city," he experienced what was perhaps "the greatest happiness" he had had in his life. "The police," he wrote, "could do nothing in the face of the perfect organization. . . . The buildings of the Banco de São Paulo, Mappin, and Sulacap were . . . submitted to careful inspection, but it was too late."[7]

One of the leaflet throwers was Paulo Zingg, who had been prohibited from writing for publication after his *Ilustração* had been closed down. He belonged to the Grupo Radical de Ação Popular (GRAP) and the leftist minority of the Frente de Resistência. His activity on December 7 resulted in his arrest for several days.[8] Carlos Eduardo de Camargo Aranha was arrested on December 8, bringing his total number of arrests to eleven.[9]

At the graduation exercises, held in the Municipal Theater on the evening of January 10, scholastic honors were showered upon Ester de Figueiredo Ferraz, one of the eight graduating young women.[10] Graduating class orator Francisco Camargo de Almeida Prado ("Chico Machão"), a former Conservador director, declared that the law students wanted "the three powers, which make up the national sovereignty, to exist in a democratic setting, incompatible with the elimination of the legislature or with a still more revolting crime, the absorption of the judiciary by the executive." "We never could understand the press being suffocated," he said.[11]

After the ceremony, students and their friends and families went to the bars. They flocked to the popular Bar Franciscano (on Líbero Badaró Street)—whose well-known fresco depicting beer drinkers in Bavaria had been painted over, on orders of the police, following Brazil's entry in the war.[12] There in the early hours of January 11, 1945, beer drinkers applauded while one of them took down the picture of Vargas and destroyed it. Although even police agents, in civilian clothes, joined in the applause, the DOPS undertook an inquiry several days later. Some law students who had been present, including first-year student Flávio Galvão (recently elected to the Centro *comissão de sindicância*), were indicted. Charges against them ("insulting the President of the Republic") were forwarded to the Tribunal de Segurança Nacional.[13]

XI

Twilight of the Estado Novo (1945)

1. Young Paulistas Favor a United Front with Eduardo Gomes (February 1945)

When approximately 250 Brazilian writers gathered in São Paulo late in January 1945 for the First Writers' Congress, they passed resolutions calling for democracy and free expression and approved a motion extending greetings to Geraldo Vidigal and other Brazilian writers who were fighting in Italy for the principles that the Writers' Congress defended in Brazil.[1]

Geraldo Vidigal, Rui Pereira de Queiroz, and Celso Braga, who would have graduated were they not in Italy, were remembered in the speechmaking at the commencement exercises on January 10 and at the Clube Comercial on February 7, when a banquet honored the recent graduates who, "while attending the São Paulo law school, distinguished themselves in the struggle for the democratization of Brazil."[2] The banquet, reflecting the reputation achieved by the democratic movement at the *arcadas*,[3] attracted more than two hundred opponents of the Estado Novo from all over Brazil, including such prominent figures as Arthur Bernardes, José Eduardo do Prado Kelly (representing Airforce Brigadeiro Eduardo Gomes), Virgílio de Melo Franco, Pedro Aleixo, Milton Campos, Gilberto Freire, Juaraci Magalhães, Dário de Almeida Magalhães, Daniel de Carvalho, José Franzem de Lima, Levi Carneiro, Mário Brant, João Mangabeira, Carlos de Lima Cavalcanti, Guilherme Flores da Cunha (representing José Antônio Flores da Cunha), and Hermes Lima. Among those in the large Paulista contingent were Paulo Duarte, Júlio Prestes de Albuquerque, and Miguel Costa.[4]

The anti-Getulistas at the Clube Comercial appreciated that the end of the Estado Novo was close at hand, for Generals Dutra and Góis Monteiro, former pillars of the Estado Novo, were calling for democracy, and Vargas was talking about holding elections. In attacking the Estado Novo, no restraint was shown by orators Luís Francisco Carvalho, who paid tribute to the honored new graduates, and Germinal Feijó, who had finally received his degree and spoke on behalf of the honored group.

Luís Francisco and Feijó delivered speeches that were strikingly similar.[5] Both gave a year-by-year review of antigovernment activities at the *arcadas* following the implantation in November 1937 ("by criminal hands" Luís Francisco said) of what they called the corrupt, impoverishing, fascist, police state. Both stressed the enormity of the task of overcoming the "sins" and "ills" stemming from the Estado Novo (Luís Francisco said that the task was too great to be completed by the sacrifices of a single generation). Both concluded that the building of "the Third Republic" would require a mighty, united front, and they urged members of the older generation to put divergences aside and follow the example of the young people, who, they declared, were united for the final overthrow of the Estado Novo and the construction of a democratic Brazil.

Feijó revealed that the university student militants, having gained political experience, were elaborating a program, not with the idea of establishing a party of their own but in order to offer "the vigorous impulse of a generation which, without connections with the old political parties, wants to be close to the people." While rejecting the pre-1937 parties as out of date, Feijó acknowledged that much had been learned from the liberals and the militants of the Left. Now he urged that ideological polemics be relegated to the future.

Feijó's program called for the establishment of diplomatic relations with the Soviet Union. Pointing out that this suggestion would lead some "spokesmen of indigenous fascism," such as *Brasil-Portugal*, to "call us Communists," the orator insisted that the "Communist danger" was always a pretext used for reactionary maneuvers. Expressing his suspicion about the government's promise to carry out elections, Feijó urged that the elections be by secret and direct vote and include an election for a constitutional assembly. "We demand," he added, "the immediate suppression of the DIP . . . and the abolishment of the Tribunal de Segurança."

In ringing words, Feijó declared that the demands he had listed had been favored by the valiant combatants of Fort Copacabana, "who, in 1922, raised the first cry of rebellion against the reactionary oligarchies" and whose survivor was "the ardent democrat Eduardo Gomes"; by those who wrote "unequalled pages of heroism, struggling against the corruption of the democratic institutions," and whose spirit would be present in the forthcoming elections in the person of Miguel Costa; by the legendary Prestes Column, which would be represented by Juarez Távora; by the great democratic revolution of 1930, whose aspirations would be renewed "in the combatants of today, Juraci Magalhães, Virgílio de Melo Franco, Manoel Rabelo, Estilac Leal, and Flores da Cunha"; by the constitutionalist revolution of 1932, whose ideal of legality would be represented by Euclides Figueiredo, Waldemar Ferreira, Aureliano Leite, and Ibrahim Nobre; by the movement of the Aliança Nacional Libertadora, whose democratic and popular vitality would live again in the names of Hercolino Cascardo and Caio Prado Júnior; by the electoral campaigns of 1937, whose hopes would be revived and reinvigorated with the return of Armando de Sales Oliveira and José Américo de Almeida to political activity; and by all those who never came to terms with the dictatorship, such as Antônio Carlos de Abreu Sodré and João Sampaio.

Late in February and early in March, Vargas took steps that spelled the demise of the Estado Novo. The first step, the end of press censorship, followed the failure of the DIP to punish *Correio da Manhã* for its publication, on February 22, of Carlos Lacerda's interview with José Américo de Almeida. The press, its freedom long crushed by the DIP, was suddenly filled with the statements of prominent Vargas haters. Many of the statements hailed the idea, advanced by José Américo, that Brigadeiro Eduardo Gomes become the anti–Estado Novo candidate for the presidency.

In São Paulo on Sunday, February 25, most of the front page of the *Diário de S. Paulo* was devoted to the "political thinking of Paulista youth"—a collection of interviews with Germinal Feijó, Luís Arrobas Martins, Paulo Emílio Sales Gomes, and Paulo Zingg.[6] None of the four liked the recent proposal of the Vargas cabinet that the 1937 Constitution be amended to provide for a presidential election and to make other changes in Brazil's political structure. Feijó, Arrobas, and Paulo Emílio declared that the "carta of 1937" should be completely abolished because it was illegal and fascist. "Only a constitutional assembly," Zingg told the *Diário de S. Paulo*, "can give the Third Republic the juridical and political structure we crave."

Paulo Emílio, pointing out that the work of a constitutional assembly would be slow, recommended the election of a provisional government because "the present government is not in a condition to preside over the assembly's work or represent Brazil at the peace conferences." He added that "the name with prestige in oppositionist circles for the provisional presidency is that of Brigadeiro Eduardo Gomes." Feijó, expressing the "enthusiasm" of the young people for the presidential candidacy of Eduardo Gomes, recommended that the government posts, during the preconstitutional phase, be in the hands of men who inspired the nation's confidence because of their fidelity to democratic ideas.

Feijó, in his interview, gave early publicity to the União Democrática Nacional (UDN), "a coalition born of the democratic forces of resistance to the Estado Novo." He said that the young people supported the UDN and that, as they had been "the most active and most consistent portion of the resistance," they could not fail to play an important role in the coalition. That role, he told the *Diário de S. Paulo*, would differ from the clandestine movement of the past, but it did not mean that "we are disregarding active resistance of what remains of the dictatorship." On the contrary, he went on to say, the young people were prepared to react against maneuvers that the government could be expected to carry out to cheat Brazil of democracy.

Arrobas Martins, warning against a new electoral law that would be a hoax, recommended using the electoral law of 1932. He added that it was therefore unnecessary for Alexandre Marcondes Filho, who had become justice minister in 1942, to work on a new law. "He must," Arrobas remarked, "already be exhausted from the effort he has expended in the thankless defense of a cause that he now has had to admit is lost."

Arrobas emphasized the need of a complete renovation in the political and social areas to allow humanity to reach a condition of life favorable to full development. Therefore, like Feijó on February 7, he pronounced the old political currents "outdated." As for the coming presidential election, he noted the wide backing for Eduardo Gomes to oppose Vargas, who, he said, "had been rejected by all good democrats and by national opinion" and who "cannot continue in office or return." Arrobas explained that, even if Eduardo Gomes were not "the unimpeachable patriot and democrat that he always revealed himself to be," the mere fact that his candidacy would be against Vargas and the principles of the Estado Novo "is enough to win our support and attract the majority of the Brazilian people."

2. Unsuccessful Student Rallies in São Paulo and Recife (early March 1945)

The enemies of Vargas had a problem because the president had gained support from the propaganda about his government's social legislation. The problem became more acute with the development, starting late in 1944, of a working relationship between the Vargas government and the Comissão Nacional de Organização Provisória (CNOP), the best organized group in the Brazilian Communist Party (PCB). The CNOP, calling for "national union with Vargas," found itself free to penetrate the officially recognized labor unions, and it was effective in this work.

The anti-Vargas law students in São Paulo were aware of the problem as they organized, with the help of the student associations at the other colleges, a "monster rally" to be held at the Praça da Sé on March 2. The rally, one of the first on a large scale in the nation since the end of censorship,[1] would extol democracy and favor the presidential candidacy of Eduardo Gomes.

The Centro Onze de Agosto, anticipating what it called "the intrigues that the government will carry out between the working class and the university student class," issued leaflets before the rally. Addressed "To the Workers," and signed "the Students of São Paulo," the wording was by fifth-year student José Bueno de Aguiar ("Chiriba"), a member of the *comissão diretora* of the Frente Acadêmica pela Democracia.[2] "The students of São Paulo," the leaflets said, "are sons of the people and struggle for Brazil together with the people. Beware of the fascist maneuvers which, at this moment, seek to create confusion and separate the workers from the students. It is for improving the people's living conditions that the students have fallen in the São Paulo streets."[3]

The custom of painting messages on walls throughout the city was begun when Flávio Galvão and some other students spent the night before the rally using this method to call on the people to be at the Praça da Sé.[4] Despite a heavy rain, the rally attracted a large crowd, including about five hundred students from all the colleges.[5] Placards proclaimed the return of liberty.

Following the opening remarks of Ruy Nazareth and the reading of a proclamation to the workers, a worker addressed the crowd in response to an appeal of the students. But heckling broke out during his speech, and it became much worse during the following speech, by anti-Vargas leftist Paulo Emílio Sales Gomes.[6] The cries of "We want Getúlio" and "Down with the students" made it almost impossible for the next two speakers (a law student and another worker) to carry on. The remaining program (which called for speakers from four colleges) was abandoned because opponents of the students, using clubs wrapped in paper, turned the rally into a battle. Flávio Galvão, describing the scene in an article in *O XI de Agosto*, wrote that "at the microphone, installed at the door of the Cathedral, the students gallantly defended their positions and sought to prevent the conflict from becoming worse. Appeals by professors and others to members of the Guarda Civil were fruitless because the guards did not try to maintain order. In view of the determination of the agitators to disturb the rally . . . , some students, using the most forceful means, tried to disperse them. Clashes occurred, with both sides using clubs and stones."

Many people were wounded, among them law school graduate Paulo Henrique Meinberg and Fernando Millan's brother Roberto. Law students, withdrawing to the *arcadas,* sang the national anthem "as a reminder that they were there to defend the democratic ideals." Their pro-Vargas foes, following them to the Largo de São Francisco, hurled stones and broke windows of the law school.[7]

Press reports said that the clash had been carried out by "provocative persons deliberately imported from the federal capital to demonstrate in favor of the President of the Republic." But the São Paulo Secretaria da Segurança Pública announced that an investigation revealed that "the people who interfered with the students' rally were, really, members of the local population, mostly workers and newspaper vendors."[8]

On March 2, the day of the clash in São Paulo, Vargas held a press conference in Rio. The journalists had many questions for the president, who had recently signed a constitutional amendment to open the way for the election of congressmen and a new president and had taken steps to replace Justice Minister Marcondes Filho and Federal District Police Chief Coriolano de Góis. In reply to questions, Vargas spoke of establishing diplomatic relations with the Soviet Union and said that he would study possible amnesty decrees, case by case. The DIP, he said, would limit itself to promoting Brazilian culture. As for a constitutional assembly, he argued that it would be unnecessary because the Congress would have the power to modify the 1937 Constitution.

On the next day, in front of the law school in Recife, students held an antigovernment rally in support of Eduardo Gomes, and then they paraded through the city to Independência Square. There they joined a crowd, which included pro-Vargas workers, to hear speeches delivered from the balcony of the *Diário de Pernambuco,* the daily that supported the students' anti-Vargas views. Shots broke out while Professor Gilberto Freire was speaking. A worker in the crowd and a student on the balcony lost their lives, and several people were wounded.[9] The student, Demócrito de Souza Filho, had been first secretary of the Union of Students of Pernambuco.

While headlines in Brazil blamed the bloodshed on Interventor Etelvino Lins and his state police, the Pernambuco Secretaria da Segurança Pública issued a statement blaming the *Diário de Pernambuco,* which, it said, had "instigated social discord by every means possible, exploiting principally the university student class, in which it has been stirring up political passions." The statement said that the first shots were fired against the pro-Vargas workers and came from the offices of the daily, and that other shots followed during the resulting "confuson."[10] Brigadeiro Eduardo Gomes sent his sympathy to the dead student's family and said that his confidence in God allowed him to feel that Brazil's honor would be upheld by the punishment of those responsible for a crime that "marks the beginning of a movement that doubtless will be one of work and suffering, sorrow and action."[11]

As a result of the student's death, Arthur José Poerner writes, the UNE "declared war on the government." A few days later, on March 8, the UNE participated in the first untroubled large-scale anti–Estado Novo rally, held in front of the Municipal Theater in Rio. Student Paulo Silveira joined with other speakers, such as José Antônio Flores da Cunha, Maurício de Lacerda, and his son Carlos Lacerda, in calling for democracy and amnesty. Following the rally, the students, singing the national anthem, marched to the UNE headquarters.[12]

3. The União Democrática Socialista (June 1945)

The UDN, formally established in Rio on April 2, represented a wide range of anti-Vargas currents. On its list of founders were ex-President Artur Bernardes, ex-Interventor Ademar de Barros, Professor Waldemar Ferreira, former presidential candidates Armando de Sales Oliveira (about to return to Brazil and die of cancer) and José Américo de Almeida, Communist Astrojildo Pereira, socialist João Mangabeira, and his brother Otávio Mangabeira (who had served in the cabinet of Washington Luís). A principal organizer was Virgílio de Melo Franco, from Minas.[1] Among the many Paulistas who helped were Roberto Victor Cordeiro and the ailing Antônio Carlos de Abreu Sodré.

In São Paulo the Frente de Resistência, which had been represented by *Resistência*, organized a provisional executive committee made up of Antônio Costa Côrrea, Antônio Cândido de Mello e Souza, Carlos Engel, Cory Porto Fernandes, Germinal Feijó, Israel Dias Novaes, José Bonifácio da Silva Jardim, José Bonifácio Coutinho Nogueira, Luís Arrobas Martins, Luís de Azevedo Soares, Paulo Emílio Sales Gomes, Paulo Zingg, Roberto de Abreu Sodré, Rômulo Fonseca, and Wilson Rahal. Alternate committee members were Celso Galvão, José Carlos Moraes Abreu, Benjamin Pereira de Queiroz, Luís Francisco Carvalho, and Renato Amaral Sampaio Coelho.[2]

These names appeared on the draft of a manifesto dated April 7 and addressed especially to urban and rural workers and young people in factories and schools. It declared that the Frente de Resistência was "to the Left" and that the signers would fight for socialism while remaining independent of the traditional Brazilian currents of leftist opinion. Democracy, the Frente de Resistência felt, could be achieved only by correcting a situation in which the big landowners, and men of industry and commerce, had spoken a great deal, while the middle class and urban workers had been limited to a few words and the rural workers had been silent. The manifesto supported Eduardo Gomes and presented a program calling for a revision of the agricultural structure (the liquidation of unproductive large landownings), free education at all levels, and state control of credit, transportation, utilities, and basic industries.

The Frente de Resistência expressed the hope of joining a national party of the Left, provided it was "sufficiently democratic internally." Its other options were to form the Left wing of a national progressive party or join with groups in other states, similar to itself, and thus form a separate party.[3]

Paulo Emílio Sales Gomes, deeply interested in the Frente de Resistência, hoped to attract Luís Carlos Prestes to the anti-Vargas movement. He was able to speak with Prestes in Rio after João Alberto Lins e Barros, the new Federal District police chief, announced that the Communist prisoner would be allowed to receive all the visitors he wanted. Paulo Emílio spent so much time with Prestes that Germinal Feijó and Cory Porto Fernandes, also visiting Rio, believed that he was giving Prestes a complete update on the situation. Later they learned from a disappointed Paulo Emílio that Prestes, listening hardly at all, had spoken for hours about the need of a union with Vargas.[4] Journalist Carlos Lacerda heard the same story from Prestes. And student leaders in Rio, such as Vítor Konder and Paulo Silveira, heard the prisoner give his support to the CNOP rather than to anti-Vargas Communists.[5]

Prestes, released with the other political prisoners on April 18, made his position clear during a conversation with Eduardo Gomes and a press interview. He rejected the candidacies of Eduardo Gomes and War Minister Dutra, whose name was being presented by politicians close to the government. Some Communist admirers of Prestes (including intellectuals Astrojildo Pereira and Mário Schemberg) withdrew support given earlier to Eduardo Gomes. But the leftists connected with the São Paulo Law School continued strongly opposed to Vargas. The pro-Vargas line adopted by the Communist Party of Brazil (PCB) was criticized by Germinal Feijó and Renato Amaral Sampaio Coelho during a call on Communist Jorge Amado, whose recent biography extolling Prestes became a best seller.[6]

Late in April, when much was heard in praise of Prestes, the Soviet Union, and Stalin, an antileftist *proclamação democrática* was released at the *arcadas* by a group that included some Libertadores who had objected earlier to the association of *democratas exaltados* with the Left. Rebutting the *proclamação*, fifth-year student Joaquim Franco Garcia told *Diário da Noite* that it was fascist and reactionary; he also accused its authors of supporting old-fashioned individualism and aiding Vargas by seeking to weaken the liberal-leftist coalition in the UDN.[7]

Joaquim Franco Garcia's description of the UDN as a liberal-leftist coalition could not hide the UDN's predominantly liberal character, and it was this character that upset the leftists. While the liberals of the Frente de Resistência, such as Arrobas Martins, Roberto de Abreu Sodré, and José Bonifácio Coutinho Nogueira, worked for the UDN[8] (Arrobas becoming a director of its state organization), Paulo Emílio organized a radical leftist São Paulo political group with Frente de Resistência leftists, such as Germinal Feijó and Antônio Costa Corrêa. This new group, the União Democrática Socialista (UDS), issued a manifesto drawn up by Paulo Emílio with assistance from Antônio Costa Corrêa, Paulo Zingg, Cory Porto Fernandes, and Antônio Cândido de Mello e Souza.[9] In many ways its program resembled that drawn up by the Frente de Resistência on April 7, but it was more forceful in calling for a socialist regime in Brazil and "democracy without classes." In discussing the contest between Dutra and Gomes, the UDS manifesto said that the Dutra candidacy attracted the most reactionary forces, whereas the Gomes candidacy, although supported by some representatives of the old conservative parties, attracted forces able to guarantee a constitutional assembly.

The manifesto was signed by Antônio Cândido de Mello e Souza, Antônio Costa Corrêa, Benedito Barbosa, Celso Galvão, Carlos Engel, Eliza Romero, Germinal Feijó, Israel Dias Novaes, Jacinto Carvalho Leal, Luís Lobato, Paulo Emílio Sales Gomes, Paulo Zingg, Renato Amaral Sampaio Coelho, and Rômulo Fonseca ("Professor Picard").[10] The UDS attracted a few Paulista leftists, such as Arnaldo Pedroso d'Horta and Febus Gikovate, a former Trotskyite.[11] But it remained infinitessimal compared with the UDN and the two national parties established by Vargas supporters. One, the Partido Social Democrático (PSD), was launched by *interventores*, such as Fernando Costa, who supported the Dutra candidacy. The second, the Partido Trabalhista Brasileiro (PTB—Brazilian Labor Party), was founded by Marcondes Filho and others associated with the Ministry of Labor. It named Vargas honorary president and remained for a while, like the Communist Party (PCB), without a presidential candidate.

In July, the UDS, to the left of the PCB, issued an internal bulletin to point out that the Communist line in Brazil and elsewhere, unmindful of the needs of the proletariat and based exclusively on Soviet foreign policy, required the proletariat to renounce the class struggle and adopt a policy of "national union" and domestic "pacification." The UDS added that the PCB policy was a negation of Marxism and would neither promote the socialist movement nor bring about the emancipation of the workers.[12]

4. The *Arcadas* and the National Election (late 1945)

Geraldo Vidigal, the first São Paulo law student to return from Italy, reached Brazil in time to attend the eighth Conselho Nacional de Estudantes, which met in Rio late in July 1945. He found that the expected winner[1] of the UNE presidential contest was another FEB veteran, Augusto Vilas-Boas,[2] a leftist supported by the Communists and Queremistas (pro-Vargas demonstrators associated with the Labor and Communist parties). However, the work of José Bonifácio Coutinho Nogueira was decisive in winning the UNE presidency for Ernesto Bagdócimo, a supporter of Eduardo Gomes.[3] Vidigal, whose publications and FEB experience brought him considerable influence, played a role in the outcome by giving a speech in favor of Bagdócimo.[4]

The UDN, thus successful in the UNE contest, was suffering from dissentions, and therefore the number of political parties (supposedly "national" in accordance with the new electoral legislation) grew. Gaúchos resurrected the Partido Libertador (PL), and Mineiros associated with Artur Bernardes founded the national Partido Republicano (PR). Haroldo Bueno Magano joined the PR because he was not on good terms with Arrobas Martins and his group, active in the UDN.[5]

In August the leftists in the UDN, such as João Mangabeira, Hermes Lima, and Eliezer Magalhães, established a new party, the Esquerda Democrática (ED—Democratic Left). The ED, with its many well-known figures—such as Miguel Costa, its leader in São Paulo—proved more attractive than the tiny, local, more radical UDS, and therefore the UDS went out of existence; its members joined the ED and so did a good many São Paulo law students.[6] In September Ademar de Barros left the UDN and played a leading role in founding the Partido Republicano Progressista, which, like the UDN, PR, PL, and ED, supported Eduardo Gomes in his race against Dutra. Ademar's new party was small—almost as small as the Partido Popular Sindicalista, the *parlamentarista* party founded at about the same time by Miguel Reale and 56-year-old José Adriano Marrey Júnior, who had been named by Vargas to the São Paulo Departamento Administrativo in 1941 and then served, from November 1943 to June 1945, as Fernando Costa's justice secretary.[7]

At the *arcadas* approximately 85 percent of the students favored Gomes, and all four student parties battling for Centro posts came out for the *brigadeiro.* Centro President Ruy Nazareth named a thirty-member Diretório Acadêmico pró-Eduardo Gomes, which included João Nery Guimarães, José Bonifácio Coutinho Nogueira, Luís Francisco Carvalho, fourth-year student Vicente Marotta Rangel, third-year student Milton Lopes de Oliveira, second-year student Heitor Mayer, and two who had been wounded in November 1943: Luís Afonso Cardoso de Melo de Alvares Otero and João Brasil Vita (a member of the PR).[8]

When the *diretório* met to choose three delegates to the first state convention of the UDN, it decided on João Nery Guimarães (who received the most votes), Heitor Mayer, and Milton Lopes de Oliveira. João Nery Guimarães, author of the pro-Gomes "O Aeronauta da Esperança" in *A Balança,* became head of the UDN work at the *arcadas.*[9] The fear that the national presidential election of December might be canceled, as in 1937, led him to reach an agreement with José Antônio Rogê Ferreira ("Toni"), head of the pro-Dutra PSD Diretório da Faculdade de Direito. Football enthusiast Rogê Ferreira, with two pro-Dutra uncles (one was José Carlos de Macedo Soares),[10] agreed with João Nery Guimarães that the rival groups should concentrate, not on attacking each other but on doing everything possible to make the national presidential election a reality in the face of the calls by Queremistas and the Communist Party leadership that Vargas remain in office.[11]

Fears of a cancellation of the presidential election were dispelled after the military, keen on the election, overthrew Vargas on October 29. The change brought Supreme Court Presiding Justice José Linhares to the interim presidency of Brazil and Professor Sampaio Dória to the post of federal justice minister. In São Paulo, José Carlos de Macedo Soares became *interventor,* 77-year-old Professor Emeritus Francisco Morato became justice secretary, and Professor Antônio de Almeida Júnior became secretary of education and public health. All these men, including Linhares, were members of the Bucha, which appeared to have regained influence,[12] especially with its top man, Macedo Soares, in the interventorship. The *arcadas'* pro-Dutra leader, "Toni" Rogê Ferreira, was given a position in the office of his uncle, the new *interventor,* and it allowed him to provide assistance to law students who returned from the FEB with financial and other problems.[13]

When Luís Carlos Prestes, after his release from prison, had addressed the Paulistas, the Pacaembu Stadium had been packed, as it had been when Vargas was there in May 1944. But little popular interest was shown when presidential aspirant Dutra spoke in the stadium, and the admirers of Eduardo Gomes had to concede that the *brigadeiro's* appearance there, after the overthrow of Vargas, was a disaster. Not only were vast sectors of the stadium empty but also the invitations had been issued so as to place the elite in the best, shady seats, thus lending credence to rumors, spread by the *brigadeiro's* foes, that the UDN candidate had expressed a lack of interest in the votes of laborers.[14] Facing this disappointing audience, law student Luís Francisco Carvalho greeted Eduardo Gomes with a speech that repeated a refrain of the Frente de Resistência about a democracy based on "the vitality of the middle class, industrial proletariat, and great rural masses."[15]

Before the national elections of December 2, Centro President Nazareth issued a reply to what he called "publications of the propaganda agents of General Dutra." Nazareth declared that the Centro, "in accordance with its tradition and the decision of the majority of the students at a general assembly, intransigently backs the candidacy of Brigadeiro Eduardo Gomes." A few days later, on the eve of the elections, some young women organized the pro-Dutra Diretório Feminino de PSD da Faculdade de Direito de São Paulo, "the only women's political *diretório* at the college."[16]

By this time Vargas, in retirement in Rio Grande do Sul, had given a late lift to the faltering Dutra campaign by placing the PTB on Dutra's side. Therefore, José Barbosa and José Gomes Talarico, early workers for the PTB, could support Dutra with the blessing of the former president. Dutra also had the backing of Plínio Salgado's Partido de Representação Popular, which was sponsoring the congressional race of law school *livre-docente* Gofredo da Silva Telles Júnior (Gofredinho).[17]

Working for Dutra in the PSD were banker Gastão Vidigal, former Partido Acadêmico Conservador leader Ulisses Guimarães, and Centro Onze de Agosto founder César Lacerda de Vergueiro.[18] Gastão Vidigal, like Horácio Lafer, became a PSD candidate for federal congressman. César Lacerda de Vergueiro entered the race as a PSD candidate for the federal senate and found himself opposing ten others, including Getúlio Vargas (PTB), Marcondes Filho (PTB), Luís Carlos Prestes (PCB), Professor Ernesto Leme (UDN), and Francisco de Paula Rodrigues Alves (UDN). Lax residence requirements allowed the name of Vargas to be presented by the PTB in the senatorial and congressional races in many states. In a similar way, the PCB used the name of Luís Carlos Prestes, who was traveling around Brazil delivering speeches on behalf of the PCB presidential candidate Iedo Fiuza, a non-Communist engineer.

Law school professors and graduates were well represented in the multitude of Paulistas running for places in the federal Chamber of Deputies. Among them the only recent graduate notable in the *resistência* work was Germinal Feijó, one of the three ED candidates who ran concurrently on the UDN and PR tickets. This arrangement allowed the PSD to describe the UDN as running "three Communists, of the Esquerda Democrática, more Marxist than Luís Carlos Prestes." Besides Feijó, they were Eliezer Magalhães, active in the Aliança Nacional Libertadora in 1935, and labor leader João da Costa Pimenta, a former Communist who had helped found the PCB in 1922. The Dutra supporters called Feijó "the perpetual student and well-known Communist."[19]

Among the UDN-PR congressional candidates, unconnected with the ED, were professor Mário Masagão, Francisco Oscar Penteado Stevenson (law school *livre-docente*), Luís Antônio da Gama e Silva (law school *livre-docente*), Paulo Nogueira Filho, Altino Arantes, Antônio Pereira Lima, Plínio Barreto, Luís de Toledo Piza Sobrinho, Aureliano Leite, Carlota Pereira de Queiroz, and Herbert Levy. Levy's father-in-law, Waldemar Ferreira, was president of the UDN state directorship.

On the list of the PDC (Partido Democrata Cristão) were law Professors Antônio Cesarino Júnior and Alvino Ferreira Lima. The PSD list included law Professors José Joaquim Cardoso de Melo Neto, José Carlos de Ataliba Nogueira, and Honório Fernandes Monteiro, as well as *livre-docente* Gofredo da Silva Telles Júnior (put up by the Partido de Representação Popular). Second-year law student Eusébio Rocha Filho, a Vargas supporter, entered the congressional race on the PTB ticket.[20]

5. Elections at the *Arcadas* (November 1945)

Naldo Caparica, having served in Italy, was back at the *arcadas* in August 1945 to complete his last year. His FEB role made it certain that he would be a popular candidate for the Centro presidency. He had been a member of the Partido Libertador *comissão diretora*, but the leftist ideas with which he returned from Italy meant that there was little accord between him and a majority of the Libertador leaders. In any event, the Left wing of the party, led by Centro President Ruy Nazareth[1] and some who had abandoned the Libertador directorship in 1944, was eager to establish a new party, the Movimento Acadêmico Renovador.

The creation of the new party was in part the work of Aloysio Ferraz Pereira, who had been president of the Partido Conservador and was its 1944 candidate for the Centro presidency. Aloysio Ferraz Pereira, attracted to the progressive wing of the Catholic Church, became the theoretician of the Movimento Acadêmico Renovador.[2] To the satisfaction of Fernando Jacob, friend of Nazareth and Caparica, the Renovadores launched the presidential candidacy of Caparica, "the former prisoner of the political police of Coriolano de Góis and brave soldier of the frozen Apennines."[3] Aloysio, who was repeating a year due to illness, became president of the new party. Among the other members of the twenty-person provisional *comissão diretora* were one young woman; three former Libertador directors; Domenico Martirani, who had been elected Centro treasurer on the Conservador slate in 1942; and Waldir Troncoso Peres, who was the Centro first orator, having been elected on the Libertador slate headed by Nazareth and who now ran for reelection as a Renovador. The Renovadores favored "a new process of electoral contest, in which debate about the problems that most disturb our times . . . replaces the method of simple academic Bohemianism of lining up votes with beer and theatrical performances."[4]

The position taken by Aloysio Ferraz Pereira brought about the death of the once powerful Partido Acadêmico Conservador.[5] Its *comissão diretora*, meeting on the night of August 23, decided to cooperate with another new party, the União Democrática Acadêmica which attracted some remnants of the liberal oligarchy (the old PRP and PD)[6] and which would offer an election slate made up in part of former Conservadores. But the withdrawal of the Conservador name from the contest drew a stiff rebuke from João Brasil Vita and five other members of the disbanding Conservador *comissão diretora*. In a printed message, these six denounced their colleagues: "On your heads will fall the tears and sweat of those who constructed, with sacrifices, the magnificent castle in which we dwelled for so long. . . . Tomorrow . . . those who were betrayed . . . will say, 'You were unworthy of our confidence.'"[7]

The new União Democrática Acadêmica rejected renovation by those who proposed experimenting with "new, imported political-social formulas" and expressed its opposition to "those who would renovate but do not first renovate themselves, and those who speak of democracy and liberty but who are, themselves, the very incarnation of arbitrariness and violence."[8] It nominated candidates for six of the ten Centro officerships, among them Haroldo Santos Abreu for president and Vicente Marotta Rangel for first orator. Rangel, instructor of the history of philosophy for prelaw students, was the member of the Diretório Acadêmico pró-Eduardo Gomes who delivered the oration at the local CPOR graduation exercises, for which Eduardo Gomes was chosen *paraninfo*.[9]

The Movimento Acadêmico Renovador and the less powerful União Democrática Acadêmica were not the only new parties. Leaders of the two-year-old Frente Acadêmica pela Democracia (among them Rui Pereira de Queiroz, back from Italy; Luís Francisco Carvalho; and Renato Amaral Sampaio Coelho) founded the Movimento Democrático Acadêmico, but they regarded the step as simply a change in the name of their party. Pointing out in their manifesto that they had participated in all the anti–Estado Novo struggles, they nominated Marcello Vidigal for the Centro presidency. Their party was weak and offered candidates for only five of the ten Centro officerships.

The Partido Acadêmico Libertador was the only party to present itself with a name used in past elections, and its leaders carried forward the program of "popularizing the party" by giving attention to the majority of students who earned a living and had devoted little time to the national political activities for which the law school was famous. Lincoln Sooma, whose parents were Japanese and who had previously shied away from student politics, gained a place on the Libertador *comissão diretora* during a party election held in August to fill vacancies.[10] Each Libertador party worker was assigned two students to turn into Libertador voters in the November Centro election.[11]

As its presidential candidate, the Partido Acadêmico Libertador selected Sílvio de Campos Melo Filho, the track star who had been taken, covered with blood, to the Santa Casa de Misericórdia on November 9, 1943. Vice-presidential candidate Salim Belfort, who spoke poorly of no one and was loyal to the Libertadores and his friends, was considered a second Cherkaski ("Menino de Ouro"). He and Sílvio de Campos Melo Filho had been among approximately twenty students who, together with Roberto Victor Cordeiro, had attended a dinner given at the Jóquei Clube de São Paulo to welcome Paulo Nogueira Filho on his return from exile. The antileftist Libertadores had been disappointed in the *progressista* position advanced that evening by Nogueira Filho, an able politician. To them it seemed excessively *progressista*.[12]

All four *partidos acadêmicos*, presenting programs for the nation, stressed the need to improve the lot of the *povo* (the common people). The thirty-five founders of the Movimento Democrático

Acadêmico (of whom two were young women) wrote that "our re-approximation with the *povo*, the true *povo* of the agricultural fields, the streets, and factories, is of transcendent importance; after our eight years of forced silence, it is natural that the proletariat believes that the law students are a part of the machine of the oppressive forces."[13]

The Renovadores, whose candidate Caparica was praised in the Communist press, offered the mildest program and warned against "extremist ideas." The other parties stressed the danger of economic power. The Libertadores, labeled "conservative" by the Communists, expressed respect for private property but called for the state to intervene to prevent the exploitation of man by man.[14] The União Democrática Acadêmica, new home of some of the Conservadores and labeled "rightist" by the Communists, presented the least conservative program. It praised the Communists for having taught (*a*) that economic liberalism left the working class destitute in the face of unbridled capitalism and (*b*) that capitalism had transformed itself into a world system in which strong, rich nations strangulated the weak, poor ones and dragged them into wars. Proclaiming that the end of the era of capitalism and economic liberalism was at hand, the União Democrática Acadêmica said that everyone had the right and duty to work, that the participation of the *povo* in the government should be concrete, and that the state was required to solve the social question.[15]

Caparica was the overwhelming favorite to win the Centro presidency. However, toward the end of the campaign, Libertadores at a Centro *assembléia* asked him if he believed in God or was a materialist.[16] Courageously, he made his leftist position clear, but in doing so he lost some support; Catholics, in particular, opposed him.[17] The balloting gave the Centro presidency to Libertador Sílvio de Campos Melo Filho.

The Libertadores won seven of the ten officerships, with the Renovadores (Caparica's party) winning the first secretaryship and *bibliotecário*, and the União Democrática Acadêmica winning the post of first orator (Vicente Marotta Rangel).

XII

Epilogue: The Post–Estado Novo Failure

1. The National Elections of 1945

With the return of Brazil to electoral democracy, veterans of the São Paulo Law School *resistência* worked for the renovation of the nation in accordance with ideas expressed at the *arcadas*, and for the defeat of Getulismo at the polls. The attention given to the *povo* in law student manifestos was inspired by both these objectives. The *resistência* enthusiasts reasoned that Vargas, maintained in power by the apparatus of a police state, had no great popular support, and this belief appeared to be confirmed by the press once it was freed of censorship. They reflected that the Estado Novo, at its zenith, had been far harsher on subversive labor leaders than on subversive students,[1] and they were convinced that pro-Vargas strongmen in officially recognized labor unions, products of Brazilian fascism, were not true representatives of their class. Workers, it was hoped, would welcome and share the *resistência*'s vision of a bright new Brazil built by a forward-looking middle class, students, and the proletariat.

The anti-Vargas forces, expecting a victory at the polls on December 2, 1945, were stunned when the returns brought defeat to Eduardo Gomes and revealed that Vargas had enormous support among the workers. José Bonifácio Coutinho Nogueira, writing in 1960 about the setback of December 1945, explained that "the first elections, characterized by demagoguery and fraudulently affected by a hasty registration, proved disappointing. The people . . . revealed that they were not prepared to use the right to vote. . . . It was as difficult for them to sign the sheets of the electoral justice system and place the ballots in the envelopes as to distinguish authentic statesmen from ordinary demagogues."[2]

The December defeat of the anti-Vargas political parties was particularly stinging in the state of São Paulo, the home of many industrial workers. There Eduardo Gomes received 377,613 votes, compared with 780,546 for Dutra (PSD-PTB), and 192,867 for Iedo Fiuza (PCB–Communist Party of Brazil). The São Paulo race for two federal senate seats was a triumph for Labor Party (PTB) candidates Marcondes Filho and Vargas, whose nine defeated rivals included Luís Carlos Prestes, in third place, and Professor Ernesto Leme, in fifth place. In the races for congressmen from São Paulo, the UDN's 285,962 votes compared with a PSD-PTB total of 717,114 (479,414 for the PSD and 237,700 for the PTB); the PCB received 189,422 votes. The results gave the PSD sixteen Paulista congressmen, the UDN seven, the PTB six, and the PCB four. The Partido Democrata Cristão (PDC) and Ademar de Barros' short-lived Partido Republicano Progressista were each awarded one seat from São Paulo.[3]

Four São Paulo Law School faculty members reached the federal Chamber of Deputies, which met with the Senate in February 1946 to work on a new constitution. Three of them won their seats on the PSD ticket (José Carlos de Ataliba Nogueira, Honório Fernandes Monteiro, and Gofredo da Silva Telles Júnior). The fourth, Mário Masagão, was far and away the UDN's leading vote getter. His six fellow *udenistas* in the *bancada paulista* were Paulo Nogueira Filho, Plínio Barreto, Aureliano Leite, Romeu de Andrade Lourenção, Altino Arantes, and Luís de Toledo Piza Sobrinho.

Vargas, who received about as many votes for congressman from São Paulo as all the other PTB candidates combined, declined the seat to which he was elected from São Paulo (becoming, instead, senator from Rio Grande do Sul). His congressional seat from São Paulo went to the PTB's first runner-up, law student Eusébio Rocha Filho.[4]

2. The Anti-Getulistas' Alliance with Quadros (1960–1961)

Less than a week after the 1945 election, *O Estado de S. Paulo* was returned to Júlio de Mesquita Filho and Francisco Mesquita. Two new reporters, Afrânio de Oliveira and Júlio de Mesquita Neto, were added to the staff of the daily,[1] which, under the Mesquitas, battled furiously in the years ahead against Vargas and his supporters.

The battle by UDN leader Antônio Carlos de Abreu Sodré was cut short by his death in November 1946. But it was carried on by other *udenistas* in São Paulo, such as Roberto de Abreu Sodré, who achieved the São Paulo governorship in 1966, and Luís Arrobas Martins. (Arrobas Martins and Luís Francisco da Silva Carvalho served in the cabinet of Abreu Sodré.)

Paulo Nogueira Filho, after his election to Congress on the UDN ticket, broke with Waldemar Ferreira and Júlio de Mesquita Filho and founded Ação Popular Renovadora. This new party soon became a part of another new party, the Partido Social Progressista (PSP), a fusion of the Partido Republicano Progressista (of Ademar de Barros), the Partido Popular Sindicalista (of Miguel Reale and Marrey Júnior), and the Partido Agrário Nacional.[2] Top officers of the PSP were Ademar de Barros (president), Miguel Reale (vice-president), and Nogueira Filho (secretary general). Renato Macedo and Jarbas Teixeira de Carvalho accompanied Nogueira Filho when he allied himself with Ademar de Barros, but many others who had been close to Nogueira Filho, such as Roberto Victor Cordeiro, refused to do so.[3] No friend of *O Estado de S. Paulo,* Ademar was elected governor in January 1947 with Communist help.

The anti-Getulistas, suffering their "glorious defeats," witnessed the return of Vargas to the Brazilian presidency "on the arms of the people" (and with the backing of Ademar and the PSP) in the elections of 1950. They witnessed also the popular support for Getulismo occasioned by the farewell message of the former dictator, made public after his suicide in August 1954.

Jânio Quadros, known at the *arcadas* for his poetry, became Brazil's most spectacular vote getter. Following his elections as PDC candidate for alderman in 1947 and state legislator in 1950, he won a landslide victory to the São Paulo mayorship in 1953 on the tickets of two small parties: the PDC and the PSB (Brazilian Socialist Party, successor of the Esquerda Democrática).

In 1954, after breaking with André Franco Montoro of the PDC, Quadros ran for the governorship with the support of the PSB, the PTN (Partido Trabalhista Nacional), and a wing of the PTB.[4] He was opposed by gubernatorial candidate Ademar de Barros, whose PSP had become the best organized party in the state, and by the governorship of Lucas Garcez, in which PSD leaders César Lacerda de Vergueiro, Antônio Sylvio Cunha Bueno, and Ulisses Guimarães were influential.[5] To oppose Jânio and Ademar, the state government launched a ticket that presented Francisco Prestes Maia for governor and Cunha Bueno for vice-governor. Their party support came from the PSD, PDC, PR, and UDN (headed in São Paulo by medical law Professor Antônio de Almeida Júnior).

The contest was another "glorious defeat" for the UDN and *O Estado de S. Paulo* because in October 1954 Quadros won a handsome victory over Prestes Maia and a narrow one over Ademar de Barros. Some analysts blamed Prestes Maia's poor showing on his connection with the UDN, said to have been partly responsible for driving Vargas to suicide in August.[6] *O Estado de S. Paulo,* lamenting the "low level" of the campaigns of Ademar and Jânio, could only conclude that "the electorate has not yet learned to distinguish between good and bad." It wrote that "an electorate with its head in place would not have hesitated a single minute in selecting Prestes Maia."[7]

In Quadros' political ascendancy prominent roles were played by some of the law students of the Estado Novo years.[8] Among his early supporters were Jair Carvalho Monteiro, Paulo Henrique Meinberg, Wilson Rahal, Gabriel Cury, Hiram Mayr Cerqueira, and federal Congressmen (or future Congressmen) Afrânio de Oliveira (who gave the popular young politician favorable press coverage), Germinal Feijó, Cory Porto Fernandes, José Antônio Rogê Ferreira, and Luís Francisco da Silva Carvalho. Another was Francisco Morato de Oliveira, who began his distinguished presidency of the Instituto de Previdência do Estado de São Paulo when Quadros was governor and who was elected federal congressman in 1962 but died before he could assume his mandate. Still others were Lenício Pacheco Ferreira, Renato Sampaio Coelho, and federal Congressman Israel Dias Novaes. Federal Congressman Auro de Moura Andrade was in Quadros' campaign for governor and was elected federal senator in the same race. Francisco de Paula Quintanilha Ribeiro joined Governor Quadros as his office chief.

Quadros, a PTB congressman in 1959, was nominated for the Brazilian presidency by the PL, PDC, PTN, and UDN, which was attracted to his gubernatorial record and ability to win votes. On October 3, 1960, he easily defeated presidential aspirants Ademar de Barros and Henrique Lott. Although Quadros, in his campaigning, revealed his independence of the UDN and called Vargas "a great patriot,"[9] and although the vice-presidency was won by a Getulista, the victory of Quadros persuaded the opponents of Getulismo that their long battle had at last been won. *O Estado de S. Paulo* declared that "the victory of Democracy has turned into a defeat of unprecedented proportions for the remains of Getulismo. These remains . . . have just been repudiated by the majority of those who, from 1945 until now, still believed in the sincerity of people who were presenting themselves in electoral contests as legitimate champions of the proletarian cause. Brazilian labor has ended up by learning its lesson. . . . The people's late but real discovery of the truth is the best reward we could have received."[10]

São Paulo Secretary of Agriculture José Bonifácio Coutinho Nogueira (who had been elected UNE president in 1946) wrote in *O Globo* in October 1960 that "we see, above all, in Quadros' campaign and victory, the triumph of the renovating message for which our generation has struggled since school days. . . . For 20 years, with their eyes and thoughts directed to the future of the Nation, a small group struggled uninterruptedly to make October 3, 1960, possible. Our mission has been accomplished."[11]

But the mission had been accomplished by an alliance with an independent politician who relied less on the "small group" than on his large personal following. An authentic member of the group would not have irresponsibly resigned the presidency after seven months in office, threatening the nation with disaster. After Quadros' resignation was accepted by Senator Auro de Moura Andrade (PSD), who was presiding over Congress, "the remains of Getulismo" recovered their traditional control of the country's executive branch.

3. The Anti-Getulistas' Alliance with the Military (1964)

A new alliance of the longtime anti-Getulistas, this one with military figures, gave promise of reversing the setback occasioned by Quadros' resignation. In 1964 the army, with considerable middle-class support, stepped in to end the exercise of federal power by those who claimed to have inherited the mantle of Vargas. *O Estado de S. Paulo* hailed the victory of "liberal democracy" over the tradition of "populism and fascism" established by Vargas and carried on by his successors. Roberto de Abreu Sodré, Herbert Levy, and the MMDC veterans described the military coup as inspired by respect for democracy and the constitution. A manifesto of "the São Paulo Law School professors and *livres-docentes*" expressed "elation for the restoration of the democratic order of the Nation." Among its signers were Law School Director Luís Eulálio de Bueno Vidigal, Ernesto Leme, Miguel Reale, Mário Masagão, Teotônio Monteiro de Barros Filho, José Carlos de Ataliba Nogueira, Noé Azevedo, and Honório Fernandes Monteiro.[1]

But the military, after taking control of Brazilian politics, hardly promoted the aims of the *resistência* students who, between 1938 and 1945, had denounced police repression and demanded democracy and freedom of expression. With the promulgation of Institutional Act Number Five in 1968, the military instituted a regime that was at least as repressive as the Estado Novo and lasted for a longer time.

Thus, during most of the post-1945 period, the anti-Getulista *bacharéis* (university graduates) lived under a regime that they described as Getulista or else under one that denied the political and individual rights for which they had struggled as students. And, during this thirty-five–year interval, not a few of these former students concluded that Vargas, as head of state, was not as bad as they had believed him to be when they resisted his dictatorship. While not condoning the repression practiced by the police during the Estado Novo, this segment of former *resistência* law students came to find reasons for approving Vargas' philosophy of governing, which, they say today, gave satisfaction, simultaneously and in an adroit manner, to the working classes and to heavy industry.[2] Some of those who have been associated with the Left have concluded critically that "we students, motivated in part by romanticism and in part by ignorance, were opposed by the working classes and a majority of the people."[3] They have faulted the student movement for having aims that were not "wide enough."

Another segment—a large one that includes men who worked for the UDN—remains faithful to arguments used against Vargas during student days. Its members maintain that any accomplishments or social reforms initiated during the Estado Novo were the result of "pragmatism"[4] or "impositions of the times,"[5] and that Vargas was a "typical *caudilho*," fundamentally opposed to democracy and "men of the law." João Nery Guimarães writes that "the legendary figure of the Gaúcho soldier, with his red neckerchief, hitching his horse in the federal senate in Rio in 1930, provides a good idea of Vargas."[6]

João Nery Guimarães, who helped build the Partido Acadêmico Libertador into a popular anti–Estado Novo party, did not have the problem that led Arrobas Martins to write in 1944 about the more activist and restricted group: "We never had the knack of winning voters. . . . We always revealed ourselves better at criticizing than pleasing. We formed a group of splendid friends and very bad *cabos eleitorais*."[7]

The problems of anti-Vargas liberal *bacharéis*, after the fall of the Estado Novo, resembled those experienced earlier at the *arcadas* by the group to which Arrobas belonged. Struggling for noble ideals, the bearers of the "renovating message" were quick to denounce dishonesty in government and trends that they considered undemocratic or demagogic. They hoped to make their campaign attractive to a wide audience, including the workers. But the UDN, to which many of the *bacharéis* belonged, had to contend, among other things, with the charge of being elitist.[8]

Arrobas in 1944 revealed skepticism about alliances and urged the exclusion from "our group" of all who were not perfectly identified with it.[9] It was inevitable, however, that the anti-Vargas liberal *bacharéis*, having found in the 1950s that their earnest message could not compete with populism, would enter into alliances, particularly when they believed that they had found outsiders who took their message seriously. The alliances, which in 1960 and 1964 seemed at long last to bring victory on a national level, proved disappointing to those who dreamed of burying Getulismo while giving life to the democratic ideals that had inspired their movement of *resistência* against the Estado Novo.

Notes

Introduction

1. Luís Arrobas Martins, "Os trinta anos do 9 de novembro," 1973 (2 pages, typewritten).

2. Ibid.

3. Naldo Caparica, letter to Ruy Nazareth, Italy, December 11, 1944, published in *Correio Paulistano*, January 23, 1945.

4. José Bonifácio Coutinho Nogueira, "Redenção Política do Brasil," *O Globo*, October 9, 1960.

I. Pre-1930 Résumé (1827–1930)

1. The First Days (1827–1831)

1. Spencer Vampré, *Memórias para a História da Academia de São Paulo*, 2d ed. (São Paulo: Instituto Nacional do Livro com a colaboração do Conselho Federal de Cultura, Ministério da Educação e Cultura, 1977), I, 13–14; Ricardo Severo, "A Casa da Faculdade de Direito de S. Paulo—1643–1937," *A Balança* (Faculdade de Direito) 7, no. 26 (January 1945); Humberto de Campos Filho, *Convento de São Francisco* (São Paulo: Convento de São Francisco, 1975), pp. 1–8. The drastic remodeling of 1934 is discussed in *A Gazeta* (São Paulo), August 11, 1954.

2. Vampré, *Memórias*, I, 14–29; Brasil Bandecchi, *A Bucha, a Maçonaria e o Espírito Liberal*, 3d ed. (São Paulo: Editora Parma Ltda., 1982), p. 63; Waldemar Ferreira, "A Faculdade de Direito na Arrancada de 9 de Julho de 1932" (lecture given in June 1957 at the Instituto Histórico e Geográfia de São Paulo, copy in the possession of Pedro Brasil Bandecchi).

3. Vampré, *Memórias*, I, 14–31.

4. Afonso Schmidt, *A Sombra de Júlio Frank* (São Paulo: Editora Clube do Livro Ltda., 1950), p. 168; Waldemar Ferreira, *A Congregação da Faculdade de Direito de S. Paulo na Centúria de 1827 a 1927* (São Paulo: Revista da Faculdade de Direito de S. Paulo, [1936?]), pp. 33–34; Vampré, *Memórias*, I, 63.

5. Vampré, *Memórias*, I, 63–71. Baiano: pertaining to Bahia.

6. Ibid., I, 39–42; Severo, "A Casa da Faculdade de Direito de S. Paulo—1643–1937"; Almeida Nogueira, *A Academia de São Paulo: Tradições e Reminiscências*, 3d ed. (São Paulo: Saraiva S.A., 1977), I, 41; Otto Cyrillo

Lehmann, *XI de Agosto: Abertura das festividades comemorativas de Sesquicentenário da Fundação dos Cursos Jurídicos no Brasil* (speech in the Brazilian Senate, August 11, 1976, published as a booklet).

7. Almeida Nogueira, *A Academia de São Paulo*, I, 228; A. Almeida Júnior, *Sob as Arcadas* (Rio de Janeiro: Centro Brasileiro de Pesquisas Educacionais, Instituto Nacional de Estudos Pedagógicos, Ministério da Educação e Cultura, 1965), p. 13.

8. Almeida Júnior, *Sob as Arcadas*, pp. 15–16, quoting José Vieira Couto de Magalhães.

9. Ibid., p. 10. Vampré, *Memórias*, II, 225.

10. Almeida Júnior, *Sob as Arcadas*, p. 11; Paulo Duarte, *Agora Nós! Chronica da Revolução Paulista, com os perfis de alguns heroes da retaguarda* (São Paulo: J. Fonseca, 1927), pp. 282–283; Glauco Carneiro, "A Bucha: Um poder secreto que mudou a História," *Manchete*, May 2, 1981, see p. 115; *Folha da Manhã* (São Paulo), August 12, 1930. "O Território Livre do Largo de S. Francisco," Arcadas, May 1942 (mimeographed Peruada paper).

11. Schmidt, *A Sombra de Júlio Frank*, p. 153.

12. Ibid., pp. 155–158, 168; Vampré, *Memórias*, I, 64–65.

13. Antônio de Toledo Piza, "Recordações históricas," *Correio Paulistano*, September 2, 1905, quoted in Almeida Nogueira, *A Academia de São Paulo*, I, 87–88.

14. Ibid., I, 85–88, 156–164; João Pandiá Calogeras, *A History of Brazil* (Chapel Hill: University of North Carolina Press, 1939), pp. 115–116.

2. The Bucha (founded in 1831)

1. Vampré, *Memórias*, I, 63; Schmidt, *A Sombra de Júlio Frank*, p. 152.

2. Bandecchi, *A Bucha*, pp. 81–82, 135–136; Gustavo Barroso, *História Secreta do Brasil* (Rio de Janeiro: Civilização Brasileira, 1937; copyright 1937, by Agência Minerva), II, 36–65; Schmidt, *A Sombra de Júlio Frank*, pp. 117–119. Barroso's contention that Frank was really Carlos Luiz Sand, assassin of Augusto Frederico Fernando de Kotzebue in Mannheim, Germany, in 1819, is refuted by Bandecchi. Schmidt, Barroso, and Afonso Arinos de Melo Franco, *Rodrigues Alves* (Rio de Janeiro: Livraria José Olympio Editora and Editora da Universidade de São Paulo, 1973), I, 24–28, contains passages about Frank's life.

3. Schmidt, *A Sombra de Júlio Frank*, p. 146. Curral dos Bichos: corral of animals.

4. Ibid., pp. 131–132, 137. Bandecchi, *A Bucha*, p. 84, gives the Bucha's founding date.

5. Schmidt, *A Sombra de Júlio Frank*, p. 171.

6. Bandecchi, interviews, São Paulo, July 2, 1981, August 9, 1982. Ernesto Leme (interview, São Paulo, August 8, 1982) said that the military wanted to investigate the Bucha and harm the tomb of Júlio Frank. Bandecchi said that soldiers of the 1930 revolution wanted to "destroy the old order."

7. Bandecchi, *A Bucha*, pp. 87, 88, 85, 86, and 82 (n. 45 quoting Ernesto Leme); Melo Franco, *Rodrigues Alves*, I, 29 (n. 20).

8. João Nery Guimarães, interview, São Paulo, August 21, 1982; Barrosa, *História Secreta*, II, 80.

9. Barrosa, *História Secreta*, II, 80; Bandecchi, *A Bucha*, p. 85; Melo Franco, *Rodrigues Alves*, I, 26 (n. 14). For founding of colleges, see Joseph L. Love, *São Paulo in the Brazilian Federation, 1889–1937* (Stanford: Stanford University Press, 1980), pp. 93–94.

10. Carlos Lacerda, *Depoimento* (Rio de Janeiro: Editora Nova Fronteira, 1977), pp. 89, 87.

3. Abolition and the Republic (1888–1889)

1. Antônio Gontijo de Carvalho, *Rui, Estudante* (Rio de Janeiro: Casa de Rui Barbosa, 1949), pp. 9–19; Vampré, *Memórias*, II, 151, 183, 26; Pedro Ferraz do Amaral, *No Sesquicentenário de José Bonifácio, o Moço* (speech of October 4, 1977, published in *Revista da Academia Paulista de Letras*, no. 93); Ferreira, *A Congregação da Faculdade de Direito de S. Paulo*, pp. 56–57.

2. Carvalho, *Rui, Estudante*, pp. 13–35; Melo Franco, *Rodrigues Alves*, pp. 19–24; Luiz Viana Filho, *A Vida de Rui Barbosa*, 7th ed. (São Paulo: Livraria Martins Editora, 1965), pp. 26–27.

3. Almeida Júnior, *Sob as Arcadas*, p. 25; Vampré, *Memórias*, II, 238–239, 243, 309–310, 317. Duílio Crispim Farina mentioned (interview, São Paulo, August 7, 1982) that Júlio Mesquita belonged to the Bucha.

4. Almeida Júnior, *Sob as Arcadas*, pp. 24–25 (with quotation of Afonso de Carvalho); Love, *São Paulo in the Brazilian Federation*, pp. 107–108.

5. Vampré, *Memórias*, II, 334–335, 333, 231; *O Estado de S. Paulo*, centenary booklet, 1976 [no title], p. 10.

6. Melo Franco, *Rodrigues Alves*, I, 30.

4. The Centro Onze de Agosto (founded in 1903)

1. Flávio de Almeida Prado Galvão, "Observações," August 1982 (typewritten for JWFD), p. 1; Almeida Júnior, *Sob as Arcadas*, pp. 23–24.

2. Pedro Dória, "Notas enviadas por Pedro Dória, referentes à fundação do Centro Acadêmico Onze de Agosto, e seus antecedentes," Jaboticabal, May 29, 1944, (8 long typewritten sheets and covering letter to Renato Pintaudi Macedo), see pp. 1–2.

3. Ibid.

4. Ibid., pp. 2–3, 5; Vampré, *Memórias*, I, 239, 401.

5. Dória, "Notas," p. 3; Faculdade de Direito da Universidade de São Paulo, Centro Acadêmico XI de Agosto, *Diretorias, 1903–1949* (booklet).

6. Dória, "Notas," pp. 3–5.

7. *O Onze de Agosto* (Faculdade de Direito de S. Paulo) 1, no. 1 (August 11, 1903); Vampré, *Memórias*, I, 185–192, II, 401; Ferreira, *A Congregação da Faculdade de Direito de S. Paulo*, pp. 19–21.

8. *O Onze de Agosto* 1, no. 1 (August 11, 1903).
9. Dória, "Notas," pp. 7–8.
10. Faculdade de Direito, *Diretorias, 1903–1949*. Waldemar Ferreira directed the student journal *O Santelmo* (see biography of Waldemar Martins Ferreira in the files of *O Estado de S. Paulo*).
11. João Nery Guimarães, interviews, São Paulo, August 16, 1981, July 31, 1982; biographical notes in the César Lacerda de Vergueiro file at *O Estado de S. Paulo*.
12. Pedro Dória, "Centro Academico Onze de Agosto," *A Balança* (Faculdade de Direito) 1, no. 2 (August 1939); "Estatutos Atuais do Centro Acadêmico 'XI de Agosto' Aprovados a 18 de Outubro de 1913 e publicados em Junho de 1914," *O "XI de Agosto,"* 1946.
13. Faculdade de Direito, *Diretorias, 1903–1949*; Vampré, *Memórias*, II, 408.
14. Trajano Pupo Netto, interviews, São Paulo, August 19, 22, 1981; biographical notes in the César Lacerda de Vergueiro file at *O Estado de S. Paulo*. Large donations of Companhia Paulista shares to the Centro Onze de Agosto by José Carlos de Macedo Soares are mentioned by José Gomes Talarico in tape recordings (1978–1979) at the Centro de Pesquisa e Documentação de História Contemporânea do Brasil (henceforth referred to as CPDOC) at the Fundação Getúlio Vargas in Rio de Janeiro.
15. Aureliano Leite, *Páginas de uma Longa Vida* (São Paulo: Livraria Martins Editôra, [1967]), pp. 33–35.
16. Ibid., pp. 35–37; Pedro Calmon, *História do Brasil* (Rio de Janeiro: Livraria José Olympio Editôra, 1961), VI, 2134–2135.
17. Câmara dos Deputados, *Deputados Brasileiros, 1826–1976* (Brasília: Câmara dos Deputados, 1976), p. 59; *Correio Paulistano*, January 8, 1947; *O Dia*, June 11, 1952; Joaquim Canuto Mendes de Almeida, interview, São Paulo, August 21, 1982.

5. The Liga Nacionalista (founded in 1917)

1. "Com Bilac, na teoria e na ação," *O Estado de S. Paulo*, July 13, 1969. Francisco Mesquita's ability at *futebol* (soccer) is mentined in *O Estado de S. Paulo*, November 8, 1979.
2. Ibid., July 13, 1969.
3. *O Estadinho*, October 10, 1915, December 28, 1918.
4. Ferreira, "A Faculdade de Direito na Arrancada de 9 de Julho de 1932."
5. Francisco Pati, *O Espírito das Arcadas* (São Paulo: Associação dos Antigos Alunos da Faculdade de Direito de São Paulo, 1950), p. 195; Calmon, *História do Brasil*, VI, 2153; Pedro Calmon writes, in n. 5, p. 2153, that "in truth Miguel Calmon was the creator of the Liga" (de Defesa Nacional).
6. "Rezenha do Mez: Liga de Defesa Nacional," *O Estadinho*, December 7, 1915; *Estatutos da Liga de Defesa Nacional*, March 24, 1924, shows the founding date in Article 1; *O Estado de S. Paulo*, December 16, 1965, states

that the army initiated recruitment on November 10, 1916 (see the Olavo Bilac file at *O Estado de S. Paulo*).

7. *O Estadinho*, March 14, April 24, 1917 (in the Liga de Defesa Nacional file at *O Estado de S. Paulo*).

8. Júlio de Mesquita Filho, "Olavo Bilac, Guia da Nacionalidade," *O Estado de S. Paulo, Suplemento Literário*, December 18, 1965.

9. Ernesto Leme, *A Sombra das Arcadas* (São Paulo: Edição Comemorativa do Sesquicentenário da Faculdade de Direito de São Paulo, 1979), p. 198; Pati, *O Espírito das Arcadas*, p. 187; Vampré, *Memórias*, II, 403; Bandecchi, *A Bucha*, pp. 92–93; Barroso, *Historia Secreta*, II, 65, says that Steidel was nicknamed "o Corvo Triste" (the Sad Crow). About the Liga Nacionalista, see also Carneiro, "A Bucha," p. 115.

10. Brasil Bandecchi, *Liga Nacionalista* (São Paulo: Editora Parma Ltda., 1980), pp. 23–24; Antônio Pereira Lima, interview, São Paulo, July 9, 1981.

11. Paulo Duarte, *Memórias* (São Paulo: Editora Hucitec, 1979), IX, 310.

12. Bandecchi, *Liga Nacionalista*, pp. 24, 59–68. About the role of Mário Pinto Serva, see Paulo Nogueira Filho, *Ideais e Lutas de um Burguês Progressista: O Partido Democrático e a Revolução de 1930* (São Paulo: Editôra Anhambi, 1958), I, 109, 144. Work of the Liga Nacionalista is discussed in José Carlos de Macedo Soares, *Justiça: A revolta militar em São Paulo* (Paris, 1925), pp. 58–68.

13. Bandecchi, *Liga Nacionalista*, pp. 33–36, 27.

14. Nogueira Filho, *Ideais . . . : O Partido Democrático*, I, 62–63; *Paulo Nogueira Filho, Cidadão Emerito de São Paulo* (São Paulo, 1961), p. 25; Comissão Promotora das homenagens ao Dr. Paulo Nogueira Filho, biography of Paulo Nogueira Filho (9 pages, typewritten) with covering letter, December 19, 1960, from Elis Antunes to the director of *O Estado de S. Paulo* (in file at *O Estado de S. Paulo*).

15. Bandecchi, *Liga Nacionalista*, pp. 45–47; Ferreira, *A Congregação da Faculdade de Direito de S. Paulo*, pp. 130–131; Love, *São Paulo in the Brazilian Federation*, p. 94.

16. Nogueira Filho, *Ideais . . . : O Partido Democrático*, I, 78, 81–87; Bandecchi, *Liga Nacionalista*, pp. 69–73.

6. Student Opposition to the Liga Nacionalista and the Bucha (1918–1927)

1. Bandecchi, *A Bucha*, p. 84.

2. Nogueira Filho, *Ideais . . . : O Partido Democrático*, I, 65–76.

3. Antônio Pereira Lima, interview, São Paulo, July 9, 1981.

4. Nogueira Filho, *Ideais . . . : O Partido Democrático*, I, 67, 79–80.

5. Ibid., I, 92–100; Bandecchi (*A Bucha*, pp. 89–92) quotes and comments on unflattering remarks about the Bucha made by Oswald de Andrade in *Um Homem sem profissão*, 3d ed. (Rio de Janeiro: Civilização Brasileira, 1976), p. 120.

6. Pati, *O Espírito das Arcadas*, p. 184.

7. *O Estadinho*, December 31, 1919 (in the Centro Acadêmico Onze

de Agosto file at *O Estado de S. Paulo*); Bandecchi, *Liga Nacionalista*, pp. 53–56.

8. Pati, *O Espírito das Arcadas*, pp. 174, 184, 187, 201, 208–210.

9. Ibid.; Hermann de Morais Barros, interview, São Paulo, August 14, 1982.

10. Pati, *O Espírito das Arcadas*, pp. 200–203; Alpheu Canniço [Paulo Duarte], *Sob as Arcadas: Chronica de um lustro academico* (São Paulo: Edição Commemorativa do Centenario da Faculdade de Direito de São Paulo, 1927), pp. 148–149, 309 (n. 1).

11. Duarte, *Memórias*, IX, 310.

12. *A Chave* 1, no. 10 (May 22, 1924): 1.

13. "Juventude Decadente," *A Chave* 1, no. 3 (January 15, 1924): 1.

14. Paulo Duarte, "O Novo Zumbi," *A Chave* 1, no. 4 (April 2, 1924): 1.

15. Duarte, *Agora Nós!*, pp. 284–287; "Festa da Banana," *A Chave* 1, no. 2 (December 19, 1923): 1, and 2, no. 19 (February 21, 1925): 1; Duarte, *Memórias*, IX, 310. Alpheu Canniço [Paulo Duarte], *Sob as Arcadas*, p. 311 (n. 21).

16. "O Voto Secreto," *A Chave* 3, no. 22 (November 18, 1925): 2; Alpheu Canniço [Paulo Duarte], *Sob as Arcadas*, p. 310 (n. 9).

17. *A Chave* 3, no. 23 (April 15, 1926): 2; Alpheu Canniço [Paulo Duarte], *Sob as Arcadas*, p. 147.

18. Hermann de Morais Barros, interview, São Paulo, August 14, 1982; *A Chave* 4, no. 29 (July 14, 1927): 1.

19. *A Chave* 4, no. 28 (April 30, 1927): 1.

7. The End of the Liga Nacionalista (1924)

1. *O Estado de S. Paulo*, centenary booklet, p. 12.

2. Macedo Soares, *Justiça*, pp. 65, 74.

3. Ibid., pp. 61, 66, 73, 79, 95, 106; Duarte, *Agora Nós!*, pp. 288–291.

4. Macedo Soares, *Justiça*, pp. 64–71, 103–111.

5. Ibid., pp. 105, 116–126.

6. Ibid., pp. 62, 134; *O Estado de S. Paulo*, centenary booklet; Carlos Guilherme Mota and Maria Helena Capelato, *História da Folha de S. Paulo (1921–1981)* (São Paulo: IMPRES, 1980), p. 13. According to Aureliano Leite (*Páginas de uma Longa Vida*, p. 41), Artur Bernardes explained later that the bombardment of São Paulo and the closing of the Liga Nacionalista were carried out by the federal government at the request of Governor Carlos de Campos.

7. Duarte, *Agora Nós!*, pp. 294–300.

8. Macedo Soares, *Justiça*, p. 187.

9. Duarte, *Agora Nós!*, pp. 291–293, 301–308.

10. Ibid., pp. 308–319.

11. Joaquim Canuto Mendes de Almeida (interview, São Paulo, August 21, 1982) mentioned Bernardes' appellation of Santo Sepulcro; Gustavo Barroso (*História Secreta*, II, 83) writes that "the macabre name of Brother Santo

Sepulcro" was assigned to one of the Bucha's Twelve Apostles who became president of Brazil.

12. Duarte, *Agora Nós!*, pp. 319–330 (n. 75).

13. Bandecchi, *A Bucha*, p. 95.

8. The Partido Democrático (1926)

1. Nogueira Filho, *Ideais . . . : O Partido Democrático*, I, 141; Bandecchi, *A Bucha*, p. 91; Bandecchi, *Liga Nacionalista*, pp. 89–93; Aureliano Leite, *Memórias de um Revolucionário*, 1st ed. (São Paulo, 1931), p. 7.

2. Nogueira Filho, *Ideais . . . : O Partido Democrático*, I, 147–151.

3. Paulo Duarte, *Júlio Mesquita* (São Paulo: Editora Hucitec, 1977), p. 161.

4. Nogueira Filho, *Ideais . . . : O Partido Democrático*, I, 153–155; Ferreira, *A Congregação da Faculdade de Direito de S. Paulo*, pp. 108–109 (about Luís Barbosa da Gama Cerqueira); Ernesto Leme, *A Casa de Bragança: Memórias* (São Paulo: Editora Parma Ltda., 1981), p. 118.

5. Ferreira, *A Congregação da Faculdade de Direito de S. Paulo*, pp. 132–133; Hermann de Morais Barros, interview, São Paulo, August 14, 1982.

6. Paulo Duarte, *Que é que há?*, 2d ed. (São Paulo, 1931), pp. 52, 50.

7. Love, *São Paulo in the Brazilian Federation*, p. 118.

8. *Jornal da Tarde*, November 13, 1976 (in Antônio Carlos de Abreu Sodré file at *O Estado de S. Paulo*).

9. Duarte, *Júlio Mesquita*, pp. 162–163.

10. Nogueira Filho, *Ideais . . . : O Partido Democrático*, I, 179, 185, 189–190; Comissão Promotora das homenagens ao Dr. Paulo Nogueira Filho, biography; Pedro Ferraz do Amaral, interview, São Paulo, July 8, 1981; *O Estado de S. Paulo*, July 4, 1971 (in Pedro Ferraz do Amaral file at *O Estado de S. Paulo*).

11. Duarte, *Que é que há?*, p. 50.

12. Joaquim Canuto Mendes de Almeida, interview, São Paulo, August 21, 1982.

13. Nogueira Filho, *Ideais . . . : O Partido Democrático*, I, 186.

14. Ibid., I, 216–238.

15. Brasil Bandecchi, *Partido Democrático de São Paulo—Sua Fundação e Seu Apoio aos Candidatos da Aliança Liberal* (Comunicação; III Encontro Regional da Associação dos Professores Universitários de História, realizado em Santos, São Paulo, de 6 a 12 de setembro de 1976).

16. João Nery Guimarães, interview, São Paulo, August 16, 1981; *O Estado de S. Paulo*, October 9, 1979 (in Roberto Victor Cordeiro file at *O Estado de S. Paulo*); Almeida Júnior, *Sob as Arcadas*, p. 36, gives the number of students in 1930.

9. Law School Reaction to João Pessoa's Assassination (August 1930)

1. Ferreira, "A Faculdade de Direito na Arrancada de 9 de Julho de 1932."

2. Hermann de Morais Barros, "Reparos a um livro de J. F. Dulles," *O Estado de S. Paulo*, June 7, 1981.

3. Ibid.; Ferreira, "A Faculdade de Direito na Arrancada de 9 de Julho de 1932," lists the student speakers: José Dias de Menezes, João Batista de Arruda Sampaio, Lauro Cerqueira César, Romeu Lourenção, Henrique Brito Viana, Fernando de Martino, Darcy Miranda, and Paulo Marzagão.

4. Morais Barros, "Reparos a um livro de J. F. Dulles."

5. Ibid.

6. Leite, *Memórias de um Revolucionário*, p. 10; Nogueira Filho, *Ideais . . . : O Partido Democrático*, II, 482; João Nery Guimarães, interview, São Paulo, August 22, 1982.

7. Morais Barros, "Reparos a um livro de J. F. Dulles"; Ferreira, "A Faculdade de Direito na Arrancada de 9 de Julho de 1932"; Nogueira Filho, *Ideais . . . : O Partido Democrático*, II, 481.

8. Morais Barros, "Reparos a um livro de J. F. Dulles."

9. Hermann de Morais Barros, interview, August 14, 1982.

10. Morais Barros, "Reparos a um livro de J. F. Dulles."

11. Ibid.; Ferreira, "A Faculdade de Direito na Arrancada de 9 de Julho de 1932."

12. "O Centro Academico 'Onze de Agosto' e o Conflicto do Largo de S. Francisco," *Folha da Manhã*, August 12, 1930.

II. São Paulo and Vargas (1930–1938)

1. An Unhappy Partido Democrático (1930–1932)

1. Leite, *Memórias de um Revolucionário*, pp. 10, 13.

2. José Gomes Talarico, interview, Rio de Janeiro, July 17, 1982.

3. Leite, *Memórias de um Revolucionário*, pp. 126, 141.

4. Ibid., p. 144; Duarte, *Que é que ha?*, pp. 70–71.

5. *O Estado de S. Paulo*, centenary booklet, p. 14; "Constituintes Brasileiros: Cardoso de Melo Neto" (a sheet in the Cardoso de Melo Neto file at *O Estado de S. Paulo*); José Joaquim Cardoso de Melo Neto, "Gastão Vidigal," *Digesto Econômico*, July 1951; *Jornal da Tarde*, March 6, 1979 (in the Antônio Pereira Lima file at *O Estado de S. Paulo*); Duarte, *Que é que ha?*, p. 67.

6. Nogueira Filho, *Ideais . . . : O Partido Democrático*, II, 583; Duarte, *Que é que ha?*, p. 81; Leite, *Memórias de um Revolucionário*, p. 176.

7. Paulo Nogueira Filho, *Ideais . . . : A Guerra Cívica, 1932: Ocupação Militar* (Rio de Janeiro: Livraria José Olympio Editôra, 1965), pp. 196–197.

8. Antônio Carlos Pereira, *Folha Dobrada: Documento e história do povo Paulista em 1932* (São Paulo: O Estado de S. Paulo, 1982), pp. 146–147; Miguel Reale, interview, São Paulo, August 16, 1982.

9. Aureliano Leite, *Martírio e Glória de São Paulo* (São Paulo, 1934), pp. 50–52.

2. São Paulo's Unsuccessful Constitutionalist Revolution (1932)

1. Leite, *Páginas de uma Longa Vida*, pp. 67–70; Paulo Nogueira Filho, *Ideais . . . : A Guerra Cívica, 1932: Insurreição Civil* (Rio de Janeiro: Livraria José Olympio Editôra, 1966), pp. 214–215.

2. Nogueira Filho, *Ideais . . . : A Guerra Cívica, 1932: Insurreição Civil*, pp. 240–241; "No 24 de Maio Fundaram a MMDC" (interview with Luiz de Toledo Piza Sobrinho), *A Gazeta* (São Paulo), July 9, 1982.

3. Nogueira Filho, *Ideais . . . : A Guerra Cívica, 1932: Povo em Armas*, (Rio de Janeiro: Livraria José Olympio Editôra, 1967), I, 34–35. Hermann de Moraes Barros, speech at the Instituto dos Advogados, São Paulo, June 24, 1982 (typewritten copy); Ferreira, "A Faculdade de Direito na Arrancada de 9 de Julho de 1932."

4. Nogueira Filho, *Ideais . . . : A Guerra Cívica, 1932: Povo em Armas*, I, 54; "Das Muitas Glórias da 'Coluna Invicta,'" (interview with Herbert Levy), *A Gazeta*, July 9, 1982; Herbert Levy, interview, São Paulo, August 18, 1982.

5. Nogueira Filho, *Ideais . . . : A Guerra Cívica, 1932: Povo em Armas*, I, 51.

6. Ibid., I, 53–54.

7. Ferreira, "A Faculdade de Direito na Arrancada de 9 de Julho de 1932"; *O Estado de S. Paulo*, July 9, 1959 (in the Antônio Pereira Lima file at *O Estado de S. Paulo*).

8. *O Estado de S. Paulo*, November 8, 1979 (in the Francisco Mesquita file at *O Estado de S. Paulo*); *O Estado de S. Paulo*, centenary booklet, p. 12; *O Estado de S. Paulo*, July 9, 1959 (in the Antônio Pereira Lima file at *O Estado de S. Paulo*).

9. *O Estado de S. Paulo*, October 9, 1979 (in the Roberto Victor Cordeiro file at *O Estado de S. Paulo*); A. Almeida Júnior, *Sob as Arcadas*, p. 33.

10. Ferreira, "A Faculdade de Direito na Arrancada de 9 de Julho de 1932."

11. *O Estado de S. Paulo*, November 8, 1979 (in the Francisco Mesquita file at *O Estado de S. Paulo*); *O Estado de S. Paulo*, June 17, 1952 (in the Vicente Ráo file at *O Estado de S. Paulo*).

12. Antônio Pereira Lima, interview, in Lourenço Dantas Mota (coordinator), *A História Vivida* (São Paulo: O Estado de S. Paulo, 1981), II, 161–174.

3. The Constitutionalization of Brazil (1934)

1. Joaquim Canuto Mendes de Almeida, interview, São Paulo, August 21, 1982; José Carlos de Ataliba Nogueira, interviews, São Paulo, August 12, 15, 1982; *71 Anos da Academia Paulista de Letras* (São Paulo: Academia Paulista de Letras, 1980), p. 147.

2. *O Estado de S. Paulo*, centenary booklet, p. 4.

3. Wanor R. Godinho and Oswaldo S. Andrade, *Constituintes Brasileiros de 1934* (Rio de Janeiro, 1934), pp. 193–218.

4. Faculdade de Direito, Universidade de São Paulo, *In Memoriam: Pro-*

fessor Alcântara Machado (São Paulo: Empresa Gráfica da "Revista dos Tribunais" Ltda., 1942), p. 18 (from speech by Levi Carneiro); João Nery Guimarães, interview, São Paulo, July 31, 1982.

5. Godinho and Andrade, *Constituintes Brasileiros de 1934*, pp. 193–218.

6. Pedro Ferraz do Amaral, interviews, São Paulo, July 8, 13, 1981; *O Estado de S. Paulo*, July 4, 1971.

7. *O Estado de S. Paulo*, June 29, 1974 (in the Henrique Smith Bayma file at *O Estado de S. Paulo*).

8. Leite, *Páginas de uma Longa Vida*, pp. 250, 258.

9. *O Estado de S. Paulo*, June 21, 30, 1936.

10. Severo Gomes, interview, São Paulo, August 25, 1981.

11. João Nery Guimarães, interview, São Paulo, August 19, 1982.

12. Ruy Martins Ferreira, interviews, São Paulo, July 26, 27, 1982; Hermann de Morais Barros, interview, São Paulo, August 14, 1982; Duílio Crispim Farina, interview, São Paulo, August 7, 1982; Pedro Brasil Bandecchi, interviews, São Paulo, August 9, 17, 1982.

13. *O Estado de S. Paulo*, October 9, 1979 (in the Roberto Victor Cordeiro file at *O Estado de S. Paulo*); Horácio Cherkaski, interview, São Paulo, August 3, 1981; João Nery Guimarães, interview, São Paulo, August 16, 1981. On his deathbed in 1979, Roberto Victor Cordeiro married his nurse (who subsequently destroyed his papers).

14. *O Estado de S. Paulo*, centenary booklet, p. 12; Ruy Mesquita, interview, São Paulo, July 25, 1981; Arthur José Poerner, *O Poder Jovem* (Rio de Janeiro: Civilização Brasileira, 1968), p. 126; Darcy Ribeiro, in Mota, *A História Vivida*, II, 335–356; Love, *São Paulo in the Brazilian Federation*, p. 96; João Nery Guimarães, interview, São Paulo, July 31, 1982.

15. Leme, *A Casa de Bragança*, pp. 126–127.

16. *A Gazeta*, August 11, 1954 (in the Faculdade de Direito file at *O Estado de S. Paulo*); Júlio de Mesquita Filho, "Onde deverá localisarse a Cidade Universitária?" (replying to an inquiry by the *Diário da Noite*), *O Estado de S. Paulo*, July 19, 1935.

4. At the *Arcadas*

1. Lauro de Barros Siciliano, interview, São Paulo, August 17, 1982.

2. Duílio Crispim Farina, interview, São Paulo, August 7, 1982; Renato P. Macedo, interview, São Paulo, July 26, 1982; João Adelino de Almeida Prado Neto, interview, São Paulo, July 27, 1982; Faculdade de Direito de São Paulo, lists of annual graduates by sex: *Anuário da Faculdade de Direito, São Paulo*, for the years 1938 and 1939.

3. João Nery Guimarães, interview, São Paulo, July 31, 1982.

4. Antônio Costa Corrêa and Germinal Feijó, interview, São Paulo, July 6, 1981; Flávio Galvão, interview, São Paulo, August 20, 1982; Antônio Sylvio Cunha Bueno, interview, São Paulo, August 19, 1981; Afrânio de Oliveira, interview, São Paulo, August 18, 1981; João Nery Guimarães, interview, São Paulo, August 16, 1981.

5. Pedro Brasil Bandecchi and Trajano Pupo Netto, interview, São Paulo Law School, August 14, 1981.
6. Roberto Whately and Luiz Alberto da Fonseca Whately, interview, São Paulo, August 6, 1981.
7. João Nery Guimarães, interview, São Paulo, July 31, 1982; José Bonifácio Coutinho Nogueira, interview, São Paulo, August 16, 1982.
8. For an earlier advocacy of this idea, see "A Casa do Estudante," *A Chave*, May 23, 1925.
9. Cicero Augusto Vieira, *Casa do Estudante: Origem e história* (São Paulo: Faculdade de Direito de São Paulo, 1942), pp. 29–73, 94.
10. *O Estado de S. Paulo*, November 23, 24, 1937, January 6, 1942 ("Dados biográficos do professor Miguel Reale"); while at the law school, Reale was vice-president of the Liga Acadêmica, a member of the Academia de Letras da Faculdade de Direito, and wrote a book, *O Estado Moderno*, which sold well. O Comitê Regional de S. Paulo do P.C.B., *Contra o Trotskismo* (March 1939); Trajano Pupo Netto, interview, São Paulo, August 22, 1981; *Frente Democrática* (Universidade de S. Paulo) 1, no. 1 (June 4, 1937), and 1, no. 4 (September 1, 1937).
11. *Revista "XI de Agosto,"* November 1937, remarks of presentation, p. 5, signed by Antônio Calvo and three other members of the Comissão de Redação of the Centro Acadêmico XI de Agosto.
12. *O Onze de Agosto*, May 13, 1937; *Revista "XI de Agosto,"* November 1937.
13. "A Associação A. Álvares de Azevedo," *A Balança* 1, no. 4 (October 1939).
14. *O Conservador* 2, no. 3 (November 1937); Rubens M. Vandoni, "Casa do Estudante," *O Conservador* 3, no. 10 (November 1938).
15. Germinal Feijó and Antônio Costa Corrêa, interview, São Paulo, July 6, 1981; Trajano Pupo Netto, interview, São Paulo, August 22, 1981.
16. *O Estado de S. Paulo*, November 23, 1937; *Terra Vermelha: Orgão da "Colonia de Ribeirão Preto,"* November 1937.
17. Transcript of José Gomes Talarico tapes at the CPDOC at the Fundação Getúlio Vargas, Rio de Janeiro.
18. Vieira, *Casa do Estudante*, pp. 75–107.

5. November 10, 1937

1. Comissão Promotora das homenagens ao Dr. Paulo Nogueira Filho, biography.
2. "Falceeu Waldemar Ferreira," *O Estado de S. Paulo*, August 11, 1964.
3. Joaquim Canuto Mendes de Almeida, interview, São Paulo, August 21, 1982.
4. Almeida Júnior, *Sob as Arcadas*, pp. 295–296.
5. Cory Porto Fernandes, interview, São Paulo, August 2, 1981; "Faleceu . . . Francisco Morato de Oliveira," *O Estado de S. Paulo*, December 20, 1962.

6. Antônio Cândido de Mello e Souza, interview, São Paulo, August 7, 1981.
7. Luís Arrobas Martins, "Notas sobre a 'resistência acadêmica' ao 'Estado Novo' (1938–1944)," November 7, 1973 (10 pages, typewritten), see p. 1.
8. Aloysio Ferraz Pereira, interview, São Paulo, August 19, 1982.
9. Almeida Júnior, *Sob as Arcadas*, p. 296.
10. Herbert Levy, interviews, São Paulo, August 16, 1981, August 18, 1982; *O Estado de S. Paulo* clipping in notebook at the Levy residence.
11. Almeida Júnior, *Sob as Arcadas*, p. 297.
12. Biography of Professor Mário Masagão in *O Estado de S. Paulo* files.

6. Reactions of Some Paulistas (1938)

1. Love, *São Paulo in the Brazilian Federation*, p. 124; *Diário da Noite*, August 3, 1960 (in the Cardoso de Melo Neto file at *O Estado de S. Paulo*); *O Estado de S. Paulo*, January 31, 1946 (in the Gastão Vidigal file at *O Estado de S. Paulo*).
2. Biography of Antônio de Sampaio Dória in the files of *O Estado de S. Paulo*, Almeida Júnior, *Sob as Arcadas*, pp. 296–297; *Anuário da Faculdade de Direito* for 1938 and 1941.
3. *Jornal da Tarde*, November 13, 1976 (in the Antônio Carlos de Abreu Sodré file at *O Estado de S. Paulo*).
4. Ruy Mesquita, interview, São Paulo, July 25, 1981.
5. Paulo Duarte, interviews, São Paulo, July 22, 23, 1981; *Brasil* (Terra de Ninguém) 1, no. 1 (January 3, 1938); *Jornal da Tarde*, July 14, 1969 (in the Júlio de Mesquita Filho file at *O Estado de S. Paulo*).
6. "A homenagem a Antônio Pereira Lima," *Jornal da Tarde*, August 12, 1978; Antônio Pereira Lima, interview, São Paulo, July 9, 1981.
7. João Batista Silva Azevedo, interviews, São Paulo, July 4, 9, 1981; José Bonifácio Coutinho Nogueira, letter to JWFD, São Paulo, July 1, 1981.
8. Pedro Ferraz do Amaral, interviews, São Paulo, July 8, 13, 1981.
9. *O Estado de S. Paulo*, October 9, 1979 (in the Roberto Victor Cordeiro file at *O Estado de S. Paulo*); *Jornal da Tarde*, July 14, 1969.
10. João Batista Silva Azevedo, interviews, São Paulo, July 4, 9, 1981.
11. Júlio de Mesquita Filho, interview, São Paulo, August 7, 1963.

III. Early Anti–Estado Novo Manifestations (1938–1939)

1. The União Cultural Brasil–Estados Unidos (established in 1938)

1. "O perfil intellectual" (one printed sheet) and "Ademar de Barros e Getúlio Vargas" (one printed sheet) [no dates shown].
2. Cory Porto Fernandes, interview, São Paulo, August 2, 1981.
3. João Nery Guimarães, letter to JWFD, São Paulo, August 13, 1982; "Faleceu . . . Dr. Roberto Victor Cordeiro," *O Estado de S. Paulo*, October 9, 1979.
4. "Faleceu . . . Dr. Roberto Victor Cordeiro."

5. Documents at the Museum da União Cultural Brasil–Estados Unidos, São Paulo; A. C. Pacheco e Silva, *Passado, Presente e Futuro da União Cultural Brasil–Estados Unidos*, reprinted from *Boletim Informativo da UCBEU*, no. 5 (São Paulo: UCBEU, 1958), pp. 3–4; Horácio Cherkaski, interview, São Paulo, August 3, 1981.

6. Antônio Carlos Pacheco e Silva, interview, São Paulo, August 2, 1982; Pacheco e Silva, *Passado, Presente e Futuro da União Cultural Brasil–Estados Unidos*, p. 4.

7. Documents at the Museu da União Cultural Brasil–Estados Unidos, São Paulo.

8. José Gomes Talarico, interviews, Rio de Janeiro, July 17, 19, 20, 1982; transcript of José Gomes Talarico tapes at the CPDOC.

9. Ibid.; *Boletim da União Cultural Brasil–Estados Unidos* 1, no. 1 (1940), see list of officers.

10. Antônio Carlos Pacheco e Silva, interview, São Paulo, August 2, 1982.

2. Hydrosulphuric Gas for the Dictator (July 23–24, 1938)

1. Trajano Pupo Netto, interview, São Paulo, August 22, 1981.

2. Germinal Feijó, interviews, São Paulo, August 16, 1979, July 6, 1981; Paulo Duarte, interviews, São Paulo, July 22, 23, 1981; João Batista Silva Azevedo, interview, São Paulo, July 4, 1981; José Bonifácio Coutinho Nogueira, letter to JWFD, July 1, 1981.

3. Germinal Feijó, interview, São Paulo, August 16, 1979; Germinal Feijó in *Tribuna da Imprensa*, November 9, 1953.

4. Germinal Feijó and Antônio Costa Corrêa, interview, São Paulo, July 6, 1981; Antônio Costa Corrêa, interview, São Paulo, July 5, 1981.

5. Germinal Feijó, interview, São Paulo, August 16, 1979.

6. *O Estado de S. Paulo*, July 24, 1938.

7. Almeida Júnior, *Sob as Arcadas*, pp. 297–298; A. Almeida Júnior, series of six articles, "A 'Resistencia Academica' e o Estado Novo," *O Estado de S. Paulo*, November 1953; Arrobas Martins, "Notas sobre a 'resistência acadêmica' ao 'Estado Novo' (1938–1944)," p. 4.

8. Germinal Feijó, interviews, São Paulo, August 16, 1979, July 6, 1981.

3. A Conservador Victory (November 1938)

1. *O Estado de S. Paulo* centenary booklet, p. 8.

2. *O Momento Acadêmico* 1, no. 2 (1938).

3. Trajano Pupo Netto, interviews, São Paulo, August 19, 22, 1981; Pedro Brasil Bandecchi and Trajano Pupo Netto, interview, São Paulo, August 14, 1981.

4. Antônio Sylvio Cunha Bueno, interview, São Paulo, August 19, 1981.

5. Trajano Pupo Netto, interview, São Paulo, August 22, 1981.

6. *O Conservador* 3, no. 10 (November 1938).

7. Afrânio de Oliveira, interview, São Paulo, August 18, 1981; Galvão, "Observacões," p. 5.

8. Vieira, *Casa do Estudante*, pp. 145–156.

9. "A nova diretoria do Centro Acadêmico 'XI de Agosto,'" *O Onze de Agosto*, December 1938, p. 28; Trajano Pupo Netto, interviews, São Paulo, August 19, 22, 1981.

10. Trajano Pupo Netto, interviews, São Paulo, August 19, 22, 1981.

11. Horácio Cherkaski, interview, São Paulo, August 3, 1981.

12. João Nery Guimarães, letter to JWFD, São Paulo, August 13, 1982.

4. The Birth of the UNE (Rio de Janeiro, December 1938)

1. *O Onze de Agosto*, December 1938, pp. 38, 32; Antônio Sylvio Cunha Bueno, interview, São Paulo, August 19, 1981.

2. João Paulo Bittencourt, "Universidade e Política," *O Onze de Agosto*, December 1938, p. 6; José Barbosa, "Balanço do Ano," *O Universitário* 1, no. 2 (November 1938).

3. For further information, see Poerner, *O Poder Jovem*, pp. 132–141, and "UNE acaba 27 anos depois de surgir combatendo a ditadura," *Jornal do Brasil*, November 8, 1964.

4. José Gomes Talarico, interview, Rio de Janeiro, July 17, 1982.

5. Poerner, *O Poder Jovem*, pp. 140–151; *O Estado de S. Paulo*, December 6–25, 1938, see especially December 21.

6. "Ata de constituição do Conselho de Presidentes dos Centros Acadêmicos de São Paulo," May 8, 1939 (copy in possession of Trajano Pupo Netto).

7. *A Balança*, June, August 1939.

5. The Dismissal of Some Law Professors (January 1939)

1. Flávio Galvão, interview, São Paulo, August 20, 1982.

2. Ernesto Leme, interview, São Paulo, August 8, 1982; Pedro Brasil Bandecchi, interview, São Paulo, July 1, 1981.

3. Almeida Júnior, *Sob as Arcadas*, p. 299.

4. O Centro Acadêmico "XI de Agosto," dinner invitation (furnished during interview with Germinal Feijó, São Paulo, August 16, 1979).

5. Almeida Júnior, *Sob as Arcadas*, p. 300.

6. Trajano Pupo Netto, interviews, São Paulo, August 14, 1981, July 27, 1982.

7. João Nery Guimarães, "Alguns Apontamentos sobre a Faculdade de Direito de São Paulo, durante o Período 1939–1945," August 1981 (typewritten notes for JWFD, São Paulo), p. 4.

6. *"folha dobrada"*

1. Armando de Sales Oliveira, letter to General Góis Monteiro, Paris, February 25, 1939, p. 8.

2. Pedro Ferraz do Amaral, interview, São Paulo, July 8, 1981.

3. Upon feeling a pounding
In the heroic stricken breast,

Leave the page turned down
While going off to die.

4. Pedro Ferraz do Amaral, interview, São Paulo, July 8, 1981; Antônio Barreto do Amaral, "Jornalismo Acadêmico," in *Revista do Arquivo Municipal* (São Paulo: Divisão de Arquivo Histórico do Departamento do Patrimônio Histórico da Secretaria Municipal de Cultura da Prefeitura do Município de São Paulo), vol. 190 (July–December 1977), pp. 9–298, see pp. 244–247.

5. *"folha dobrada"* (Arcadas) 1, no. 1 (May 23, 1939).

6. Ibid.; Antônio Costa Corrêa, interview, São Paulo, July 5, 1981.

7. The "Friends of Rui Barbosa" Denounce Vargas (May 21, 1939)

1. Germinal Feijó, interview, São Paulo, August 16, 1979; Roberto de Abreu Sodré, interview, São Paulo, August 13, 1981; Israel Dias Novaes, interview, São Paulo, July 13, 1981.

2. José Bonifácio Coutinho Nogueira, interview, São Paulo, July 6, 1981.

3. "Treze de Maio," *"folha dobrada"* 1, no. 1 (May 23, 1939), p. 2.

4. Almeida Júnior, "A 'Resistencia Academica' e o Estado Novo," see second article.

5. Ibid.; see also Arrobas Martins, "Notas sobre a 'resistência acadêmica' ao 'Estado Novo' (1938–1944)," p. 4.

8. Pupo Netto, UNE President (1939–1940)

1. Joaquim Canuto Mendes de Almeida, interview, São Paulo, August 21, 1982; Gofredo da Silva Telles Junior, interview, São Paulo, August 9, 1982; *A Balança* 1, no. 2 (August 1939); *O Estado de S. Paulo,* June 2, 1939.

2. *O Estado de S. Paulo,* May 19, 1939.

3. Trajano Pupo Netto, interview, São Paulo, August 24, 1981.

4. Ibid., July 27, 1982; Vieira, *Casa do Estudante,* pp. 184–191.

5. "União Nacional dos Estudantes," *O "XI de Agosto,"* August 1939, p. 36; *Relatórios da União Nacional dos Estudantes, 1939, 1940* (Rio de Janeiro: U.N.E., July 1940), pp. 39–40; Celso Peçanha, interview, Brasília, August 27, 1981, and notes provided by him; Trajano Pupo Netto, letter to JWFD, São Paulo, January 11, 1982.

6. *Relatórios da União Nacional dos Estudantes, 1939, 1940,* pp. 109–112.

7. Ibid., pp. 117–152, 49; see also Poerner, *O Poder Jovem,* pp. 150–152.

IV. The Libertadores' First Year (1940)

1. *Resistência* Activists Promote Party Schisms (August–November 1939)

1. "O Partido Académico Conservador e a Candidatura de José Maria Ribeiro de Barros," *O Libertador* (Arcadas) 1, no. 1 (November 1939): 2.

2. Antônio Costa Corrêa, interviews, São Paulo, July 5, 6, 1981.

3. Antônio Cândido de Melo e Souza, interview, São Paulo, July 8, 1981.

4. *A Urna* (Arcadas) 1, no. 2 (November 10, 1939); "Manifesto da Dissidência da 'Reação Acadêmica,'" *O Libertador* 1, no. 1 (November 1939): 7.

5. Horácio Cherkaski, interview, São Paulo, August 3, 1981.

6. Manifesto: Partido Acadêmico Reformador; *O Reformador* (Arcadas) 1, no. 1 (November 1939).

7. *A Urna* 1, no. 2 (November 10, 1939).

8. "Os Paulistas e a Democracia—Reflexões que sugere o último discurso do grande Presidente Roosevelt," *O Libertador* 1, no. 1 (November 1939): 5.

9. Astolfo Pio Monteiro da Silva, "Ao Primeiro Ano," ibid., p. 4.

10. *O Combate* (Jaboticabal newspaper), June 28, July 23, 1936.

11. Paulo Henrique Meinberg, interviews, São Paulo, July 8, August 1, 1981.

12. Luís Arrobas Martins, curriculum vitae (typewritten).

2. A Defeat for the *Resistência* Activists (November 18, 1939)

1. Arrobas Martins, "Notas sobre a 'resistência acadêmica' ao 'Estado Novo' (1938–1944)," p. 4; "Centro Acadêmico XI de Agosto," *O Estado de S. Paulo*, November 1, 1939, and another newspaper clipping in the collection at the residence of Maria Alice Arrobas Martins.

2. *O Estado de S. Paulo*, November 1, 18, 1939, and other newspaper clippings at the residence of Maria Alice Arrobas Martins; Ulisses Silveira Guimarães, "Colegas da Faculdade, ouvintes desta Hora Acadêmica," *O Libertador* 1, no. 1 (November 1939): 4.

3. *O Estado de S. Paulo*, October 28, 1939.

4. Ibid., October 28, November 1, 1939.

5. Péricles Eugênio da Silva Ramos, interview, São Paulo, August 18, 1982.

6. "O Partido Acadêmico Libertador aos Estudantes de Direito: Manifesto," April 23, 1940.

7. Luís Arrobas Martins, "Notas sobre a 'resistência acadêmica' ao 'Estado Novo' (1938–1944)," p. 5; Renato Amaral Sampaio Coelho, interview, São Paulo, July 8, 1981.

8. "Bacharelandos de Direito homenageados pelos seus colegas," *Diário da Noite*, January 4, 1940; "Homenagem a bacharelandos," *O Estado de S. Paulo*, January 5, 1940; "A Fundação do Partido Acadêmico Libertador," *O Libertador* 1, no. 2 (June 1940).

3. The Woes of *O Estado de S. Paulo* and *Revista Universitária* (March–April 1940)

1. Newspaper clipping, no date or publication shown, in file about Júlio de Mesquita Filho at *O Estado de S. Paulo*; *O Estado de S. Paulo* centenary booklet, pp. 5–14.

2. Ibid.

3. *O Estado de S. Paulo* centenary booklet, pp. 14–15; Ruy Mesquita, interview, São Paulo, July 25, 1981.

4. *Diário da Noite,* April 11, 1940 (in the collection at the residence of Maria Alice Arrobas Martins), and another newspaper clipping, no date or publication shown (in the collection of José Bonifácio Coutinho Nogueira); Arrobas Martins, "Notas sobre a 'resistência acadêmica' ao 'Estado Novo' (1938–1944)," p. 6.

4. Launching of the Partido Acadêmico Libertador (April–June 1940)

1. "O que o Partido Acadêmico Libertador tem feito," *O Libertador* 1, no. 3 (August 1940).
2. João Nery Guimarães, interviews, São Paulo, July 31, August 21, 1982.
3. Israel Dias Novaes, *Papel de jornal* (São Paulo: Revista de Poesia e Crítica, n.d.), p. 31.
4. Arrobas Martins, "Notas sobre a 'resistência acadêmica' ao 'Estado Novo' (1938–1944)," pp. 4–5.
5. "O que o Partido Acadêmico Libertador tem feito."
6. O Partido Acadêmico Libertador aos Estudantes de Direito: Manifesto, April 23, 1940.
7. "O que o Partido Acadêmico Libertador tem feito"; Projeto de Estatutos do Partido Acadêmico Libertador.

5. The *Arcadas* during the Presidency of Quintanilha Ribeiro (1940)

1. Antônio Sylvio Cunha Bueno, interview, São Paulo, August 19, 1981.
2. Arrobas Martins, "Notas sobre a 'resistência acadêmica' ao 'Estado Novo' (1938–1944)," p. 6; *Diário da Noite,* May 14, 1940, and another clipping (no publication or date shown) in the collection at the residence of Maria Alice Arrobas Martins.
3. Arrobas Martins, "Notas sobre a 'resistência acadêmica' ao 'Estado Novo' (1938–1944), p. 5.
4. Broadside about MUN, title illegible (1 page, mimeographed).
5. *O Libertador* 1, no. 2 (June 1940).
6. "O que o Partido Acadêmico Libertador tem feito," *O Libertador* 1, no. 3 (August 1940).
7. União Nacional dos Estudantes, *IV Conselho Nacional de Estudantes: Relatório, Julho 1940* (Rio de Janeiro: U.N.E., December 1940), pp. 31–34.
8. *O Libertador* 1, no. 3 (August 1940).
9. *Diário de S. Paulo,* July 19, 25, 1940.
10. Sociedade Acadêmico "Amigos de Ruy Barbosa": Eleição da nova diretoria (1 page, typewritten); newspaper clipping (no source shown), August 20, 1940, about the installation of the officers (in the collection at the residence of Maria Alice Arrobas Martins); invitation to the installation ceremony (*solenidade de empossamento*).
11. Arrobas Martins, "Notas sobre a 'resistência acadêmica' ao 'Estado Novo' (1938–1944)," p. 6; Aureliano Leite, "Minhas recordações de Monteiro Lobato," *O Estado de S. Paulo,* October 10, 1948; Raimundo de Menezes, "Lobato na Cadeia," *O Estado de S. Paulo,* September 12, 1948;

Diário de S. Paulo, May 21, 1941, p. 3; José Bento Monteiro Lobato, letter to Getúlio Vargas, São Paulo, August 5, 1940 (mimeographed copy).

12. Vieira, *Casa do Estudante*, pp. 195–204; *O "XI de Agosto"* 37, no. 2 (September 1940): 59–60; *A Balança* 2, no. 7 (August 1940): 16. About Cásper Libeiro, see A. Melo Franco, *Rodrigues Alves*, I, 30.

13. "Baile das Américas," *O Libertador* 2, no. 8 (October 1941); invitation to the Baile of 1940; Vieira, *Casa do Estudante*, pp. 196–199.

6. Kidnapping of Chico Elefante (September 1940)

1. Germinal Feijó, interview, São Paulo, July 6, 1981; Israel Dias Novaes, interview, São Paulo, July 5, 1981; Antônio Costa Corrêa, interview, São Paulo, July 5, 1981; Dias Novaes, *Papel de jornal*, p. 31; "Israel Dias Novaes lembra um seqüestro," *Diário de S. Paulo*, November 29, 1973.

2. Note about the *capivara* (capybara) in João Nery Guimarães, letter to JWFD, São Paulo, August 13, 1982, p. 5.

3. Israel Dias Novaes, interview, São Paulo, July 5, 1981; *Diário da Noite*, September 27, 1940.

4. Newspaper clipping (without date or source) in the collection at the home of Maria Alice Arrobas Martins.

5. *Diário da Noite*, September 27, 1940; *A Gazeta*, November 15, 1940.

6. Printed invitation addressed to "Acadêmico de Direito."

7. Renato Amaral Sampaio Coelho and Hiram Mayr Cerqueira, interview, São Paulo, August 4, 1981; Trajano Pupo Netto, interviews, São Paulo, August 14, 22, 1981, July 27, 1982; João Nery Guimarães, interview, August 21, 1982; Bandecchi, *A Bucha*, p. 97.

8. "Colegas!" (broadside furnished by Renato Pintaudi Macedo, bearing date—October 30, 1940—in ink).

9. Flávio Galvão, "Observações."

7. An Anti-Vargas Victory, Thanks to Pavan and Cherkaski (November 1940)

1. João Nery Guimarães, letter to JWFD, São Paulo, August 13, 1982.

2. "Cópia da Acta das Eleições Prévias do Partido Acadêmico Libertador," *O Libertador* 1, no. 4 (September 1940).

3. Flávio Galvão, interview, São Paulo, August 20, 1982.

4. José Vasques Bernardes, interview, São Paulo, August 20, 1982.

5. *O Conservador* (Arcadas) 5, no. 9 (October 1940): 3; Antônio Sylvio Cunha Bueno, interview, São Paulo, August 19, 1981.

6. *O Universitário* (Faculdade de Direito) 3, no. 8 (November 1940): 4–5; *A Balança* 2, no. 9 (November 1940): 3.

7. Rivaldo de Assis Cintra, interview, São Paulo, August 5, 1981.

8. *O Conservador* 5, no. 9 (October 1940).

9. Rivaldo Assis Cintra, interview, São Paulo, August 5, 1981.

10. *O Conservador* 5, no. 9 (October 1940): 5, 16.

11. *Diário da Noite*, November 13, 1940; *O Libertador* 1, no. 5 (November 1940).
12. "Basta!" (1 page, mimeographed broadside); *Folha da Noite*, November 13, 1940.
13. *Plataforma de Luiz Leite Ribeiro*, November 1940.
14. *Folha da Noite*, November 13, 1940; *O Libertador* 2, no. 5 (November 1940).
15. *Folha da Noite*, November 13, 1940.
16. Jarbas Teixeira de Carvalho, interview, Rio de Janeiro, July 19, 1982; Horácio Cherkaski, interview, São Paulo, August 3, 1981; Arthur Octavio de Camargo Pacheco, interview, São Paulo, August 6, 1981.
17. Newspaper clipping (no date or source) in the collection at the home of Maria Alice Arrobas Martins.
18. Faculdade de Direito, *Diretorias, 1903–1949*.
19. *O Libertador* 2, no. 6 (December 1940).

V. The Centro in Libertador Hands (1941)

1. *Trote, Peruada*, and *Caravanas* (April–July 1941)

1. Anacleto de Oliveira Faria, *A Geração Acadêmica de 1941/1945* reprinted from *Revista da Faculdade de Direito da Universidade de São Paulo*, vol. 69 [1974]), pp. 294–295.
2. Antônio Cândido de Mello e Souza, interview, São Paulo, July 8, 1981.
3. Oliveira Faria, *A Geração Acadêmica de 1941/1945*, p. 295.
4. Invitation, signed by "Je Victor Tieghi De La Barbiche Rosé," announcing the "Perruade" offered by "la faculté de droit de la Université de Saint Paul," Arcadas, June 1941. João Nery Guimarães, letter to JWFD, August 13, 1982, and interview, São Paulo, July 31, 1982.
5. Joaquim Rui Gonçalves, "Peruada de 1941," *Tribuna Acadêmica* (Arcadas) 2, no. 3 (August 1941): 5.
6. Ibid.
7. "Sessões do Centro Acadêmico 'XI de Agosto' em 1941," *O Libertador* 2, no. 7 (June 1941): 7, see also p. 4 of the same number; Portaria Número 2, Centro Acadêmico 'XI de Agosto,' signed by Luiz Leite Ribeiro, April 3, 1941, establishing "*missão cultural*" to Goiás; *Jornal da Manhã*, April 4, 1941; *O Estado de S. Paulo*, April 3, 1941.
8. *A Tarde* (Salvador), July 19, 1941; *Estado de Baia*, July 19, 1941; program: Festival Artistico do Centro Acadêmico "XI de Agosto" . . . a realisarse nos salões da Associação Atlética da Bahia, July 26, 1941.

2. The Return of the Dismissed Professors and Other Changes (May–June 1941)

1. "Voltam à Faculdade os Profs. Vicente Ráo, Waldemar Ferreira e Sampaio Dória," *A Balança* 3, no. 10 (June 6, 1941): 8; *O Libertador* 2, no. 7 (June 1941): 7; *O Conservador* 6, no. 10 (October 1941).

2. *Diário de S. Paulo,* May 29, 1941.

3. *A Balança,* June 6, 1941, October 1940; *Folha da Manhã,* April 11, 1941; *O Estado de S. Paulo,* June 6, 1942; Miguel Reale, interview, São Paulo, August 16, 1982; Miguel Reale, *O Concurso de Filosofia do Direito* (São Paulo: E. G. "Revista dos Tribunais," 1940).

4. "Sociedade Acadêmica 'Amigos de Rui Barbosa,'" *O Libertador* 2, no. 7 (June 1941).

5. Ibid.; Israel Dias Novaes, interview, São Paulo, August 18, 1982; Péricles Eugênio da Silva Ramos, interview, São Paulo, August 18, 1982.

6. Roberto de Abreu Sodré, interview, São Paulo, August 13, 1981.

7. "Sociedade Universitária 'Amigos da Itália,'" *A Balança* 3, no. 10 (June 6, 1941).

8. "União Cultural Brasil–Estados Unidos," *O Libertador* 2, no. 7 (June 1941).

9. *Diário da Noite,* July 23, 1941.

10. "As taxas escolares serão rebaixadas," newspaper clipping (apparently June 1941) in the collection at the residence of Maria Alice Arrobas Martins.

11. *O Estado de S. Paulo,* June 11, 1941; clippings in the Cardoso de Melo Neto and Abelardo Vergueiro César file at *O Estado de S. Paulo*; Duarte, *Memórias,* IX, 314.

12. Antônio Sylvio Cunha Bueno, interview, São Paulo, August 19, 1981. curriculum vitae of Antônio Sylvio Cunha Bueno (10 pages, typewritten).

13. *O Estado de S. Paulo,* January 6, 1942; Miguel Reale, interview, São Paulo, August 16, 1982.

3. Conservadores Infiltrate the Libertadores' *Prévia* (August 30, 1941)

1. Vieira, *Casa do Estudante,* p. 207.

2. Antônio Costa Corrêa, interview, São Paulo, August 14, 1982.

3. Antônio Sylvio Cunha Bueno, interview, São Paulo, August 19, 1981. "Conversa com Roberto Sodré," *Tribuna Acadêmica* (Arcadas) 2, no. 3 (August 1941); *O Estado de S. Paulo,* May 22, 1941.

4. Jorge Carneiro, "Fernando José Fernandes e a letra 'V,'" *O Libertador* 2, no. 8 (October 1941).

5. *O Estado de S. Paulo,* May 22, 1941; *O Libertador* 2, no. 7 (June 1941).

6. "Em torno da prévia," *Tribuna Acadêmica* 2, no. 3 (August 1941).

7. Antônio Costa Corrêa, "Alguma coisa sôbre o Libertador e a candidatura Roberto Sodré," *Tribuna Acadêmica* 2, no. 3 (August 1941).

8. Antônio Sylvio Cunha Bueno, interview, São Paulo, August 19, 1981.

9. Arthur Octavio Camargo Pacheco, interview, São Paulo, August 6, 1982.

10. "Prévia do Partido Acadêmico Libertador," *A Gazeta,* September 2, 1941.

11. João Nery Guimarães, interview, São Paulo, August 21, 1982.

4. An Honorary Doctorate for Vargas (September 1941)

1. José Gomes Talarico, interview, Rio de Janeiro, July 17, 1982; Poerner, *O Poder Jovem*, pp. 178–179.

2. José Gomes Talarico, interview, Rio de Janeiro, July 17, 1982; José Gomes Talarico tapes at the CPDOC. Germinal Feijó declares (*Tribuna da Imprensa*, November 9, 1953) that by 1941 Talarico had become connected with the Rio police and the DIP (the federal Department of the Press and Propaganda).

3. José Gomes Talarico, interview, Rio de Janeiro, July 17, 1982; João Nery Guimarães, interview, São Paulo, August 22, 1982; Poerner, *O Poder Jovem*, p. 178.

4. Poerner, *O Poder Jovem*, p. 179; José Gomes Talarico, interview, Rio de Janeiro, July 17, 1982; Luís Leite Ribeiro, letter to J. J. Cardoso de Melo Neto, São Paulo, September 25, 1941 (revealing the position of some Grêmio Politécnico members).

5. José Gomes Talarico, interview, Rio de Janeiro, July 17, 1982.

6. Ibid.

7. Fernando Costa, letter to Vargas, São Paulo, September 24, 1941 (CPDOC).

8. Ibid.; Almeida Júnior, *Sob as Arcadas*, p. 304; Jorge Americano, letter to Vargas, São Paulo, September 23, 1941 (CPDOC).

9. "Ata da 3ª Sessão Extraordinária do Centro Acadêmico 'XI de Agosto,'" September 23, 1941 (in the handwriting of Renato Macedo).

10. Lenício Pacheco Ferreira, "Concessão de título de doutor Honoris Causa a Getúlio Vargas," August 12, 1981 (3 pages, handwritten, with covering letter to JWFD, Catanduva, S.P.); Arrobas Martins, "Notas sobre a 'resistência acadêmica' ao 'Estado Novo' (1938–1944)," pp. 7–8; Renato Pintaudi Macedo, interviews, São Paulo, August 5, 20, 1981; Paulo Henrique Meinberg, Renato Amaral Sampaio Coelho, and Hiram Mayr Cerqueira, interview, São Paulo, July 8, 1981.

11. Arrobas Martins, "Notas sobre a 'resistência acadêmica' ao 'Estado Novo' (1938–1944)," pp. 7–8; Renato Pintaudi Macedo, interviews, São Paulo, August 5, 20, 1981.

12. Arrobas Martins, "Notas sobre a 'resistência acadêmica' ao 'Estado Novo' (1938–1944)," pp. 7–8; "Greve na Faculdade de Direito pela concessão do título de doutor 'honoris causa' ao Ditador Getulio Vargas" (2 pages, typewritten, in the collection at the residence of José Bonifácio Coutinho Nogueira); Fernando Costa, letter to Vargas, São Paulo, September 24, 1941 (CPDOC).

5. The Indefinite Suspension of Classes (September 29, 1941)

1. Oliveira Faria, *A Geração Acadêmica de 1941/1945*, p. 299; Arrobas Martins, "Notas sobre a 'resistência acadêmica' ao 'Estado Novo' (1938–

1944)," pp. 7–8; Pacheco Ferreira, "Concessão de título de doutor Honoris Causa a Getúlio Vargas," Catanduva, August 12, 1981.

2. Fernando Costa, letter to Vargas, September 24, 1941 (CPDOC).

3. Renato Pintaudi Macedo, interview, São Paulo, August 20, 1981.

4. Luís Leite Ribeiro, letter to J. J. Cardoso de Melo Neto, São Paulo, September 25, 1941.

5. Arthur Octavio de Camargo Pacheco, interviews, São Paulo, August 6, 1981, August 6, 1982.

6. Ibid.; Arrobas Martins, "Notas sobre a 'resistência acadêmica' ao 'Estado Novo' (1938–1944), p. 2.

7. Poerner, *O Poder Jovem*, pp. 179–180; Roberto Whately, interview, São Paulo, August 6, 1981.

8. Israel Dias Novaes, interview, São Paulo, July 31, 1981.

9. Almeida Júnior, *Sob as Arcadas*, p. 304.

10. Poerner, *O Poder Jovem*, pp. 179–180.

11. Jarbas Teixeira de Carvalho, inscription on the back of a photograph.

12. Oliveira Faria, *A Geração Acadêmica de 1941/1945*, pp. 299–300.

13. Ibid.; Agência Nacional news release, São Paulo, September 30.

6. Capanema, Tactful Conciliator (early October 1941)

1. *Diário de S. Paulo*, October 3, 1941; *O Estado de S. Paulo*, October 3, 1941.

2. Germinal Feijó, interview, São Paulo, August 16, 1979.

3. Arthur Octavio de Camargo Pacheco, interview, São Paulo, August 6, 1981.

4. Germinal Feijó, interview, São Paulo, August 16, 1979.

5. Ibid.

6. "Greve na Faculdade de Direito pela concessão do título de doutor 'honoris causa' ao Ditador Getulio Vargas" (2 pages, typewritten, in collection at the residence of José Bonifácio Coutinho Nogueira); Poerner, *O Poder Jovem*, p. 180.

7. Gustavo Capanema, letter to Sr. Reitor da Universidade de São Paulo, São Paulo, October 3, 1941 (CPDOC); *Diário de S. Paulo*, October 4, 1941, p. 6.

8. *Diário de S. Paulo*, October 4, 1941, p. 6; "Greve na Faculdade de Direito pela concessão do título . . ."

9. *O Estado de S. Paulo*, October 4, 5, 1941.

10. Almeida Júnior, *Sob as Arcadas*, p. 305.

11. José Gomes Talarico tape at the CPDOC.

7. Conservadores Overwhelm Dispirited Libertadores (November 1941)

1. "Onde Estão os Nossos Ideais?" (1 page, typewritten, with the following handwritten notation: "Copy of an anonymous bulletin distributed at the College on September 24, 1941").

2. Fernando José Fernandes, letter to JWFD, São Paulo, August 31, 1984; *O Libertador* 2, no. 8 (October 1941).

3. "Nosso Manifesto," *O Conservador* 6, no. 10 (October 1941); it appeared also as a brochure with a photograph of Bressane.

4. "Merecida homenagem à memória do dr. Oscar Augusto de Barros Bressane," *A Gazeta*, January 9, 1949; Roberto de Abreu Sodré, interview, São Paulo, August 13, 1981.

5. *O Libertador* 2, no. 8 (October 1941).

6. *O Conservador* 6, no. 10 (October 1941).

7. A Comissão Diretora do Partido Acadêmico Conservador, "Desespero ou Má Fé?," 1942; see also A Comissão Diretora do Partido Acadêmico Conservador, "Acautelando a Opinião Acadêmica," September 14, 1942; Fernando José Fernandes, letter to JWFD, August 31, 1984.

8. Fernando José Fernandes, letter to JWFD, August 31, 1984.

9. Ênio de Novais França, Germinal Feijó, Luís Gonzaga Arrôbas Martins, Renato Amaral Sampaio Coelho, "Aos Estudantes de Direito," June 1943 (printed manifesto).

VI. Brazil Enters the War

1. The Liga Acadêmica de Defesa Nacional (May–June 1942)

1. Arthur Octavio de Camargo Pacheco, interviews, São Paulo, August 6, 1981, August 6, 1982.

2. "A mocidade paulista despertou e luta pela democracia!," *Folha da Tarde* (Porto Alegre), June 27, 1942.

3. *Diário da Noite*, April 8, 1942; *peruada* invitation of the Território Livre do Largo de S. Francisco, May 1942; Arrobas Martins, "Notas sobre a 'resistência acadêmica' ao 'Estado Novo' (1938–1944)," p. 8.

4. "A mocidade paulista despertou e luta pela democracia!"; "À Mocidade Brasileira" (printed manifesto launching the Liga Acadêmica de Defesa Nacional).

5. "À Mocidade Brasileira."

6. A Liga Acadêmica de Defesa Nacional, "Grandes Manifestações Públicas dos Acadêmicos Baianos pela Defesa Nacional e Contra o Eixo" (1 page, printed).

7. "A mocidade paulista despertou e luta pela democracia!"

2. A New Libertador Manifesto (August 11, 1942)

1. "O Partido Acadêmico Libertador aos Estudantes de Direito," August 11, 1942 (4 pages, printed).

2. "O Partido Acadêmico Libertador aos Estudantes de Direito" (10 pages, typewritten).

3. The Rally at the Praça da Sé (August 18, 1942)

1. *Correio Paulistano*, August 19, 1942; *O Estado de S. Paulo*, August 19, 1942; Poerner, *O Poder Jovem*, pp. 169–170; José Gomes Talarico, interview, Rio de Janeiro, July 17, 1982.

2. Arrobas Martins, "Notas sobre a 'resistência acadêmica' ao 'Estado Novo' (1938–1944)," p. 8; *Folha da Noite*, August 18, 1942; *O Estado de S. Paulo*, August 19, 1942; Almeida Júnior, *Sob as Arcadas*, p. 307; Oliveira Faria, *A Geração Acadêmica de 1941/1945*, p. 303.

3. *O Estado de S. Paulo*, August 19, 1942; Almeida Júnior, *Sob as Arcadas*, pp. 307–308; A Comissão Diretora do Partido Acadêmico Libertador, "A bem de verdade," October 1942 (6 pages, typewritten).

4. Almeida Júnior, *Sob as Arcadas*, pp. 307–308; Arrobas Martins, "Notas sobre a 'resistência acadêmica' ao 'Estado Novo' (1938–1944)," p. 8.

5. "Campanha nacionalista do Centro Acadêmico 'XI de Agosto,'" *Diário da Noite*, August 22, 1942.

6. Arthur Octavio de Camargo Pacheco, interview, São Paulo, August 6, 1982.

7. *Folha da Noite*, August 18, 1942; "Merecida homenagem à memória do dr. Oscar Augusto de Barros Bressane," *A Gazeta*, January 9, 1949.

8. "De São Paulo," *Nação Brasileira* (Rio de Janeiro), September 1942; *Folha da Noite*, August 18, 1942; *O Estado de S. Paulo*, August 19, 1942.

9. Horácio Cherkaski, interview, São Paulo, August 3, 1981; *O Estado de S. Paulo*, August 19, 1942; *Correio Paulistano*, August 19, 1942.

10. "Merecida homenagem à memória do dr. Oscar Augusto de Barros Bressane."

11. *O Estado de S. Paulo*, August 19, 1942.

4. The Campanha Nacionalista and Its *Caravana* (September–October 1942)

1. "Campanha nacionalista do Centro Acadêmico 'XI de Agosto,'" *Diário da Noite*, August 22, 1942; "Os estudantes de Direito ao povo de São Paulo," *A Gazeta*, August 21, 1942.

2. Arrobas Martins, "Notas sobre a 'resistência acadêmica' ao 'Estado Novo' (1938–1944)," p. 8.

3. "Merecida homenagem à memória do dr. Oscar Augusto de Barros Bressane," *A Gazeta*, January 9, 1949; Oscar Bressane, telegram to Vargas, August 25, 1942 (and handwritten note on copy of it).

4. "Perfeita identificação dos universitários paulistas com o governo," *O Estado de S. Paulo*, September 9, 1942.

5. Horácio Cherkaski, interview, São Paulo, August 3, 1981.

6. Arrobas Martins, "Notas sobre a 'resistência acadêmica' ao 'Estado Novo' (1938–1944)," p. 9; *Diário de S. Paulo*, September 26, 1942; "Ao Povo de Cedral" (1-page notice), Cedral, September 29, 1942; "Campanha Nacionalista" (1-page notice), Catanduva, October 2, 1942; *Folha da Manhã*, Oc-

tober 6, 1942; Horácio Cherkaski, interview, São Paulo, August 3, 1981.

7. *Diário de S. Paulo*, October 17, 1942.

5. The Fifth Conselho Nacional de Estudantes (September 1942)

1. *O Estado de S. Paulo*, September 17, 1942; *A Noite*, October 3, 1942; "Solucionando o 'caso' Miguel Reale," *Correio Paulistano*, August 1, 1943; Carlos Eduardo de Camargo Aranha, interview, São Paulo, August 5, 1982; José Bonifácio Coutinho Nogueira, interview, São Paulo, August 3, 1982.

2. *O Estado de S. Paulo*, September 16, 1942.

3. Ibid.; José Gomes Talarico, interview, Rio de Janeiro, July 17, 1982.

4. *O Estado de S. Paulo*, September 16–23, 1942.

5. Poerner, *O Poder Jovem*, pp. 172–173.

6. José Gomes Talarico, tapes at the CPDOC.

7. Hélio de Almeida, interview, Rio de Janeiro, July 20, 1982.

8. Poerner, *O Poder Jovem*, pp. 172–173.

9. Ibid.

10. Hélio de Almeida, interview, Rio de Janeiro, July 20, 1982.

11. Poerner, *O Poder Jovem*, p. 173.

12. Luís de Azevedo Soares, interviews, São Paulo, August 20, 1981, August 11, 1982.

6. Another Libertador Defeat (November 1942)

1. Domenico Martirani, interview, São Paulo, August 25, 1981.

2. Trajano Pupo Netto, interview, São Paulo, July 27, 1982; João Nery Guimarães, interview, São Paulo, July 31, 1982; Arthur Octavio de Camargo Pacheco, interview, São Paulo, August 6, 1982.

3. Luís de Azevedo Soares, interview, São Paulo, August 11, 1982.

4. Re name of Jequiti Bar, Trajano Pupo Netto, interview, São Paulo, July 27, 1982.

5. José Vasques Bernardes, interview, São Paulo, August 20, 1982.

6. *A Noite*, October 3, 1942.

7. Re *solicitador-acadêmico*, Renato Pintaudi Macedo, interview, São Paulo, July 26, 1982, and João Adelino de Almeida Prado Neto, interview, São Paulo, July 27, 1982.

8. "Nosso Manifesto" (October 1942), *O Conservador* 7, no. 11 (November 1942); also published separately.

9. "Aos Estudantes de Direito" (pro-Arrobas Martins, 4 pages, printed); "A bem da verdade" (Libertador Party propaganda, 6 pages, typewritten).

10. A Comissão Diretora do Partido Acadêmico Conservador, "Desespero ou Má Fé?"; see also A Comissão Diretora do Partido Acadêmico Conservador, "Acautelando a Opinião Acadêmica," September 14, 1942.

11. Ibid.

12. João Nery Guimarães, interview, São Paulo, August 16, 1981; "A bem da verdade."

13. Oliveira Faria, *A Geração Acadêmica de 1941/1945*, p. 305.
14. *A Gazeta*, November 17, 1942, p. 5.

VII. Arrobas and the Front for Democracy (1943)

1. Arrobas Addresses the Sociedade Amigos da América (May 22, 1943)

1. José Bonifácio Coutinho Nogueira, "1943," São Paulo, November 12, 1943 (1 page, handwritten).
2. *O "XI de Agosto,"* 1943, p. 35; *O Onze de Agosto*, 1946, p. 118; Paulo Henrique Meinberg, interview, São Paulo, August 2, 1982.
3. Domenico Martirani, interview, São Paulo, August 25, 1981.
4. Arrobas Martins, "Notas sobre a 'resistência acadêmica' ao 'Estado Novo' (1938–1944)," p. 5.
5. Germinal Feijó, interview, São Paulo, August 16, 1979; Paulo Silveira, interview, Rio de Janeiro, November 28, 1967.
6. *Jornal do Brasil*, January 1, 1943; *O Estado de S. Paulo*, January 1, 1943; *A Sociedade Amigos da América em 1943*, Rio de Janeiro, 1944 (20 pages, booklet); Eurico Gaspar Dutra, letter to Vargas, Rio de Janeiro, January 12, 1943 (Vargas papers, CPDOC); Manoel Rabelo, "Exposição de Motivos" to Vargas (printed, Vargas papers, CPDOC).
7. Sociedade Amigos da América, invitation issued by Hélio Mota and others, May 21, 1943.
8. Maria Alice Arrobas Martins, interview, São Paulo, July 4, 1981.
9. *Diário de S. Paulo*, May 23, 1943; *Correio Paulistano*, May 23, 1943.
10. Ibid.
11. Small sheet giving notice of the Departamento Universitário da Sociedade Amigos da América; *O Libertador* 4, no. 9 (September 1943).

2. The Partido Libertador Schism (June 1943)

1. João Adelino de Almeida Prado Neto, interview, São Paulo, August 26, 1981.
2. Haroldo Bueno Magano, interview, São Paulo, July 27, 1981.
3. João Nery Guimarães, interviews, São Paulo, August 16, 1981, August 21, 1982.
4. Galvão, "Observações," pp. 24–25.
5. Geraldo de Camargo Vidigal, "Um Estudante Paulista na FEB" (manuscript of book), pp. 39–40; idem, typed notes for JWFD, São Paulo, July 1981, and interview, São Paulo, August 3, 1982.
6. João Nery Guimarães, interviews, August 16, 1981, August 21, 1982.
7. Renato Amaral Sampaio Coelho, interview, São Paulo, July 8, 1981.
8. Partido Acadêmico Libertador, "Manifesto," Arcadas, June 1943 (3 pages, printed).
9. Ênio de Novais França, Germinal Feijó, Luís Gonzaga Arrôbas Martins,

and Renato Amaral Sampaio Coelho, "Aos Estudantes de Direito," São Paulo, June 1943.

10. Partido Acadêmico Libertador, "Manifesto," Arcadas, June 1943.

11. João Nery Guimarães, "A Democracia e os democratas," *O Libertador* 4, no. 9 (September 1943).

3. Hélio Mota, UNE President (July 1943)

1. *O Estado de S. Paulo*, April 4, 1943; Poerner, *O Poder Jovem*, pp. 175–178.

2. Hélio de Almeida, interview, Rio de Janeiro, July 20, 1982; idem, letter to the minister of education, Rio de Janeiro, April 3, 1943, and one-page mimeographed sheet, "Histórico Sucinto dos Motivos que Levaram o Acadêmico Hélio de Almeida a Solicitar Sua Demissão do Cargo de Presidente da União Nacional dos Estudantes" (copies of these papers were furnished by Hélio de Almeida following the interview of July 20, 1982).

3. Poerner, *O Poder Jovem*, pp. 175–178; Hélio de Almeida, interview, Rio de Janeiro, July 20, 1982.

4. *O Estado de S. Paulo*, July 20, 1943.

5. Arrobas Martins, "Notas sobre a 'resistência acadêmica' ao 'Estado Novo' (1938–1944)" pp. 9–10; Paulo Henrique Meinberg, Renato Amaral Sampaio Coelho, and Hiram Mayr Cerqueira, interview, São Paulo, July 8, 1981.

6. *O Estado de S. Paulo*, July 20–27, 1943.

7. *Diário de S. Paulo*, August 1, 1943.

8. Luís Arrobas Martins, notes about "candidatos à Diretoria da União Nacional dos Estudantes, lançados por mim em nome da bancada paulista" (in papers at the residence of Maria Alice Arrobas Martins).

9. Paulo Silveira, interview, Rio de Janeiro, October 29, 1967.

10. Hélio Mota and Luís Arrobas Martins in *O Jornal*, July 27, 1943.

11. Hélio Mota and twenty-two other São Paulo students, "Voto de Louvor," Rio de Janeiro, July 26, 1943 (typewritten).

12. Hélio Mota and Luís Arrobas Martins in *O Jornal*, July 27, 1943.

13. Arrobas Martins, "Os trinta anos do 9 de novembro."

4. Reale Faces the Students (July 21, 1943)

1. Israel Dias Novaes, interview, São Paulo, July 5, 1981; Paulo Henrique Meinberg, Renato Amaral Sampaio Coelho, and Hiram Mayr Cerqueira, interview, São Paulo, July 8, 1981.

2. Renato Pintaudi Macedo, interview, São Paulo, August 20, 1981.

3. Murillo Antunes Alves (a fifth-year student), stenographic notes of lecture of Miguel Reale, São Paulo, July 21, 1943. A longer version, without showing the interruptions, is in *O Estado de S. Paulo*, July 29, 1943.

4. Alves, stenographic notes.

5. Reale's Declarations End a Strike (July 31–August 2, 1943)

1. See Noberto Villela, "O Retôrno" (verse) and "Dois Retratos de um Homem" (mimeographed sheets).
2. Miguel Reale, interview, São Paulo, August 16, 1982.
3. Arrobas Martins, "Notas sobre a 'resistência acadêmica' ao 'Estado Novo' (1938–1944)," p. 10.
4. *Diário da Noite,* July 31, 1943; *Diário de S. Paulo,* August 1, 1943.
5. Os Universitários do Rio de Janeiro, letter to Caros colegas de S. Paulo, Rio de Janeiro, July 31, 1943 (original at the residence of Maria Alice Arrobas Martins).
6. Hildeberto Vieira de Melo, interview, São Paulo, August 5, 1981.
7. Luís Arrobas Martins, "Questionário por mim formulado e submetido ao Sr. M. Reale pelo Superintendente de Ordem Política e Social" (handwritten sheets, at the residence of Maria Alice Arrobas Martins).
8. *Diário da Noite,* July 31, 1943; *Diário de S. Paulo,* August 1, 1943.
9. Miguel Reale, interview, São Paulo, August 16, 1982.
10. "Solucionando o 'caso' Miguel Reale," *Correio Paulistano,* August 1, 1943.
11. *Diário de S. Paulo,* August 1, 1943.

6. The Frente Acadêmica pela Democracia's Incisive Manifesto (September 1, 1943)

1. Geraldo de Camargo Vidigal, interview, São Paulo, August 3, 1982; José Vasques Bernardes, interview, São Paulo, August 20, 1982.
2. José Bonifácio Coutinho Nogueira, "1943."
3. José Carlos Moraes Abreu, interview, São Paulo, August 4, 1982; Geraldo de Camargo Vidigal, interview, São Paulo, August 3, 1982, typewritten notes for JWFD, São Paulo, July 1981, and letter to JWFD, São Paulo, September 11, 1984.
4. Frente Acadêmica pela Democracia, "Aos Acadêmicos de Direito," São Paulo, September 1, 1943 (2 pages, printed); the manifesto erroneously speaks of the founding of the Partido Acadêmico Conservador as being in 1937.
5. Arrobas Martins, "Os trinta anos do 9 de novembro."

7. Prelude to the Centro Elections (September–October 1943)

1. Roberto Fleury Meirelles, interview, São Paulo, August 20, 1981.
2. "Version taquiligrafica del discurso del señor Luís Gonzaga Arrobas Martins, delegado por Brasil, en la sesión inaugural del Congresso Latinoamericano de Estudiantes (18 de Stbre. de 1942)" (copy at the residence of Maria Alice Arrobas Martins; the year is in error). For other information, see *La Fronda, El Diario, El Mundo,* and *El Nacional,* all of Buenos Aires, September 9, 1943.

3. José Bento Monteiro Lobato, letter to Prezados Colegas, September 7, 1943; for date, see Almeida Júnior, *Sob as Arcadas*, p. 309.

4. Rui Pereira de Queiroz, interview, São Paulo, August 17, 1982.

5. *Diário da Noite*, October 28, 1943; *O Estado de S. Paulo*, October 30, 1943; Arrobas Martins, "Notas sobre a 'resistência acadêmica' ao 'Estado Novo' (1938–1944)," p. 10.

6. João Nery Guimarães, interview, São Paulo, August 21, 1982.

7. Galvão, "Observações," p. 33; Brasil Bandecchi, "Ode aos Moços," *O "XI de Agosto,"* 1943.

8. Page of propaganda of the Partido Acadêmico Conservador.

9. Haroldo Bueno Magano, interview, São Paulo, July 22, 1981.

10. João Nery Guimarães, interview, São Paulo, August 21, 1982.

11. Eduardo Gomes Freitas Martins, "Aos colegas, amigos e correligionários políticos" (1 page, mimeographed, in the collection of Paulo Nogueira Neto).

12. Haroldo Bueno Magano, interview, São Paulo, July 27, 1981; idem, interview ("A Verdade Histórica do '9 de Novembro'"), *Diário de S. Paulo*, November 29, 1973.

13. José Vasques Bernardes, interview, São Paulo, August 20, 1982.

14. Flávio Galvão, letter to JWFD, São Paulo, March 9, 1983.

15. Renato P. Macedo, interview, São Paulo, August 5, 1981.

16. João Nery Guimarães, interview, São Paulo, August 21, 1982.

17. "O Partido Acadêmico Libertador e seu candidato," October 1943.

18. José Gonçalves Santana, interview, São Paulo, August 16, 1982.

19. We are against submissive inaction,
Our people are of great value,
Liberty, Law, and Justice
Are principles of the Libertador.

VIII. Repression by the Special Police (1943)

1. The Baile das Américas (October 30–31, 1943)

1. "Ao Povo Mineiro," Belo Horizonte, October 24, 1943.

2. Documento XLII-41 in CPDOC (Ref. GV 43.11.08).

3. Lenício Pacheco Ferreira, "Baile das Américas—31/X/43," Catanduva, August 12, 1981 (10 pages, handwritten, with covering letter from Lenício Pacheco Ferreira to JWFD).

4. Oh! valiant legionary
Of the Expeditionary Corps:
Why do you wander abroad to fight
If the bloody and cold
Struggle is for Democracy.
Let us carry it on here at home!

5. Wilson Rahal, interview, Campinas, July 11, 1981.

6. Paulo Henrique Meinberg, interviews, São Paulo, July 8, August 1, 1981; Ferreira, "Baile das Américas."

7. Paulo Henrique Meinberg, Renato Amaral Sampaio Coelho, and Hiram Mayr Cerqueira, interview, São Paulo, July 8, 1981.

8. Ferreira, "Baile das Américas"; "Breve relato das atrocidades policiais, praticados em São Paulo, nos primeiros dias de Nov. de 1943" (3 pages, typewritten, no author shown).

9. "Breve relato das atrocidades policiais."

10. Ferreira, "Baile das Américas."

2. Arrobas' Manifesto Condemning the Estado Novo (November 1, 1943)

1. Renato Amaral Sampaio Coelho, interviews, São Paulo, July 8, August 4, 1981; Document XLII-41 in CPDOC (Ref. GV 43.11.08); Almeida Júnior, *Sob as Arcadas*, p. 310.

2. "Breve relato das atrocidades policiais, praticadas em São Paulo, nos primeiros dias de Nov. de 1943"; Hildeberto Vieira de Melo, interview, São Paulo, August 5, 1981.

3. Presidents of the associations of college students of São Paulo, "Relatório sôbre o incidente havido entre os estudantes de direito de São Paulo e o Sr. Secretário da Segurança Pública," São Paulo, November 8, 1943 (4 pages, typewritten, Document XLII-38a in CPDOC—Ref. GV 43.11.08).

4. Luís de Azevedo Soares, interview, São Paulo, August 11, 1982.

5. Roberto Fleury Meirelles, interview, São Paulo, August 20, 1981.

6. Presidents of the associations of college students of São Paulo, "Relatório sôbre o incidente."

7. Renato Amaral Sampaio Coelho, interviews, São Paulo, July 8, August 4, 1981; João Batista Silva Azevedo, interview, São Paulo, July 9, 1981.

8. "Os Estudantes de Direito de São Paulo à Nação Brasileira" (typed copy with handwritten signatures, at the residence of Maria Alice Arrobas Martins).

3. The Special Police Invade the Centro (November 2, 1943)

1. José Henrique Turner, interview, São Paulo, July 13, 1981.

2. "Os Estudantes de Direito de São Paulo à Nação Brasileira."

3. Renato P. Macedo, interview, São Paulo, August 5, 1981.

4. Presidents of São Paulo university student organizations, "Relatório sôbre o incidente."

5. Geraldo Vidigal and Rui Pereira de Queiroz, interview, São Paulo, August 17, 1982.

6. Antônio Cláudio Fernandes Rocha, interview, Rio de Janeiro, August 26, 1982.

7. Cory Porto Fernandes, interviews, São Paulo, August 2, 5, 20, 1981.

8. Presidents of São Paulo university student organizations, "Relatório sôbre o incidente."

9. Renato P. Macedo, interview, São Paulo, August 5, 1981.

10. Ferreira, "Baile das Américas," see p. 4.

11. Hildeberto Vieira de Melo, interview, São Paulo, August 5, 1981.

12. Document XLII-41 in CPDOC (Ref. GV 43.11.08).

13. Galvão, "Observações," p. 12.

14. Presidents of São Paulo university student organizaions, "Relatório sôbre o incidente"; "Breve relato das atrocidades, praticadas em São Paulo, nos primeiros dias de Nov. de 1943"; São Paulo Law School faculty members, "Moção endereçada ao Sr. Presidente da República, aos Srs. Ministros da Educação e Justiça, ao Sr. Interventor Federal em São Paulo e ao Sr. Secretário da Educação do Governo do Estado de São Paulo," São Paulo, November 8, 1943; Centro Acadêmico XI de Agosto (and lawyers) petition to Exmo. Sr. Dr. Juiz de Direito da Vara dos Feitos da Fazenda do Estado; report of judicial sentence, signed by *escrivão* Affonso Botelho de Abreu Sampaio, July 19, 1944; Ferreira, "Baile das Américas"; "Manifesto aos estudantes de direito de São Paulo" (2 pages, mimeographed, signed "Viva a Democracia," no date shown); Renato P. Macedo, interview, São Paulo, August 5, 1981; conversation at the residence of Geraldo Vidigal, August 6, 1981 (Gabriel Cesário Cury and Arthur Octavio de Camargo Pacheco also present).

4. Days of Imprisonment (November 2–5, 1943)

1. "Breve relato das atrocidades policiais, praticadas em São Paulo, nos primeiros dias de Nov. de 1943"; São Paulo Law School faculty members, "Moção endereçada ao Sr. Presidente da República," November 8, 1943.

2. Geraldo Vidigal, typewritten notes for JWFD, São Paulo, July 1981.

3. Almeida Júnior, *Sob as Arcadas*, p. 313.

4. "Breve relato das atrocidades."

5. Ferreira, "Baile das Américas"; Renato P. Macedo, interview, São Paulo, August 5, 1981; Sylvio de Campos Mello Filho, "A Luta pela volta de Democracia," *O "XI de Agosto,"* 1946, pp. 13–18, see p. 17.

6. Ferreira, "Baile das Américas."

7. Document XLII-41 in CPDOC (Ref. GV 43.11.08).

8. Diretoria do Centro Acadêmico Cândido de Oliveira, communication to the minister of education and public health, Rio de Janeiro, November 1 (*sic*), 1943.

9. Presidents of university student *grêmios* and *centros*, "Ao Povo de São Paulo," São Paulo, November 4, 1943; manifesto of the Alunos da Escola Politécnica de São Paulo; Grêmio da Faculdade de Filosofia, resolutions, Sala do Grêmio, São Paulo, November 4, 1943; Centro Acadêmico da Faculdade de Filosofia de São Bento, "Amigos e Colegas"; resolutions of the Alunos da Faculdade de Medicina da Universidade de São Paulo; Centro Acadêmico de Economia, Finanças e Administração, São Paulo, November 5, 1943; declaration of the Centro Acadêmico Luiz de Queiroz of the Escola Superior de Agricultura, Piracicaba, November 4, 1943; Centro Acadêmico Horacio Lane (Escola de Engenharia Mackenzie), letter to Fernando Costa, November 4, 1943.

10. Ferreira, "Baile das Américas."

11. Arthur Octavio de Camargo Pacheco, interview, São Paulo, August 6, 1981.
12. Ferreira, "Baile das Américas."

5. Reactions to the Assaults and Jailings (November 5–8, 1943)

1. José Bonifácio Coutinho Nogueira, handwritten notes on the margins of an anti–Estado Novo item in *Diário da Noite,* March 14, 1945, showing photograph of the parade of November 5, 1943.
2. Cory Porto Fernandes, interview, São Paulo, August 2, 1981.
3. Hélio Mota, letter to Exmo. Sr. Interventor Federal no Estado de São Paulo (copy in the collection at the residence of Maria Alice Arrobas Martins).
4. Luís de Azevedo Soares, interview, São Paulo, August 20, 1981; copy of judicial sentence, condemning the São Paulo state finance secretaryship to make payment to the Centro XI de Agosto, July 19, 1944, with handwritten notes by José Bonifácio Coutinho Nogueira; Cory Porto Fernandes, interview, São Paulo, August 2, 1981.
5. Marcello Vidigal, interview, São Paulo, August 17, 1982; José Bonifácio Coutinho Nogueira, handwritten notes adjoining a copy of the invitation to the rally of November 9, 1943, and "Os fatos falam por si só" (handwritten, in a notebook at his residence).
6. Ruy Mesquita, interviews, São Paulo, July 25, 1981, August 5, 1982; Severo Gomes, interview, São Paulo, August 25, 1981.
7. Ferreira, "Baile das Américas."
8. Mimeographed sheet with twelve stanzas, headed by newspaper item; João Nery Guimarães, interview, São Paulo, August 16, 1981.
9. It is said and it is proved
That a government makes a people.
If we are a backward people
It is because the *estado novo* lives.
10. And the rats of the vessel,
Perceiving that the ship was sinking,
"Solved" the situation
By giving the order to jump overboard.
11. "É o que ele quer. . . . Paródia do samba do mesmo nome" (2 pages, mimeographed); sheet of verses in the handwriting of Renato P. Macedo, dated November 8, 1943; Renato P. Macedo, letter to JWFD, São Paulo, August 18, 1981.
12. São Paulo Law School professors, "Moção endereçada ao Sr. Presidente da República, aos Srs. Ministros da Educação e Justiça, ao Sr. Interventor Federal em São Paulo e ao Sr. Secretário da Educação do Governo do Estado de São Paulo."
13. "Manifesto aos estudantes de direito de São Paulo" (2 pages, mimeographed, signed "Viva a Democracia!").
14. Presidents of twelve São Paulo university student associations and the

student representative on the University of São Paulo Conselho, "Relatório sôbre o incidente havido entre os estudantes de direito de São Paulo e o Sr. Secretário da Segurança Pública," São Paulo, November 8, 1943.

6. The March of Silence (November 9, 1943)

1. Laudelino de Abreu, "Relatório do inquerito policial instaurado sobre a chacina do Largo de São Francisco," São Paulo, May 20, 1944 (published, thanks to Flávio Galvão, in *O Estado de S. Paulo*, November 9, 16, 1958). Coriolano de Góes, *Entrevista concedida à imprensa . . . no dia 5 de Dezembro de 1943* (6 pages, booklet, copy at residence of José Bonifácio Coutinho Nogueira).

2. Ibid.

3. José Bonifácio Coutinho Nogueira, handwritten notes next to newspaper clipping ("Proibidos os comícios") in one of his notebooks.

4. Abreu, "Relatório do inquerito policial"; Jussieu da Cunha Batista, "A verdade sobre a chacina do Largo de S. Francisco," *Jornal de São Paulo*, May 19, 1946.

7. Coriolano de Góis Dispatches the Special Police (November 9, 1943)

1. Abreu, "Relatório do inquerito policial"; Cunha Batista, "A verdade sobre a chacina."

2. Ibid.; João Brasil Vita, interview, São Paulo, August 17, 1981.

3. Abreu, "Relatório do inquerito policial."

8. Shootings by the Special Police (November 9, 1943)

1. Abreu, "Relatório de inquerito policial."

2. Fernando Jacob, interview (by telephone), Fernandópolis, S.P., August 25, 1981; João Nery Guimarães, interview, São Paulo, August 16, 1981.

3. Cunha Batista, "A verdade sobre a chacina"; Almeida Júnior, *Sob as Arcadas*, p. 316.

4. Abreu, "Relatório do inquerito policial."

5. Ferreira, "Baile das Américas."

6. Fernando Jacob, interview (by telephone), Fernandópolis, S.P., August 25, 1981.

7. Renato P. Macedo, interview, São Paulo, August 5, 1981.

8. Aloysio Ferraz Pereira, interview, São Paulo, August 19, 1982.

9. João Brasil Vita, interview, São Paulo, August 17, 1981.

10. João Nery Guimarães, interview, São Paulo, July 31, 1982.

11. João Brasil Vita, interview, São Paulo, August 17, 1981.

12. Almeida Júnior, *Sob as Arcadas*, p. 317.

13. Haroldo Bueno Magano, interviews, São Paulo, July 22, 27, 1981.

14. Flávio Galvão (another member of the *pré-jurídico* "grupo do cursinho do Azevedinho"), "Observações," p. 17.

15. Aloysio Ferraz Pereira, interview, São Paulo, August 19, 1982.
16. Arrobas Martins, "Os trinta anos do 9 de novembro."

IX. Aftermath of the Shootings (1943–1944)

1. Resignations and Dismissals (November 9–13, 1943)

1. João Nery Guimarães, letter to JWFD, São Paulo, August 13, 1982.
2. Document XLII-41 in CPDOC (Ref. GV 43.11.08); Almeida Júnior, *Sob as Arcadas*, p. 317.
3. *O Dia* (São Paulo), November 10, 1943.
4. *O Estado de S. Paulo*, November 11, 1943.
5. Newspaper clippings in the collections at the residences of Maria Alice Arrobas Martins and José Bonifácio Coutinho Nogueira; "Breve relato das atrocidades policiais, praticadas em São Paulo, nos primeiros dias de Nov. de 1943."
6. "Traços Rápidos" (verse on mimeographed sheet); "M.M.D.C.J." (verse on mimeographed sheet), with handwritten notes by José Bonifácio Coutinho Nogueira.
7. Fernando Barjas Millan, interview, São Paulo, August 10, 1982.
8. Severo Gomes, interview, São Paulo, August 25, 1981.
9. "Ao povo de S. Paulo," São Paulo, November 11, 1943, with handwritten notes by José Bonifácio Coutinho Nogueira.
10. Roberto Barbosa, José Botelho Filho, Oswaldo Barros, and Arnaldo G. Senna, "Aviso ao Povo."
11. *Diário da Noite*, November 13, 1943; *Folha da Noite*, November 13, 1943; *O Estado de S. Paulo*, November 13, 1943.
12. Hildeberto Vieira de Melo, interview, São Paulo, August 5, 1981.

2. Law Student Reactions (November 13–16, 1943)

1. *Diário da Noite*, November 13, 1943.
2. "Explicação Necessária" (1 page, mimeographed).
3. Document XLII-41 in CPDOC (Ref. GV 43.11.08).
4. "Comentários sôbre o movimento estudantil em São Paulo, feitos por co-participante do mesmo," Segurança Nacional report in CPDOC, Vargas papers (Document XLII-38C, "Examined November 20, 1943," Censor No. 412).
5. "Breve relato das atrocidades policiais, praticadas em São Paulo, nos primeiros dias de Nov. de 1943."
6. Ibid.; newspaper clippings in the collections at the residences of Maria Alice Arrobas Martins and José Bonifácio Coutinho Nogueira.
7. Ibid.
8. Afrânio de Oliveira, interview, São Paulo, August 18, 1981; idem, speech at the grave of Martinico Prado, São Paulo, November 17, 1943 (typewritten).

3. Magano, Centro President-Elect (late November 1943)

1. Pedro Brasil Bandecchi, interview, São Paulo, August 9, 1982; João Nery Guimarães, interview, São Paulo, August 21, 1982.
2. Haroldo Bueno Magano, interviews, São Paulo, July 22, 27, 1981; idem, "A Verdade Histórico do '9 de Novembro,'" interview in *Diário de S. Paulo*, November 29, 1973.
3. Pedro Brasil Bandecchi, interview, São Paulo, August 17, 1982.
4. Haroldo Bueno Magano, interview, São Paulo, July 27, 1981, and papers in his scrapbook.
5. Fernando Jacob, interview (by telephone), Fernandopolis, S.P., August 25, 1981.
6. Renato Pintaudi Macedo, letter to JWFD, São Paulo, August 18, 1981.
7. Haroldo Bueno Magano in *Diário de S. Paulo*, November 29, 1973.
8. Hildeberto Vieira de Melo, interview, São Paulo, August 5, 1981.
9. José Carlos Moraes Abreu, interview, São Paulo, August 4, 1982.
10. Péricles Eugênio da Silva Ramos, interview, São Paulo, August 18, 1982 (Péricles Eugênio da Silva Ramos held an important editorial post at *Correio Paulistano*).
11. Hildeberto Vieira de Melo, interview, São Paulo, August 5, 1981.

4. Closing Out the School Year (December 1943–March 1944)

1. José Barbosa, "Mensagem ao Presidente do C.A. 'XI de Agosto,'" São Paulo, December 27, 1943 (1 page, printed).
2. Newspaper clipping (no source shown), December 29, 1943 (in the collection of José Bonifácio Coutinho Nogueira).
3. Geraldo de Camargo Vidigal, "Um Estudante Paulista na FEB," p. 39.
4. João Adelino de Almeida Prado Neto, interview, São Paulo, July 27, 1982; Arthur Octavio de Camargo Pacheco, interviews, São Paulo, August 6, 1981, August 6, 1982; Paulo Henrique Meinberg, interview, São Paulo, August 1, 1981.
5. Mimeographed sheet, signed Os CONTRA-DIP.
6. *O Estado de S. Paulo*, August 20, 1943; *A Gazeta*, November 29, 1943; biography of Mário Masagão and autobiographical notes in the files of *O Estado de S. Paulo*; Flávio Galvão, "Mário Masagão, advogado, professor, juiz, e político," *O Estado de S. Paulo*, March 21, 1980.
7. "Discurso de Rivaldo de Assis Cintra, Orador da Turma de 1943, da Faculdade de Direito do Largo de São Francisco" (printed copy).
8. Paulo Henrique Meinberg, Renato Amaral Sampaio Coelho, and Hiram Mayr Cerqueira, interview, São Paulo, July 8, 1981.
9. "Discurso do Professor Mário Masagão, Paraninfo da Turma de Bacharéis de 1943, da Faculdade de Direito da Universidade de São Paulo" (printed and mimeographed copies).
10. Galvão, "Mário Masagão, advogado, professor, juiz, e político."
11. "Jantar . . . No salão de festas do Esporte Clube Pinheiros, Dia 29 de Fevereiro" (invitation, on card); "Ao povo brasileiro" (1 page, printed) and

8-page typewritten document describing the Clube Pinheiros banquet of March 3, 1944. The banquet honored Alceu Dias de Aguiar, Anésio Abadio de Paula e Silva, Arlindo de Camargo Pacheco Filho, Celso Galvão, Cory Porto Fernandes, Hélio Mota, Hiram Mayr Cerqueira, Inês Bustamente Guil, Israel Dias Novaes, João José Pereira Ferraz, João Sanchez Postigo, Joaquim Gomes dos Reis Neto, José Carlos Pereira Geribelo, José Vasques Bernardes, Lenício Pacheco Ferreira, Luís Gonzaga Arrobas Martins, Osvaldo Reverendo Vidal, Paulo Henrique Meinberg, and Rômulo Fonseca.

X. The Resistance in High Gear (1944)

1. Calls for Army Service (1944)

1. Maria Alice Arrobas Martins, interview, São Paulo, July 4, 1981; Luís Arrobas Martins, letter (handwritten draft without date) to the British council.

2. "Chamada de reservistas," *Folha da Manhã*, January 27, 1944; Maria Alice Arrobas Martins and son Luís, interview, São Paulo, July 4, 1981.

3. Luís Arrobas Martins, letter to Professor Reynaldo Saldanha da Gama, São Paulo, January 31, 1944.

4. Luís Arrobas Martins, handwritten letter to José Bonifácio Coutinho Nogueira, Santos, S.P., July 12, 1944; correspondence between Arrobas Martins and the British council, 1944, and letters to Arrobas Martins, September 29, October 4, 1944, about Brazilian army officers and his scholarship (in the collection at the residence of Maria Alice Arrobas Martins).

5. Almeida Júnior, *Sob as Arcadas*, pp. 317–318.

6. "Oração do Professor Ernesto Leme, que paraninfou o 'expedicionário,'" *Diário de S. Paulo*, January 28, 1945.

7. List furnished by José Vasques Bernardes, São Paulo, August 1982.

8. Flávio Galvão, "Observações."

9. Geraldo Vidigal, interviews, São Paulo, August 3, 17, 1982.

10. Geraldo Vidigal typewritten notes for JWFD, São Paulo, July 1981; *Correio Paulistano*, September 13, 1944; Carlos Lacerda, "Retratos do DIP," *Correio da Manhã*, March 11, 1945.

11. *E a cobra fumou!* (Acampamento em Tarquínia) 1, no. 1 (August 17, 1944); "E a Cobra Fumou!," *Diário Carioca*, July 21, 1945; Geraldo Vidigal, *Predestinação*, introduction by Mário de Andrade (São Paulo: Livraria Martins Editora, 1944), and reviews of it in *O Globo*, February 24, 1945, *Jornal do Commercio*, March 25, 1945, and *A Gazeta*, January 16, 1945.

12. Paulo Nogueira Neto, "Geraldo Vidigal," *Mocidade Paulista*, January 1945; "Enviaram seus votos da frente de batalha," *Folha da Noite*, October 20, 1944; "Os estudantes de direito combatem valiosamente na Itália," *Correio Paulistano*, January 23, 1945.

2. *Resistência* and the Proletariat (April–August 1944)

1. Paulo Duarte, "Cento e vinte e sete anos da imprensa paulista," *O Estado de S. Paulo*, January 25, 1954, p. 85, quoted in Antônio Barreto do Amaral, "Jornalismo Acadêmico," reprinted from *Revista do Arquivo Municipal* 190 (1977): 266.
2. Barreto do Amaral, "Jornalismo Acadêmico," p. 266.
3. "Resistência, o nosso jornal," *Resistência* 1, no. 1 (April 1944).
4. Ibid.
5. "Atentado à Inteligência," *Resistência* 1, no. 1 (April 1944).
6. "O massacre de 9 de Novembro," "Antevéspera da Chacina—Baile das Américas," and "O Comício," *Resistência* 1, no. 1 (April 1944).
7. "O Comício."
8. "Getúlio Vargas em São Paulo" (1 page, mimeographed).
9. *O Estado de S. Paulo*, April 30, May 3, 1944; *New York Times*, May 2, 1944.
10. "Getúlio Vargas versus Democracia," *Resistência* 1, no. 4 (August 1944).
11. Antônio Cândido de Mello e Souza, interviews, São Paulo, July 8, August 7, 1981; Paulo Zingg, interview, São Paulo, July 9, 1981.
12. "Proletariado brasileiro," *Resistência* 1, no. 4 (August 1944).

3. The Pursuit of Democracy by Libertadores and the Frente (April–August 1944)

1. Haroldo Bueno Magano, interview, São Paulo, July 27, 1981; newspaper clipping (April 1944) in the collection at the residence of João Nery Guimarães.
2. João Nery Guimarães, *Discurso Proferido na homenagem prestada pelo Partido Acadêmico Libertador aos seus antigos diretores, Astolfo Pio Monteiro da Silva, Jarbas Teixeira de Carvalho e Zwinglio Ferreira, no dia 20 de Abril de 1944, na Casa Anglo-Brasileira* (São Paulo, 1944).
3. Gabriel Cesário Cury, interview, São Paulo, August 6, 1981; Mello Filho, "A Luta pela volta de Democracia."
4. Severo Gomes, interview, São Paulo, August 25, 1981.
5. José Bonifácio Coutinho Nogueira, handwritten notes on a copy of "Mensagem dos paulistas ao povo do Rio de Janeiro."
6. Ibid.; Fernando Barjas Millan, interview, São Paulo, August 10, 1982.
7. "Mensagem dos paulistas ao povo do Rio de Janeiro," São Paulo, August 1944 (1 page, mimeographed).
8. Ruy Mesquita, interviews, São Paulo, July 25, 1981, August 5, 1982; Afrânio de Oliveira, interview, São Paulo, August 18, 1981.

4. The Mota Filho Case (June–August 1944)

1. *A Manhã*, March 18, 1944.
2. "Traços biográficos do Professor Cândido Motta Filho," in the files at *O Estado de S. Paulo*.
3. Almeida Júnior, "A 'Resistência Acadêmica' e o Estado Novo," see second article.
4. Haroldo Bueno Magano, interview, São Paulo, July 27, 1981; Renato P. Macedo, interviews, São Paulo, August 5, 20, 1981.
5. "Colegas!" (1 page, mimeographed).
6. Renato Amaral Sampaio Coelho and Hiram Mayr Cerqueira, interview, São Paulo, August 4, 1981; Renato P. Macedo, interview, São Paulo, August 20, 1981; Haroldo Bueno Magano, interview, São Paulo, July 27, 1981.
7. Almeida Júnior, "A 'Resistência Acadêmica' e o Estado Novo," see second article.
8. Luís de Azevedo Soares, interview, São Paulo, August 11, 1982; Hermann de Morais Barros, interview, São Paulo, August 14, 1982.
9. Renato P. Macedo, circular letter, São Paulo, July 27, 1944, and 6-page attachment (Affonso Botelho de Abreu Sampaio, escrivão do cartório do primeiro ofício privativo dos feitos da fazenda estadual desta comarca e capital do estado de São Paulo, etc., São Paulo, July 19, 1944); see also legal presentation of the Centro Acadêmico XI de Agosto (copy in the collection at the residence of Maria Alice Arrobas Martins).

5. Advice from Arrobas (July 1944)

1. Luís Arrobas Martins, letter to José Bonifácio Coutinho Nogueira, Santos, S.P., July 12, 1944.
2. Luís Francisco da Silva Carvalho, interview, São Paulo, August 15, 1982.
3. Arrobas Martins, letter to José Bonifácio Coutinho Nogueira, July 12, 1944.
4. Flávio Galvão, "Observações."
5. Arrobas Martins, letter to José Bonifácio Coutinho Nogueira, July 12, 1944.

6. Authorities React to Centro Electioneering (October–November 1944)

1. Luís Francisco da Silva Carvalho, interview, São Paulo, August 15, 1982.
2. "Processo de seleção de candidatos," *O Libertador* 5, no. 10 (November 10, 1944).
3. Flávio Galvão, "Observações," p. 29.
4. José Gonçalves Santana, interview, São Paulo, August 16, 1982.
5. Aloysio Marcondes Barbosa Ferreira, Cicero de Toledo Piza, Fernando

Jacob, José Gonçalves Santana, Ruy Junqueira de Freitas Camargo, and Victor Tieghi, "Aos Colegas da Faculdade de Direito," Arcadas, November 1944.

6. José Gonçalves Santana, interview, São Paulo, August 16, 1982.

7. *Folha da Noite*, October 5, 1944, p. 2.

8. Partido Acadêmico Conservador, Manifesto, Arcadas, November 1944.

9. Newspaper clipping (without source or date) in the collection of Antônio Cláudio Fernandes Rocha (Rio de Janeiro).

10. Luís Francisco da Silva Carvalho, interview, São Paulo, August 15, 1982.

11. Newspaper clippings, October 30, 1944 (no source shown), in the collections of Luís Francisco Carvalho and Antônio Cláudio Fernandes Rocha.

12. Luís Francisco Carvalho, interview, São Paulo, August 15, 1982; "Uma velha lição de Ruy," *Diário da Noite*, October 13, 1944.

13. "Enviaram seus votos da frente de batalha," *Folha da Noite*, October 20, 1944; "Um brasileiro votando da frente de batalha," *Diário da Noite*, September 9, 1944.

14. Handwritten notes by José Bonifácio Coutinho Nogueira on a copy of "Manifesto Político da Frente Acadêmica pela Democracia"; José Carlos Moraes Abreu, interview, São Paulo, August 4, 1982.

15. "Manifesto Político da Frente Acadêmica pela Democracia," São Paulo, November 5, 1944.

16. "O Partido Acadêmico Libertador aos Estudantes de Direito," Arcadas, October 12, 1944.

17. Handwritten notes by José Bonifácio Coutinho Nogueira on a copy of "Manifesto Político da Frente Acadêmica pela Democracia"; Luís Francisco Carvalho, interview, São Paulo, August 15, 1982; Mello Filho, "A Luta pela volta da Democracia," pp. 13–18.

18. Mello Filho, "A Luta pela volta da Democracia."

7. The Centro Elects Nazareth and Expels Celio Costa (November 1944)

1. Clippings in notebook of João Nery Guimarães.

2. Ibid.

3. *Correio Paulistano*, January 23, 1945 (in notebook of Geraldo Vidigal).

4. Paulo Henrique Meinberg and Renato Amaral Sampaio Coelho, interview, São Paulo, July 8, 1981; Paulo Henrique Meinberg, interview, São Paulo, August 1, 1981; João Nery Guimarães, interview, São Paulo, August 21, 1982.

5. "Os Processos Nazistas do 'Estado Novo'" (1 page, printed).

6. Flávio Galvão, "Observações," p. 20.

7. Ibid. (re Quintino Ferreira Millás).

8. Célio de Oliveira Costa, "Aos meus amigos e colegas," São Paulo, December 1, 1944 (2 pages, printed).

9. Ibid.

8. Anti-Vargas Activities (December 1944–January 1945)

1. José Bonifácio Coutinho Nogueira, "Um baptismo de fogo," São Paulo, December 7, 1944 (2 pages, typed).
2. "Povo de São Paulo" (1 page, mimeographed, copy at residence of José Bonifácio Coutinho Nogueira).
3. Coutinho Nogueira, "Um baptismo de fogo."
4. "Povo de São Paulo" (copy in the collection of Antônio Cláudio Fernandes Rocha, Rio de Janeiro); letters to JWFD from José Bonifácio Coutinho Nogueira (São Paulo, September 9, 1982) and Antônio Cláudio Fernandes Rocha (Rio de Janeiro, October 21, 1982).
5. José Carlos Moraes Abreu, interview, São Paulo, August 4, 1982; Antônio Cláudio Fernandes Rocha, interview, Rio de Janeiro, August 26, 1982.
6. Coutinho Nogueira, "Um batismo de fogo."
7. Ibid.
8. Paulo Zingg, interview, São Paulo, July 9, 1981.
9. Carlos Eduardo de Camargo Aranha, interview, São Paulo, August 5, 1982.
10. *O Estado de S. Paulo*, December 29, 1944, January 11, 1945.
11. Francisco Camargo de Almeida Prado, "Discurso do Orador da Turma de 1944," *O "XI de Agosto,"* 1946, pp. 49–57.
12. Re fresco, João Nery Guimarães, interview, São Paulo, August 21, 1982.
13. Flávio Galvão, "Observações," pp. 31–33.

XI. Twilight of the Estado Novo (1945)

1. Young Paulistas Favor a United Front with Eduardo Gomes (February 1945)

1. *O Estado de S. Paulo*, January 28, 1945.
2. In addition to Rui Pereira de Queiroz, Celso Braga, and Geraldo Vidigal, the honored students were Afrânio de Oliveira, Aluísio Alvares Cruz, Cícero de Toledo Piza, Domingos Marmo, Francisco Camargo de Almeida Prado, Germinal Feijó, José Carlos Moraes Abreu, José Gonçalves Santana, Nasser Bussamra, and Vítor Tieghi.
3. Luís Francisco da Silva Carvalho, interview, São Paulo, August 15, 1982.
4. A fuller list, including many eminent Paulistas, is given in the handwriting of Germinal Feijó on copy of his speech of February 7, 1945 (given to JWFD).
5. "Discurso pronunciado por Luís Francisco Carvalho no Club Comercial, dia 7 de Fevereiro de 1945" (9 pages, typewritten); Germinal Feijó, "Discurso pronunciado por Germinal Feijó no banquete em homenagem aos jovens advogados formados em 1944 e que durante o curso da Faculdade de Direito de S. Paulo mais se destacaram na luta pela democratização do

Brasil, realizado nos salões do Clube Comercial em 7 de fevereiro de 1945" (8 pages, mimeographed).

6. "Pensamento político da mocidade paulista," *Diário de S. Paulo*, February 25, 1945.

2. Unsuccessful Student Rallies in São Paulo and Recife (early March 1945)

1. Flávio Galvão, "Observações," p. 35.
2. José Bonifácio Coutinho Nogueira, handwritten notes on leaflet "Aos Trabalhadores."
3. "Aos Trabalhadores," mimeographed leaflet signed "Os Estudantes de São Paulo."
4. Flávio Galvão, "Observações," p. 35.
5. Duílio Crispim Farina, interview, São Paulo, August 7, 1982.
6. Flávio Galvão, "Abrindo Fogo," *O "XI de Agosto,"* 1946, pp. 91–92.
7. Ibid.
8. *O Estado de S. Paulo*, March 4, 1945.
9. Ibid., March 6, 1945; see also Virgílio A. de Mello Franco, *A Campanha da U.D.N. (1944–1945)* (Rio de Janeiro: Livraria Editora Zelio Valverde, 1946), pp. 176–183, and Etelvino Lins, *Um depoimento político: Episódios e observações* (Rio de Janeiro: Livraria José Olympio Editora, 1977), p. 23.
10. *O Estado de S. Paulo*, March 6, 1945.
11. Ibid.
12. Poerner, *O Poder Jovem*, pp. 183–184.

3. The União Democrática Socialista (June 1945)

1. Maria Victoria de Mesquita Benavides, *A UDN e o Udenismo: Ambigüidades do Liberalismo Brasileiro (1945–1965)* (Rio de Janeiro: Paz e Terra, 1981), pp. 27–28.
2. "Ante-projeto do Manifesto da Frente da Resistência," São Paulo, April 7, 1945 (7 pages, mimeographed).
3. Ibid.
4. Cory Porto Fernandes, interview, São Paulo, August 5, 1981; Ruy Mesquita, interview, São Paulo, July 25, 1981.
5. Moacir Werneck de Castro, interview, Rio de Janeiro, July 2, 1979; Paulo Silveira, interviews, Rio de Janeiro, October 29, November 28, 1967, June 20, 1979.
6. Renato Amaral Sampaio Coelho, interview, São Paulo, August 4, 1981.
7. Flávio Galvão, interview, São Paulo, August 20, 1982; idem, "Observações," pp. 26–27; declaration of Joaquim Franco Garcia in *Diário da Noite*, May 3, 1945.
8. Jair Carvalho Monteiro, interview, São Paulo, August 4, 1982.
9. Antônio Cândido de Mello e Souza, interviews, São Paulo, July 8, August 7, 1981.
10. *Manifesto da União Democrática Socialista* (15 pages, printed).

11. Antônio Cândido de Mello e Souza, interviews, São Paulo, July 8, August 7, 1981.

12. União Democrática Socialista, *Boletim Interno*, no. 1 (July 1945).

4. The *Arcadas* and the National Election (late 1945)

1. Geraldo Vidigal, interview, São Paulo, August 17, 1982.

2. Poerner, *O Poder Jovem*, p. 182.

3. Geraldo Vidigal, typewritten notes for JWFD, São Paulo, August 1982.

4. Geraldo Vidigal, interview, São Paulo, August 6, 1981.

5. Haroldo Bueno Magano, interview, São Paulo, July 27, 1981.

6. Benjamin Pereira de Queiroz, interview, São Paulo, August 10, 1982; Paulo Henrique Meinberg, Renato Amaral Sampaio Coelho, and Hiram Mayr Cerqueira, interview, São Paulo, July 8, 1981; Antônio Cândido de Mello e Souza, interview, July 8, 1981; Wilson Rahal, interview, Campinas, July 21, 1979; Afrânio de Oliveira, interview, São Paulo, August 18, 1981; Paulo Zingg, interview, São Paulo, July 9, 1981.

7. Regina Sampaio, *Ademar de Barros e o PSP* (São Paulo: Global Editora, 1982), p. 51; Miguel Reale (interview, São Paulo, August 16, 1982) explained that the Partido Popular Sindicalista was *parlamentarista*; "José Adriano Marrey Júnior," *Ordem* (Publicação reservada a Maçons) 1, no. 5 (March 1974); articles about José Adriano Marrey Júnior in *Correio Paulistano*, June 15, 19, 1941; *Diário Popular*, November 22, 1943, and *A Gazeta*, November 22, 1943, June 4, 1945, April 14, 1953.

8. "Diretorio da U.D.N. pró-Brigadeiro Eduardo Gomes na Faculdade de Direito de S. Paulo" (newspaper clipping in the notebook of João Nery Guimarães).

9. Ibid.; João Nery Guimarães, "O Aeronauta da Esperança," *A Balança* 7, no. 27 (July–August 1945).

10. Renato P. Macedo, interview, São Paulo, July 26, 1982; José Antônio Rogê Ferreira, interview, São Paulo, July 26, 1982.

11. José Antônio Rogê Ferreira, interview, São Paulo, July 26, 1982; João Nery Guimarães, interview, São Paulo, August 16, 1981.

12. João Nery Guimarães, interview, São Paulo, July 31, 1982.

13. Geraldo Vidigal, interview, São Paulo, August 3, 1982.

14. João Nery Guimarães, letter to JWFD, São Paulo, August 13, 1982; Luís Francisco Carvalho, interview, São Paulo, August 15, 1982; Antônio Cláudio Fernandes Rocha, interview, Rio de Janeiro, August 26, 1982.

15. Luís Francisco Carvalho, speech (10 pages, typewritten, original in the collection of Luís Francisco Carvalho).

16. Ruy Nazareth, "A Mocidade com o Brigadeiro," São Paulo, November 28, 1945, reprinted in *O Onze de Agosto*, 1946, p. 92; *O Estado de S. Paulo*, December 1, 1945.

17. Hélio Silva, *1945: Porque despuseram Vargas* (Rio de Janeiro: Editora Civilização Brasileira, 1976), p. 278; *O Onze de Agosto*, 1946, p. 46; *O Estado de S. Paulo*, October 26, 1945.

18. Cardoso de Melo Neto, "Gastão Vidigal"; *Tribuna da Imprensa*, July 2, 1956; *Correio Paulistano*, January 8, 1947.
19. *O Estado de S. Paulo*, November 22, 29, 1945.
20. About Eusébio Rocha Filho, see Flávio Galvão, "Observações," pp. 38–39.

5. Elections at the *Arcadas* (November 1945)

1. Aloysio Ferraz Pereira, interview, São Paulo, August 19, 1982.
2. Ibid.
3. João Nery Guimarães, interviews, São Paulo, August 16, 1981, August 21, 1982; Movimento Acadêmico Renovador, "Manifesto Programa: A Luta da Nossa Geração," Arcadas, October 1945 (4 pages, printed).
4. Movimento Acadêmico Renovador, "Manifesto Programa."
5. Aloysio Ferraz Pereira, interview, São Paulo, August 19, 1982.
6. Ibid.
7. Humberto da Silva Ramos, João Brasil Vita, José Cabral, José Roberto Siqueira, Laercio de Oliveira Lima, Manoel Pedro Pimentel, and Waldemar Maricondi, "Mensagem aos colegas membros do Partido Acadêmico Conservador," Arcadas, August 1945 (1 page, printed).
8. "Plataforma Político-administrativa de Haroldo Santos Abreu, candidato à Presidência do Centro Acadêmico 'XI de Agosto' pela União Democrática Acadêmica" (2 pages, printed).
9. Invitation to the "solenidade de Declaração de Aspirantes ao Oficialato da Reserva . . . na Praça de Esportes do Club Atlético Paulistano," October 20, 1945.
10. *O Estado de S. Paulo*, August 4, 1945; João Nery Guimarães, interview, São Paulo, August 21, 1982.
11. João Nery Guimarães, interview, São Paulo, August 16, 1981.
12. Flávio Galvão, "Observações," p. 28.
13. "Nós, Estudantes de Direito," announcing the founding of the Movimento Democrático Acadêmico, bearing 35 signatures (4 pages, printed, no date).
14. "O Partido Acadêmico Libertador aos Estudantes de Direito," Arcadas, October 12, 1945 (4 pages, printed, signed by twelve members of the *comissão diretora*).
15. "Aos Acadêmicos de Direito," presenting the candidacy of Haroldo Santos Abreu (2 pages, printed, no date or party name shown).
16. João Nery Guimarães, interviews, São Paulo, August 16, 1981, July 31, 1982.
17. Aloysio Ferraz Pereira, interview, São Paulo, August 19, 1982.

XII. Epilogue: The Post–Estado Novo Failure

1. The National Elections of 1945

1. José Carlos Moraes Abreu, interview, São Paulo, August 4, 1982.
2. José Bonifácio Nogueira, "Redenção Política do Brasil."
3. *Anuário Estatístico do Brasil* (Rio de Janeiro: Serviço Gráfico do Instituto Brasileiro de Geografia e Estatística, 1947) 7 (1946): 516–518; *O Estado de S. Paulo*, January 8, 1946.
4. Flávio Galvão, "Observações," p. 38.

2. The Anti-Getulistas' Alliance with Quadros (1960–1961)

1. Afrânio de Oliveira, interview, São Paulo, August 18, 1981; Ruy Mesquita, interview, São Paulo, August 5, 1982.
2. Sampaio, *Ademar de Barros e o PSP*, p. 51.
3. José Bonifácio Coutinho Nogueira, interview, São Paulo, August 3, 1982; Renato P. Macedo, interviews, São Paulo, August 5, 20, 1981; João Nery Guimarães, interviews, São Paulo, August 16, 1981, August 21, 1982.
4. Viriato de Castro, *O Fenômeno Jânio Quadros*, 3d ed. (São Paulo: Palácio do Livro, 1959), pp. 86–109.
5. Castilho Cabral, *Tempos de Jânio e outros tempos* (Rio de Janeiro: Editôra Civilização Brasileira, 1962), p. 54.
6. Castro, *O Fenômeno Jânio Quadros*, pp. 104–106.
7. *O Estado de S. Paulo*, October 1, 6, 1954.
8. A helpful contribution to the list that follows was furnished by Jair Carvalho Monteiro (interview, São Paulo, August 4, 1982).
9. Thomas E. Skidmore, *Politics in Brazil, 1930–1964: An Experiment in Democracy* (New York: Oxford University Press, 1967), pp. 190–191; Vladimir Reisky de Dubnic, *Political Trends in Brazil* (Washington, D.C.: Public Affairs Press, 1968), p. 111.
10. *O Estado de S. Paulo*, October 6, 1960.
11. José Bonifácio Nogueira, "Redenção Política do Brasil."

3. The Anti-Getulistas' Alliance with the Military (1964)

1. *O Estado de S. Paulo*, April 2, 3, 1964.
2. Paulo Henrique Meinberg, interview, São Paulo, August 1, 1981; Fernando Barjas Millan, interview, São Paulo, August 10, 1982; Paulo Henrique Meinberg, Renato Amaral Sampaio Coelho, and Hiram Mayr Cerqueira, interview, São Paulo, July 8, 1981.
3. Wilson Rahal, interview, Campinas, July 21, 1979; Antônio Costa Corrêa, interview, São Paulo, August 14, 1982; Fernando Barjas Millan, interview, São Paulo, August 10, 1982.
4. José Bonifácio Coutinho Nogueira, interview, São Paulo, August 9, 1982.
5. João Nery Guimarães, letter to JWFD, São Paulo, August 13, 1982, p. 9.

6. Ibid.

7. Luís Arrobas Martins, letter to José Bonifácio Coutinho Nogueira, Santos, S.P., July 12, 1944.

8. Benjamin Augusto Pereira de Queiroz, interview, São Paulo, August 10, 1982.

9. Arrobas Martins, letter to José Bonifácio Coutinho Nogueira, July 12, 1944.

Index